Be a Bum — Tour the USA in a
1919 Model T Ford with the Ford Tramps

Seegar Swanson

— One of the Tramps

Ford Tramps

by

Seegar Swanson

Life in the United States during the Not-So-Roaring Mid-1920s, seen through the eyes of two Wisconsin youths working at odd jobs while on an adventurous tour of the country in a secondhand 1919 Model T Ford. They became known as Ford Tramps. Oddly enough, about the same time, Henry Ford himself and his close friends, Thomas Edison and Harvey S. Firestone, toured together in one of Henry's Fords, calling themselves Ford Vagabonds.

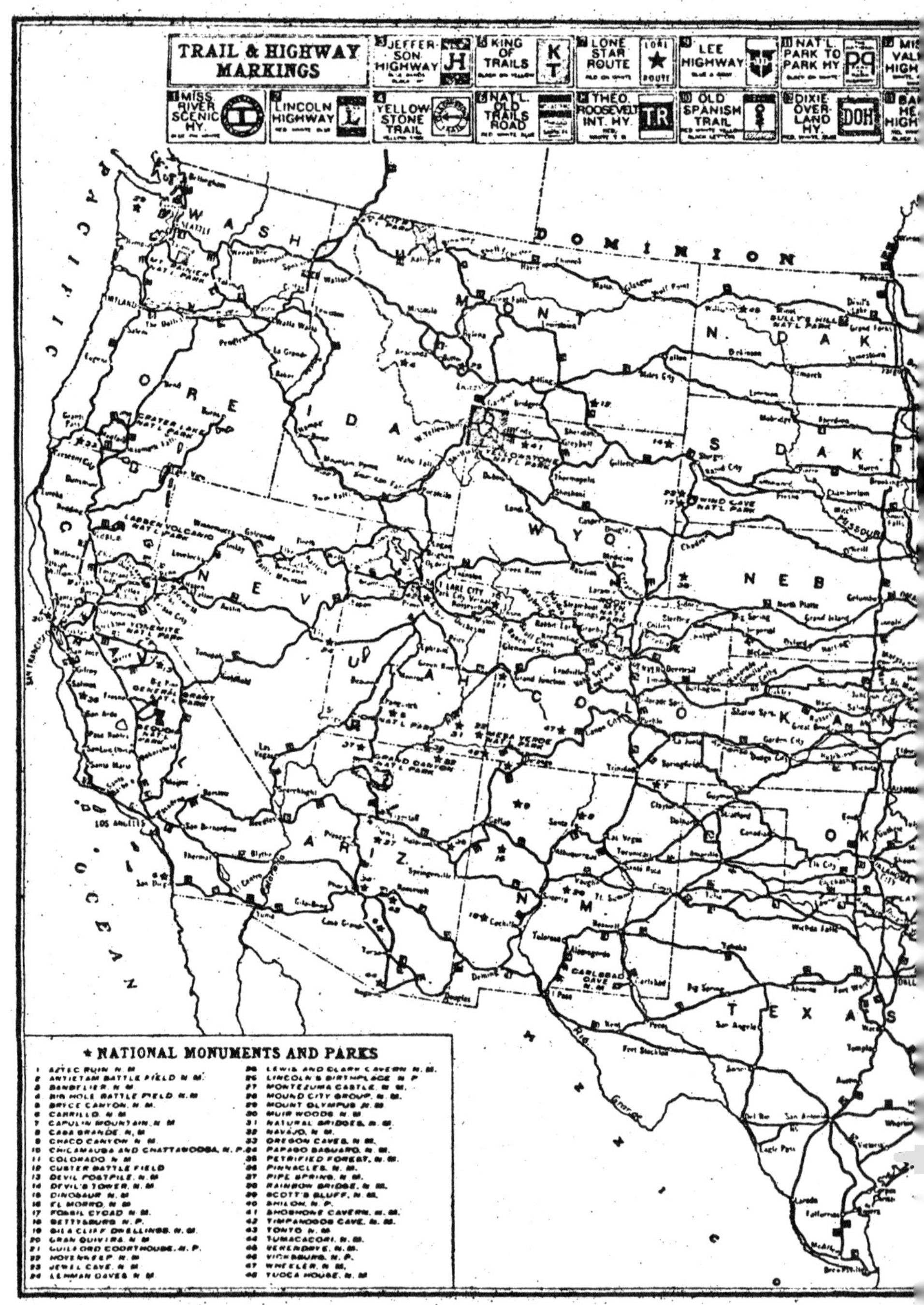

A brief description of the special characteristics of all National Parks and Monuments administer

eparlments of Interior, War and Agriculture will be found on pages 4 to 7 inclusive.

ISBN: 0-9671882-0-2

Library of Congress Number: 99-90537

Seegar
Company

2865 113th Avenue N.W.
Coon Rapids, MN 55433

Printed in the United States of America by
Palmer Publications, Inc.
318 North Main Street
Amherst, WI 54406

Dedication

*Dedicated to the memory of Elliott Nystrom, my
Ford Tramp partner who made this book possible,
and to the memory of my wife Ruth and our
daughter Jennett Hoff, who urged me to write it.*

Table of Contents

Acknowledgements

Gratefully acknowledged is the cooperation of others in preparation of this book, including my daughters Jean Cross and Doris Wattman, my son Seegar Swanson, Jr., Marian Wattman Oshima, Clarence Cross, Jane and Clarence Cross, Jr., David and Mary Blink, David Cross, Timothy Cross and Rick Wattman.

Preface

Seegar Swanson and Elliott Nystrom were friends from elementary grade school through and beyond their graduation from Ashland High School in 1922. They obtained employment immediately after graduation. They were both first generation Americans of Scandinavian descent.

Ashland is a port city located on Lake Superior in northern Wisconsin. Iron ore and coal docks as well as a blast furnace were located there. The city also had saw mills, a paper mill, an iron works factory, other small industries and was a railroad center. Many of their classmates attended Northland College in Ashland and other colleges and universities.

The two heroes of this book appreciated having jobs but gave them up and postponed attending college to make an adventurous trip. They were undecided about life and sought an opportunity to broaden their viewpoints.

They came up with the idea of buying a car and traveling around the perimeter of the then 48 United States of America. Elliott talked it over with some of his neighborhood friends who thought it was a great scheme but decided not to go along. Only Elliott and Seegar had the courage to make the undertaking.

They began preparing for the trip in the spring of 1924. In mid-summer they found a for sale ad for a used 1919 Model T Ford touring car in Duluth. Because neither could drive, they recruited Seegar's older cousin Olaf Olson of Mason to take the train to Duluth and check out the car. After its purchase, Olaf drove the three of them back to Ashland.

Duluth is about 75 miles west of Ashland, which was a long trip in those days. Seldom had either of the future country wide tourists been more than 30 miles from home. Most of the author's traveling had been done by bicycle or freight train. It was a three hour bike ride to his uncle's farm at Mason. His father worked for the railroad, enabling his son to take a train to go fishing or berry picking.

Unlike young people of today, the pair had no urge to use their new purchase before they started on the long journey. The car sat in front of the Swanson house except when it was at the garage being checked and modified for the tour. The author drove just enough to teach himself how to drive.

The day the trip was to begin, Elliott, suitcase in hand, walked six and a half blocks to Seegar's house rather than being picked up at his own. He had all he needed for a year's journey.

There was no requirement for a drivers license at this time. Elliott didn't even try to drive until after they were on their trip. Wisconsin and some other states had begun numbering highways but the numbering of Federal routes wasn't started until 1926. Instead, longer routes were given names, like the Lincoln Highway or the Yellowstone Trail.

Crude route maps were available at service stations which served for the start of the trip. The first edition of the Rand McNally & Company road atlas was prepared for the S.S. Kresge Company and copyrighted in 1924. Entitled *Official Automobile Road Maps of the United States,* a copy was obtained somewhere en route and used to guide the remainder of the trip. A reproduction of the only known first edition copy was furnished for this book by THE NEWBERRY LIBRARY, Chicago, Illinois.

During this time frame, almost all roads were built and maintained by local government jurisdictions i.e. towns, cities, villages and counties. The quality varied from jurisdiction to jurisdiction. Bridges were expensive so river crossings were often by ferry boat or driving through a shallow spot. These travelers selected a route through central Alabama, Mississippi and Louisiana, well inland from the Gulf of Mexico, on advice that river crossings were difficult near the coast.

Motels were nonexistent at this time. However, motor car

touring had grown in popularity to the extent that many communities encouraged tourism by providing parks for overnight camping.

There was no way to lock this open-sided car. Packed with their gear and food, it often was left standing on public streets, in tourist camps, in school yards and open fields. Sometimes neighboring campers were hungry and hard pressed. Yet, never was anything stolen.

After completing their ten month circle tour of the United States, neither Seegar nor Elliott drove the car much. They did feature it in the Northland College homecoming parade that fall.

They never obtained a Wisconsin title or license for the car. When their Florida plates expired December 31, they chose to give the car away for parts rather than keep it unlicensed.

Most of the photographs in this book came from an album the author has treasured for 75 years. They are faded two by three inch contact prints. In a few cases, the original negatives were available. The back home photo was professionally taken by C. W. Pfefferkorn of Pfefferkorn Studios and was reproduced on a picture post card and published in the *Milwaukee Journal* and the *Superior Evening Telegram*.

Following the adventure, the author spent four years at Northland College, working his way through as a newspaperman. He continued his journalism career to his retirement at age 72. He moved from Ashland to Superior in 1936 to become editor of the *Superior Evening Telegram* and later worked in the newsroom of the *Duluth News-Tribune*. He started writing this book at age 90 and spent three years perfecting the manuscript.

His wanderlust spirit remains. At 94 he and I made a motor car trip up the Alcan highway and toured Alaska. He still is traveling to this day.

Seegar Swanson, Jr.
July 4, 1999

Chapter I
A Shaky Start

THE AFTERNOON of September 20 was placidly sunny and warm, the clear blue sky dotted with fleecy white clouds. We, however, were filled with excitement and anticipation as a sizable crowd of neighbors waited expectantly in front of my home in Ashland, Wisconsin. They had gathered to give us a hearty send-off for what we hoped would be a happy-go-lucky year's tour around the United States in a secondhand 1919 Model T Ford, working at odd jobs as we traveled.

Nowadays such a journey would lift few eyebrows, but in the mid-1920s, cars, roads, a sluggish economy, and conditions in general being what they were, it was a different matter. Our departure was front-page news in the *Ashland Daily Press*.

It all began early in June when Elliott Nystrom, my close friend and classmate throughout elementary and high school days, suggested we buy a car and take a year off to explore the country, touching each corner state: Maine, Florida, California, and Washington.

"We can easily find jobs to pay expenses," Elliott assured me. He raised his voice to emphasize the point.

The suggestion, of course, hit me like the proverbial bolt out of the blue. It was fantastic, I thought. After thinking it over, however, I was skeptical, doubting feasibility of the idea. After all, I reasoned, the year was 1924. True, we were in the midst of what was supposed to be the "Roaring 20s." Yet the economy was anything but roaring. It was, in fact, in a slump, a letdown from the boom period of World War I. I debated, was this an appropriate time to set forth on a trip as extensive as this? My early skepticism soon vanished, however, but it was echoed by friends around town. Our parents, on the other hand, said nothing to discourage our dream.

E.P. Christensen, general secretary of the YMCA, questioned whether Elliott should give up his position at the Ashland National Bank, with its promise of a future banking career. Others stressed the nationwide scarcity of jobs, the bleak prospect of working our way around the country during a presidential election year.

The consensus was we would return to Ashland within a month. Oscar King, managing secretary of the Ashland Chamber of Commerce, for whom I had worked as office assistant, was more optimistic. He gave us six weeks!

As might be expected, Elliott and I discussed these predictions. With a determined look, Elliott exploded, "Six weeks! They'll never see us *that* soon! We'll either make it around the country, or we won't come home for at least a year!"

By now, we were well into plans for our adventure. First we had to earn money to buy a secondhand car, and have enough left over to begin our journey. We had the summer months to do this, and knew September weather still would be warm enough to start traveling.

Elliott went on working at the bank. I had just finished my first year at Northland College, and rather than continue part-time secretarial employment at the Chamber of Commerce, decided on manual labor to gain weight and to get more physically fit.

For three months I worked on the Frank Shefchik farm in the Marengo Valley. I helped harvest peas for the Marengo pea cannery, mowed and stacked many tons of hay, spread fertilizer over fields to be cultivated, and performed invigorating chores. By late August, I was pleased my weight had climbed to 142 pounds, my muscles had hardened, and that I felt stronger than ever.

Not so with Elliott. His work required little physical effort. He didn't gain a pound and remained as lean as ever, weighing only 130 pounds.

During the summer we accumulated sufficient money to begin negotiations for a car. Our fund received an unexpected boost of $48 when we were hired to sell tickets at the Ashland County Fair. This, we figured, was a bonanza.

Unable in Ashland to find a suitable car at an affordable price, we finally bought the Ford touring car advertised by its owner in Duluth, Minnesota. The cost was $125. The seller assured us it was in excellent running condition, pointing out that this 1919 Model T had a self-starter and a foot accelerator, introduced that year by Henry Ford.

He grinned. "No more cranking," he said.

We soon discovered, however, that the Ford had some short-comings. Trial runs by friends who knew more about cars and driving than we did, convinced us considerable overhauling was necessary. That made quite a dent in our limited resources.

The author worked for money and muscles doing farm work, including operating a hay mower.

Most disturbing was the need to tighten connecting rods on several occasions. We suspected the repairing overlooked other faults too, but at the time had no way of knowing what they might be. With so many problems, I wondered if this Ford could take us to the four corners of the United States.

We finally drove off at 2:40 P.M. the scheduled day of our leaving, with slightly more than $100 cash and provisions for a week. The neighbors waved and shouted good-byes, only to show dismay when the Ford stalled twice a few yards away.

"Wouldn't you know," Elliott groaned as he waved back at the crowd. "Here comes our pal Bill Lynch. Bet he's going to give us the business."

"Hey, you guys," chortled Bill, "how far do you think you'll get with this heap of junk?" He patted the Ford, and grinningly leaned toward us in the front seat.

I knew, of course, he was joshing. It was his Irish way of cheering us on. But inwardly, I felt he was putting into words what I had wondered about. Elliott, however, had expressed no doubts about the Ford's capability of getting us around the country, but it seemed to me he now also was beginning to wonder.

Chagrined when the car stalled, I wasn't sure whether the car was behaving like a stubborn mule, or if my inexperienced driving should be blamed for the Ford's stalling. I was thankful, though, for the self-starter. It saved Elliott or me the embarrassment of getting out to crank the motor.

Finally under way, we passed Ashland High School where we believed we had spent the happiest days of our young lives. As we drove past the Northland College campus at the edge of town, I had a momentary feeling I should be enrolling for the fall semester instead of embarking on an unpredictable tour around the country.

We intended to drive south on State Highway 13 through the center of Wisconsin, roughly 450 miles, and then to head eastward for Maine. This, we knew, was contrary to most advice offered by our friends. The logical thing would be to go west, they said, and not until the coming spring. Winter soon would hit the mountains, they cautioned.

Although the temperature still retained its summer warmth, leaves already displayed hints of autumn colors as soon as we passed the farm lands of the Marengo Valley. In the valley I looked in the direction of the Shefchik farm, recalling the summer days I had worked there to earn some of the money that put the Ford on the road.

About eight miles from Mellen, the car refused to climb in high gear to the top of a long hill. After it stopped, I realized I should have stepped on the low gear pedal, according to the rules of operation laid down by the originator of the car, Henry Ford. Another driving lesson had come the hard way.

While we drove on admiring the northern Wisconsin hardwoods, I apprehensively spoke about possible tornadoes we might encounter on our trip.

Elliott scoffed at the idea. "Why worry about that now?" he asked. "We aren't in tornado country yet."

He was right, I thought. There was no immediate cause for concern. We had a long way to go.

As we approached the Glidden-Butternut area, we anticipated the novelty of seeing the world's largest broom-handle factory.

"We're starting out big," Elliott said.

By early evening we arrived at Marion Park just outside of Glidden. The park was attractive, an alluring grove of hardwoods centered with a spacious pavilion. We were tempted to camp there for our first night out.

"But we've traveled only 50 miles," Elliott protested. "We ought to drive a bit farther."

I was hungry, however, so Elliott finally decided a few more miles wouldn't make that much difference. We parked the Ford by a tall maple near the edge of the park, and ate our first outdoor meal of potted meat sandwiches and sweet rolls.

"This is the life," Elliott said. He sat contentedly on a log strumming a ukulele. His deep bass voice harmonized with the peaceful surroundings while he sang "In the Good Old Summer Time," "There's a Long, Long Trail," and "Carry Me Back to Old Virginny." I hummed the familiar melodies in my own peculiar way.

For an evening stroll we visited downtown Glidden and, with darkness fast approaching, returned to the park to roll out blankets for our first night's sleep.

"I'm glad we don't have to pitch a tent," Elliott said. "Thank goodness we can sleep in the Ford."

Sleeping in the car was possible because, at a cost of six dollars, an auto mechanic in Ashland ingeniously had contrived a bed in the car. He sawed through the ends of the front seat, and hinged the seat so its cushioned backrest could be lowered against the rear seat cushion. In the morning the backrest could be raised to its normal position, to be held in place by hooks at both ends.

When I suggested we might feel cramped curling up on the cushions night after night, Elliott promptly solved the problem.

"If we put our suitcases on the floor ahead of the front seat, we'll have plenty of room to stretch out," he said.

Elliott, a trifle over six feet tall, needed leg room. So we decided he should sleep on the right side of our outdoor Pullman. Two inches shorter, I would have less trouble coping with the steering wheel.

As the Romans would say, *Ah, Morpheus!*

Our initial night's sleep was interrupted about 5 A.M. "It's raining," Elliott said. "Water's coming through the side of the car."

He got out of the Ford and groped in the dark for side curtains stored under our bed, struggling to fasten them to his side of the car. I did the same on my side. We were glad to have the side curtains, made with heavy rubber-coated auto cloth, and equipped with Celluloid windows for visibility during daytime driving. Since our Ford was a touring model, not a sedan, its sides were open and needed side curtains to keep out rain and other weather disturbances. Chilled and wet from our inexperienced maneuvering, we eventually crawled back under our blankets. The soothing patter of raindrops on top of the car soon lulled us to sleep. When we arose shortly after 10 o'clock, rain still fell and increased in intensity throughout most of the day.

"No use traveling," Elliott said. He shrugged his shoulders, resigned to the hopelessness of the weather.

We spent much of the day in the car, speculating about travel plans. We hiked to a Glidden confectionery where we splurged 30 cents for two dishes of ice cream.

Shortly after we retired for the night, rain suddenly slashed against the side curtains. The wind gusted so violently it seemed as if the curtains would rip off and blow away. We heard a steady roar through the tree tops and the crackle of dead branches hurled along the pathways.

All in all, this was hardly a night to be wandering around, we agreed. We felt safe in the car, though. Elliott said the next morning he heard two trees crash to the ground, but I had dozed off, comforted by the thought we weren't yet in tornado country.

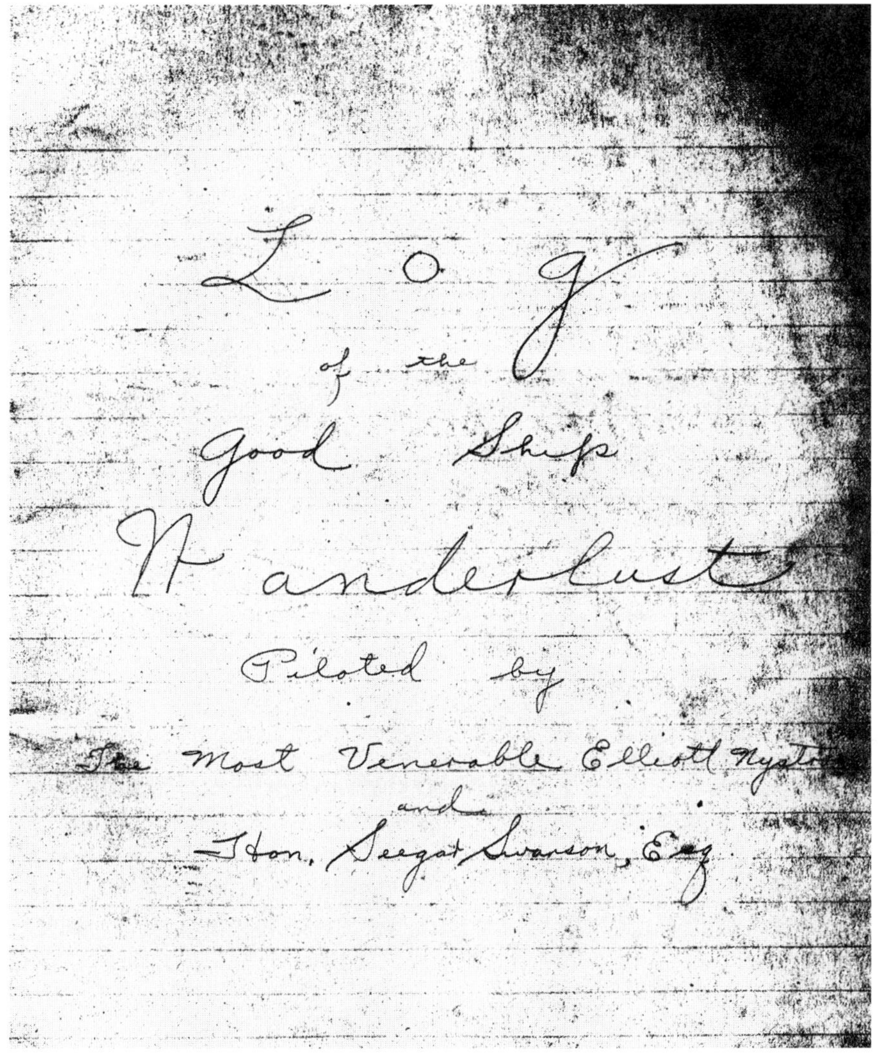

Log of the Good Ship Wanderlust.

Monday morning we left Glidden under clearing skies, only to be annoyed by loud knocks in the Ford's engine. I suspected they were caused by loose connecting rods, but had no idea why they should be loose. Three miles beyond

ASHLAND DAILY PRESS

A NEWSPAPER DEVOTED TO THE INTERESTS OF NORTH WISCONSIN, THE FOUR-SEASONS TOURIST PLAYGROUND.

THE WEATHER

Strong west winds. Northwest winds tonight diminishing. Generally fair tonight and Tuesday.—Donnell.

Maximum 60 above
Minimum 42 above

ASHLAND, WISCONSIN, MONDAY SEPTEMBER 22, 1924

42 LIVES LOST IN STORMS

Death List Remains at Six; More Are Injured

MCKINNON, MAKI FARMS, ALSO STRUCK

Mrs. Jacob Holma, Unconscious Since Cyclone Struck Hill Farm, Killing Other Four People Outright, is at General Hospital But is Not Expected to Live.—Storm Played Gruesome Tricks.

The death list in the Marengo valley cyclone remained at six this afternoon, though officials at the Ashland General hospital held slight hope for Mrs. Jacob Holma, unconscious since the Hill farm was struck, and suffering multiple injuries.

TWO ASHLAND BOYS WILL SEE AMERICA FIRST

"See America First" has become the motto of two local boys, who left Saturday morning for an extended tour to the four corners of the United States. The two boys are Elliott Nystrom, formerly employed at the Ashland National Bank, and Seegar Swanson, formerly connected with the Chamber of Commerce.

No definite itinerary has been established, but the two young men expect to direct their course to the eastern states first, and will probably winter in Florida.

The trip will be made in an antiquated Ford touring car, so arranged that sleeping at night may be done in the car itself.

The total resources of the two youths aggregate slightly more than $100, and provisions for a week. The young travelers hope to keep in funds by securing employment while enroute.

Under the circumstances, it is believed that the trip will extend over a period of six months or a year.

Ashland Daily Press considered the Seegar Swanson – Elliott Nystrom tour front page news. "Ford Tramps" was the title given the pair by John B.Chapple, city editor of the paper. Progress of the trip appeared periodically when letters written by the author to Oscar King his former employer found their way to the paper.

Butternut the car's engine smoked like a smoldering fire. That explained the loose connecting rods. The Ford was low on oil. Elliott hiked back to Butternut to purchase two quarts.

We drove slowly to Park Falls, further frustrated when we had to buy a three-inch tire to replace the badly worn one on the left front side. We parted with $6.65.

In Park Falls we stopped in a tourist camp where there was free wood, water and an outdoor stove for cooking meals. Here I removed the pan under the Ford's engine to tighten the first three rods, but lacked a tool to get at the fourth. I was only guessing. My previous experience with tightening connecting rods was watching others do it.

Despite the Ford's problems, we already had developed a feeling of affection for our car. We were depending upon it to get us from state to state. It was an integral part of a U.S. touring team: Elliott, the Ford, and I. We held to the prevailing philosophy that with some baling wire and a bit of tinkering the Ford would get us there.

Elliott said the car deserved a name. I thought so, too. We named it Wanderlust.

In Park Falls we decided to record our daily adventures. With a Tom Sawyer flourish, we each titled our record books, "Log of the Good Ship Wanderlust," designating ourselves as pilots.

Elliott said we ought to keep track of expenses, too. As a banker, he kept close tab of our daily cash flow, but left the book work to me. My first entry was:

> 5 gallons gasoline, $.85

The night in Park Falls was cold. Frost, and the brilliant hues of the leaves, were reminders autumn had arrived.

Elliott said, "We'd better be on our way. Winter will be here before we know it."

By the time we reached nearby Phillips, the Ford's motor acted up again. In my log I wrote that the noise "sounded like a village blacksmith shop with hammers pounding its anvils with terrific force." We steered directly to the nearest garage.

After tightening the connecting rods, including the fourth one requiring a special tool, the garage mechanic sympathetically said, "I hate to tell you, boys, but there's a crack in the crankcase. That's where you're losing oil."

There was no way to seal the crack, he told us. "You will have to get a new crankcase," he said. He thumbed through a book to quote us a price. Detecting our looks of dismay, the mechanic consoled us.

"You don't have to get a new crankcase right away," he said. "You can add a quart of oil every time you buy five gallons of gas. That way the oil won't drip too low." With that, we decided to move on. Better that a new crankcase be purchased later, "whenever we earn the money to pay for it," Elliott said.

As we were leaving the garage, Elliott spotted a copy of the *Ashland Daily Press* lying on a counter. "Look," he exclaimed, pointing at glaring headlines.

Amazed, we read that 6 persons were killed and 11 injured, one critically, and scores of buildings were leveled by a cyclone which ripped through the Marengo Valley on Sunday. Among the places hit was the Shefchik farm where I had recently worked. The statewide death toll during scattered weekend tornadoes and violent windstorms, most within 50 to 100 miles of our Glidden campsite, was reported as 46.

We stood speechless. "It seems only a few hours since we were in the Marengo Valley," Elliott said.

We both realized it was only 30 miles or so from Marion Park where we awoke at 5 a.m. to rain the first night and were pelted by wind and rain the second night.

— The Log, October 2, 1924

Chapter II
Big City Driving

UNLIKE MODERN freeway motorists, we didn't zip
through Wisconsin's captivating scenery, nor by-pass
towns and cities. This wasn't a matter of choice, though. The
Good Ship Wanderlust couldn't travel much faster than 25
miles per hour.

Turning onto State Highway 64, we planned to visit Elliott's
sister Helen in Wausau. Up to this time, I had done all the
driving, not expertly, but well enough to get us out of our
home county. Elliott now made his first attempt to drive a car.
I told him he did very well.

By observing me at the wheel, Elliott had familiarized
himself with all the essential gadgets, the starter button on the
floor, the hand lever, three foot pedals, and the foot accelerator.

Requiring three manipulations, the clutch pedal at the left

was quite complicated for a beginner, but Elliott quickly got the knack of it. He was aware that when this pedal was pressed halfway forward the driving mechanism was in neutral, was in low gear when the pedal was pushed to the floor, and in high gear when released. He knew the hand lever had to be pushed forward once the car was in low or high gear, and that the reverse pedal was in the center and the brake pedal at the right.

Before long we had our first difficulty with poor roads, one of the obstacles of which our skeptics back home had warned us. For fully two miles I drove the car in low gear, trying desperately to hold it in a zigzag rut, up to the hub caps in soggy mud. The Ford became hectic, inching forward by jerks.

Once out of the mud, we had to stop every few miles. If the exhaust pipe didn't come loose, something else did. The engine hit on three cylinders, and the radiator overflow pipe came in noisy contact with the fan. To top it all, the right front tire blew out.

By late afternoon we reached Wausau. There we drove into a beautiful and spacious park to camp for the night. Hungry for a cooked meal, we hiked downtown to purchase necessary kitchenware, kettles, a coffeepot, a galvanized pail, and a few smaller utensils.

Returning to camp, we started a fire in a grill to cook supper. As shifting smoke forced us to move from one side of the grill to the other, a young couple from Shelbyville, Indiana, Mr. and Mrs. Russell Ray, came over.

Mrs. Ray swished an arm to brush aside a puff of smoke. "What you need is a camp stove," she said.

Her husband rubbed his eyes. Waving his broad-brimmed hat, he, too, whiffed a puff of smoke. "We're going to quit

A page from the Ford operation manual. (opposite)

THE CAR AND ITS OPERATION

How do the Foot Pedals operate?

Answer No. 10

The first one toward the left operates the clutch. When pressed forward the clutch pedal engages the low speed. When half-way forward the clutch is in neutral (i. e., disconnected from the driving mechanism of the rear wheels), and the releasing of this pedal engages the high-speed clutch. The center pedal operates the reverse. The right-hand pedal operates the transmission brake.

How is the Car started?

Answer No. 11

Slightly accelerate the engine by opening the throttle, press the clutch pedal half way forward, thereby holding the clutch in a neutral position while throwing the hand lever forward; then press the pedal forward into slow speed and when under sufficient headway (20 to 30 feet), allow the pedal to drop back slowly into high speed, at the same time partially closing the throttle, which will allow the engine to pick up its load easily. With a little practice, the change of speeds will be easily accomplished, and without any appreciable effect on the smooth running of the machine.

How is the Car stopped?

Answer No. 12

Partially close the throttle, release the high speed by pressing the clutch pedal forward into neutral; apply the foot brake slowly but firmly until the car comes to a dead stop. Do not remove foot from the clutch pedal without first pulling the hand lever back to neutral position, or the engine will stall. To stop the motor, open the throttle a trifle to accelerate the motor and then throw off the switch. The engine will then stop with the cylinders full of explosive gas, which will naturally facilitate starting.

Endeavor to so familiarize yourself with the operation of the car that to disengage the clutch and apply the brake becomes practically automatic—the natural thing to do in case of emergency.

How is the Car reversed?

Answer No. 13

It must be brought to a dead stop. With the engine running, disengage the clutch with the hand lever and press the reverse pedal forward with the left foot, the right foot being free to use on the brake pedal if needed. Do not bring the hand lever back too far or you will set the brakes on the rear wheels. Experienced drivers ordinarily reverse the car by simply holding the clutch pedal in neutral with the left foot, and operating the reverse pedal with the right.

How is the Spark controlled?

Answer No. 14

By the left-hand lever under the steering wheel. Good operators drive with the spark lever advanced just as far as the engine will permit. However, advancing the spark too far will cause a dull knock in the motor, due to the fact that the explosion occurs too early. The spark should only be retarded when the engine slows down on a heavy road or steep grade, but care should be exercised not to retard the spark too far as this will result in late ignition, which causes loss of power and overheating of the motor and may also result in warped, burned or cracked valves. Learn to operate the spark as the occasion demands. The greatest economy in gasoline consumption is obtained by driving with the spark advanced sufficiently to obtain the maximum speed.

How is speed of Car controlled?

Answer No. 15

The different speeds required to meet road conditions are obtained by opening or closing the throttle. Practically all the running speeds needed for ordinary travel are obtained on high gear, and it is seldom necessary to use the low gear except to give the car momentum in starting. The speed of the car may be temporarily slackened in driving through crowded traffic, turning corners, etc., by "slipping the clutch," i. e., pressing the clutch pedal forward into neutrral. When doing this the throttle lever should be nearly closed.

camping," he said. "Would you like to buy our stove?"

To our elated surprise, the couple offered us their portable Coleman camp stove, almost new, for $2.50. Certain such a stove would cost considerably more in a sporting-goods store, we bought it. At a ridiculously low price of 25 cents, the couple generously tossed in additional camp supplies, including a can opener.

After several futile attempts to contact Elliott's sister, we concluded she was out of town. We explored Wausau's famed Rib Mountain, and enjoyed the hilly countryside surrounding the city. We noted that trees in the area still were green, untouched by early autumn frost. We moved on, glad there would be more summer weather ahead.

A few miles south of Marshfield the Ford rebelled again, hitting on three cylinders. We stopped at a roadside garage for gasoline and oil, and asked the mechanic to adjust the miss in the car's engine.

Lifting the hood, he detected nothing wrong. He next looked under the dashboard. Here he pushed down one of four coil boxes which had crept slightly upward in the compartment containing the boxes. He started the engine. Instantly it "hit on all four." The entire procedure took about two minutes. I made an entry in our expense book:

Mechanic's time, $.10

We felt the dime was well spent. Now we knew one more place to look should the Ford fail to hit on all its four cylinders. No one had told us what a key element those coil boxes were for operation of the car.

Now that we were out of the wooded region of Upper Wisconsin, but still driving through comparatively small cities, we realized we were getting closer to Chicago, the nation's second largest city. With our limited driving experience, and the unpredictable antics of the Ford, we felt concern about driving through the metropolitan city. Elliott said he would delay learning to drive to give me more practice in handling the car.

Stopping for the night at a campsite adjoining the schoolhouse in Friendship, we had a touch of homesickness. Watching students entering the school building early in the morning, I suddenly felt a pang. Recalling my own school days, I again had the notion that I, too, should be starting a new school year back home.

The feeling of homesickness intensified when the school janitor came over to talk with us. We were flattered when the school principal called upon us. The schoolmen eyed the pancakes frying on a stove provided for campers. Elliott later said the two men seemed to envy us, free to travel without everyday concerns.

Maybe we should envy them, I thought.

The Ford purred smoothly that morning. We reached Wisconsin Dells well before noon. Here was our first opportunity to tour a world famous wonderland, right in our home state. For more than an hour we motored in and about the city of perhaps 1,500 inhabitants. This, we perceived, was a community thriving on tourism, its atmosphere being distinctly different. The city, however, wasn't the main attraction.

Parking the Ford against a curb in downtown Wisconsin Dells, we boarded a nearby river boat together with about 20 other passengers. Most preferred the upper deck to get better views and to relax in the warm afternoon sun. So did we.

When the craft had pulled away from the boat landing, a guide told us we were embarking on a remarkable journey through the deep narrows of the Wisconsin River, an area of great historical interest. In this region, he said, Indians, fur traders, and loggers had left their marks.

As the trip progressed, the guide fed us more bits of information, adding significance to the marvelous sights we beheld.

Our cruise took us through the brownish waters of the Upper Dells, a distance of roughly five miles. The fantastic contours of water-eroded and weather-beaten rocks impressed us immensely. Chimney Rock and Black Hawk's Head were among the first of nature's handiwork to draw our attention. Our guide explained that Black Hawk Rock derived its name from a face etched on the wall of the cliff. The face resembled that of Chief Black Hawk, captured by Indians of the Dells region, he said. Chief Black Hawk had been in hiding after the defeat of his tribe along the Mississippi River in 1832.

The boat made the first of three stops at Cold Water Canyon. The passengers got off to hike up a narrow gorge, its steep sides flanked by tall straight trees reaching for the sky. The gorge was delightfully cool, and the air we breathed was fragrant with the scent of ferns and flowers. The Devil's Bath Tub, one of the sights we viewed, must have held allure for serpents. Startled, a woman screamed, "It's a snake!"

Picking up a broken tree branch, the guide rushed toward the Bath Tub. Quickly he allayed the woman's fright. He swung the branch forcefully, killing the reptile.

"It's a blue racer," he said. "He's harmless."

Apparently, the time hadn't yet arrived when guides or park rangers, rather than kill a snake, poisonous or not, would prod him into a bag to be released in some remote area to continue his role in the balance of nature.

"Are there rattlesnakes around here?" a woman fearfully asked.

"Not in this gorge. It's too cold," the guide responded.

"There are a few back of the cliffs where it's warmer." He paused, then added a reassuring thought. "I've never heard of anyone getting bit by one."

On the way upstream, our guide pointed out more sculptured wonders, notably Alligator's Head and Steamboat Rock. At Witches Gulch the boat made its second stop. Here again the passengers disembarked to walk up a gorge similar to Cold Water Canyon, except that in places it was narrower, scarcely two feet wide, a tight squeeze for stoutly-built hikers. Like Cold Water Canyon, the gulch was pleasantly cool.

We now were at the headwaters of the Dells where the river widened substantially and was devoid of rapids. As the boat chugged toward the western bank of the stream, our guide briefed us on the logging activities that glamorized the Dells around the turn of the century.

Having grown up in a part of Wisconsin which long had buzzed with the sound of sawmills, some still operating, Elliott and I listened with rapt attention. I also was intrigued because during two summer vacations I had peeled cedar bark at a White River logging camp near Ashland, and caught edgings in the Odanah sawmill on the Bad River Indian Reservation.

Our guide described the narrows of the Dells as a dangerous bottleneck for loggers. He said huge rafts of logs which had been floated down the Wisconsin River were held in the wide waters we were facing. Loggers split the large rafts into smaller ones, the guide said, so lumberjacks could steer them through the narrows. It was hazardous work, he stressed, with rafts colliding with rocks, logs churning in the rapids, and men drowning. Particularly ominous was Devil's Elbow, bent, extremely narrow, and filled with swirling water.

As if the struggles through the narrows weren't enough, the loggers, weighed down by heavy caulked boots, had to hike back to the headwaters to bring down more rafts. When enough had accumulated, they were reassembled so the logs could continue drifting with the slower flowing stream below the dells, our guide said.

We noticed a couple, the young man a blond, and the girl a brunette, seated on a bench, oblivious to the passengers and the enchanting scenery. Exchanging frequent amorous glances, the couple cuddled and smooched.

"Newlyweds," our guide said, lowering his voice. "Honeymooners," he added, with a knowing wink.

On the western shore of the river, the boat made its third stop. With cameras clicking all about, we were amazed by the rigid stance of Stand Rock, "the most photographed formation in the Dells," the guide said.

What we gazed at was a wide circular sandstone table top held nearly 50 feet above ground by a slender, but sturdy, pillar of rock. Separating the table top from an overhanging cliff was a gap of five and a half feet. We regretted this wasn't a day we would see a man or dog daringly leap from the cliff to the table top, "but they do it," our guide said.

He lavishly lauded the Palisades, next on the trip agenda, and pointed out more spectacular sights as the boat continued downstream on its return to the landing dock. We stored these in our memory banks, but knew we would have difficulty recalling them in chronological order.

Little imagination was required to know all were named appropriately. Noteworthy were such self-evident spectacles as the Demon's Anvil, Luncheon Hall, Visor Ledge, Toadstool Rock, Hornet's Nest, Giant's Shield, Navy Yard, and Swallows' Nest, diminutive caves on sandstone cliffs, pecked by beaks of the birds.

We wondered, "Who did the naming?" Did some individual

jot the names in a notebook while making a cruise for that purpose? Or did the names gradually evolve, in folklore fashion, with many persons recognizing the obvious similarities to well-known persons or things, handing them down for others to corroborate and pass on?

The boat docked at four o'clock. We felt richly rewarded by the three hour tour. For just a dollar and a half each, we had the benefit of all that scenic, geological, and historic education. For this I could thank Elliott. Although he never had been there, he was a one-man Chamber of Commerce, extolling the Dells of Wisconsin ever since we left Ashland.

South of Wisconsin Dells we drove close to the Baraboo area, home of the celebrated Ringling Brothers Circus. I recalled the one and only appearance the circus made in Ashland during my boyhood days. I remembered the throngs that gathered to watch the dazzling parade. The heavy wagons conveying bands, show people, lions, tigers and many other jungle animals, made such deep ruts and otherwise damaged Ashland's unpaved main street, that the city fathers deemed it unwise to allow the Ringling Brothers future return engage-ments. This suited taxpayers, but didn't please circus lovers.

The days were getting shorter. By "stepping on the gas" we reached Madison, the imposing state capital of Wisconsin. As darkness enveloped the city, we cruised about the well-lighted

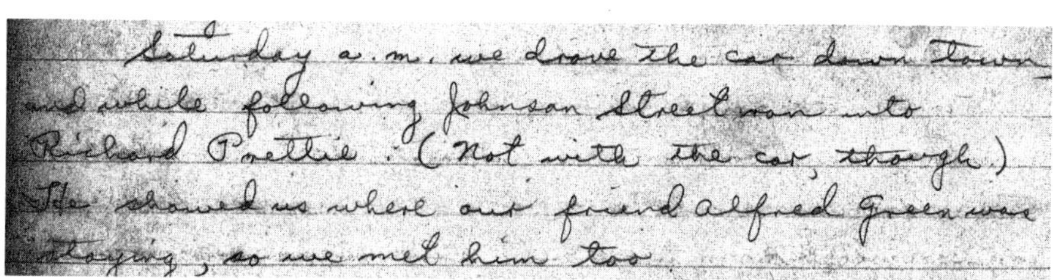

From the Log.

streets. Encountering three friends from Ashland, we obtained directions to Madison's tourist camp.

Next morning, after refreshing ourselves with showers and shaves in Madison's YMCA, we roamed the streets again, happy to run into three more hometown friends. (Not with the car, though, I noted in my log.) All were enrolled at the University of Wisconsin, and were anxious to show us through campus buildings where they attended classes.

We devoted the afternoon, a rainy one, to a tour of the state capitol, completed just seven years earlier, replacing the previous capitol, damaged by fire. The building, with its magnificent dome, was a scaled down model of the nation's Capitol, we were told, giving us a preview of what we would see in Washington, D.C., if we ever got there.

Inside, we joined a guided tour, which gave us a better understanding of our state government. The guide escorted us into the four wings of the capitol utilized by the governor, the state supreme court, the senate, and the assembly.

He explained that most of the interior's imposing marble and granite was quarried in European countries, ranging from Norway in the north to Italy in the south. Granite from Vermont was used for the capitol's exterior, he said. From the guide we learned the capitol's site was between two inland lakes, Mendota and Monona, and formed the hub for streets radiating from it, many named after signers of the United States Constitution.

Elliott and I roamed about on our own after the tour ended.

Elliott had a happy solution for the dreary evening. We attended a movie in the Strand Theater where *The Hunchback of Notre Dame* was featured.

Reluctant to leave Madison with all its appealing attractions, we spent the next morning walking up and down streets radiating from the capitol, concentrating on University Avenue. We met three more Ashland student friends there. Elliott remarked somewhat regretfully, "This probably will be the last time we'll see anyone from home."

It was one o'clock before we finally broke away from Madison. As we intermittently looked back, the capitol, with its enthralling dome, stared at us until we were well beyond the city limits. Madison, we reflected, had an air of elegance, endowed with both natural and man-made beauty in the midst of rolling hills and four exquisite lakes.

Chilled by the sudden coolness of a shifting wind, I stopped the car so we could get out our suitcases to put on more clothes. I reached for a jacket while Elliott slipped on a sweat-shirt, ruffling his blond hair. He quickly smoothed it as we hopped back into the car, and were on our way.

When I had opened my suitcase, I noticed a two-pound box of chocolates my sister Myrtle had given me before we left Ashland. Now would be a good time to sample the chocolates, I told Elliott.

Oh, oh, we left our suitcases standing on the highway, I suddenly remembered.

After pressing hard on the brake pedal, I hurriedly turned the Ford around, and bore down on the accelerator. We reached the suitcases in time to see a motorist putting them into his car. "I'm glad you returned to claim them. I didn't know how I would find the owners," he said.

By late afternoon we were pleased to reach the Wisconsin-Illinois border a few miles north of Harvard, happy because our home state was behind us and that now we really were on the way to untold adventures ahead.

In Harvard we had the feeling we were running out of the

free tourist camps generously provided by Wisconsin communities. We took the liberty of setting up camp in the Harvard city park. This drew quite a bit of attention.

"You going to sleep in this tin Lizzie?" an inquisitive onlooker asked as we unhooked the backrest of the Ford to form our bed. "A puff of wind will blow you clean out of the park," he added.

We weren't concerned about puffs of wind. We let the man know our Ford had stood its ground in Ashland County's tornado belt.

The next day we drove through busy, but contented-looking Illinois towns and small cities. We stopped at Woodstock, and learned about the Woodstock typewriter manufactured there. Our experience with typewriters was limited to Remingtons and Underwoods. We were surprised they had competition.

Traffic increased noticeably and moved faster as we drew closer to Chicago. Rather than plunge into difficult driving conditions, we parked the Ford on Dempster Street a couple of blocks from the business district of Evanston, and hiked there to get our bearings. We learned the two of us could ride the elevated railway line into Chicago for a one-way fare of 25 cents.

"That settles it," Elliott said. "Let's leave the car in Evanston and take the elevated into Chicago tomorrow morning."

After lunch in an Evanston restaurant, we spent most of the afternoon wandering about the Northwestern University campus, watching students and faculty members going in and out of buildings, or walking along the pathways, carrying books and intently engaged in conversation. We also strolled through residential areas, impressed by the many beautifully-landscaped homes.

Emerging from a restaurant after a suppertime snack, we

approached a policeman to ask whether we could sleep in our Ford that night in the city park.

"Sure," he said, with a grin, "but the night patrol will come by. They'll wake you up."

The prospect of being aroused by suspicious police wasn't appealing, but when we returned to our car after dark we agreed to take a chance. We left the Ford where it was, and slept in it on Dempster Street, disturbed by some passing cars, but not by police.

Boarding the crowded elevated railway early the next morning, we soon were aware of the vastness of Chicago, with its population of more than two million. The maze of factories, warehouses, apartment houses, skyscrapers, cars and trucks zooming along a network of cluttered streets, seemed endless. We were surprised to learn that the first skyscraper did not originate in New York City as we supposed, but was built in Chicago during the 1880s.

Elliott said the best place to begin the day's tour would be the Field Museum of Natural History. We found it so absorbing we spent most of the morning viewing but a few of its countless exhibits. We noted their educational significance. The real thrill, though, was observing the dinosaur displays. We hated to leave, but realized days would be required to see and study all the museum offered.

Although our feet got tired, later we visited Chicago's famous Lincoln Park Zoo. Invigorated by the brisk wind off Lake Michigan, we then began an exploratory ramble in Chicago's Loop, so named, we learned, because the elevated railway forms a U-shaped curve around the area.

During the noon hour rush, our attention was drawn to an unending stream of pedestrians. As we saw them jostle through the crowded sidewalks, their scurrying pace seemed like the rush of children let out of school. Their faces tense and determined, the pedestrians bolted across intersections, anticipating the shrill blast of a policeman's whistle signaling a change in traffic.

We were watching human beings like ourselves, yet among the hundreds of faces, did not recognize one that resembled anyone we knew. How could so many people be so alike, but still so different?

As the afternoon wore on, we entered several of the Loop's large business establishments, and were awed by the vast amount of merchandise in the mammoth Marshall-Field and Company Department Store, window-shopped other huge stores on State Street, and visited the lobbies of several multi-storied hotels.

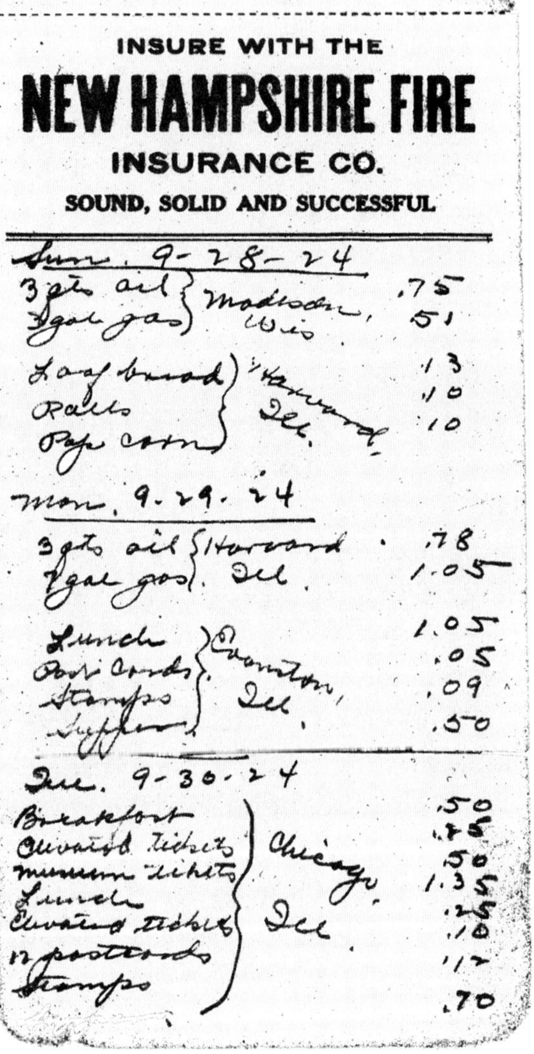

Page from Expense Book.

Gazing up at one of the tall hotels, we shuddered at the thought of having to descend the rickety-looking fire escape we saw extending from the top floor to the ground below.

Bewildered by the cars and trucks mysteriously finding their way in the Loop, we asked people if there were an easier way to drive a Ford through Chicago. No one seemed to know.

"I take the elevated," was the general response. Or, "I call a taxi."

Elliott queried a robust, intelligent-looking man who appeared knowledgeable about car driving.

"Don't get tangled up with all this traffic," he counseled. "Stay out of the Loop. Take Western Avenue," he said. "Just follow the streetcars. You won't get lost."

Satisfied with this advice, we continued our exploration of the Loop, ultimately ending up on Michigan Avenue. It was getting late, but in a final fling at culture, we breezed through the Art Institute of Chicago, then returned to the Loop to catch the elevated for Evanston. It was jammed with commuters.

We had experienced an enlightening and rewarding day, we thought. Entries in our expense book indicated how minimal the cost was:

> Breakfast $.50, elevated tickets $.50,
> museum tickets $.50, lunch $1.35, 12
> postcards $.10, 12 stamps for postcards $.12,
> supper $.70

As we walked toward the Ford parked on Dempster Street, we suddenly realized how odd and conspicuous it was, standing alone by the curb. Nothing had been disturbed though. Nevertheless, it had been our plan to move the car to a new spot, fearing that by now police were bound to question us.

But we were so tired we went to sleep without moving the Ford a foot. We doubted whether anyone ever had slept in camp-style so close to Evanston's main streets, except possibly in earlier years when Indians may have set up a wigwam in that vicinity.

Wakened by early morning traffic, we walked to an Evanston restaurant for breakfast, and then asked a police officer how we could reach Western Avenue to drive our Ford south through Chicago.

"Why don't you just go straight down Michigan Avenue?" the affable officer asked. "It's the shorter way to Indiana, and it will take you out of town without your having to worry about streetcars."

Elliott said we weren't sure whether the Ford could make it through all the traffic we had seen the day before.

"Get in the second lane from your right," the officer said, "and keep pace with the traffic. You don't have to turn right or left. It's only 25 miles along the lakeshore. You'll be in Indiana before you know it."

Elliott thanked the policeman for his help, but I expressed doubt as we proceeded toward Dempster Street.

I was dubious because on several occasions the Ford's engine had died when I took my foot off the accelerator to press the brake. I didn't relish the idea of either of us getting out on Michigan Avenue to crank the car in the midst of relentless traffic in the event the starter didn't work.

But Elliott offered a solution. He pointed out that our 1919 Ford still was equipped with a feature all previous models had, a throttle lever under the steering wheel. To make sure the engine didn't stall, he said he could give it gas by pulling down the throttle.

When we got to the Ford, a kindly man who said he lived in

the neighborhood, told us policemen had checked our car, and had indicated they were going to headquarters to summon a tow truck.

We made a sudden departure, directing the Ford straight ahead toward the lakeshore.

The time had come for our dash through Chicago, down Michigan Avenue, as recommended by the police officer. We both tensed as we drew nearer the heavy traffic. The Ford chugged along in fine shape, although it took the two of us to operate it. While I manipulated the foot levers, Elliott held the hand throttle down to make certain the engine would keep running at the stop signs.

It was raining, which didn't help matters. Taxi drivers darted in front of us at every stop, squeezing into the narrow space between our car and the stop line. Cars whizzed by in other lanes, while our slower-moving Ford seemed to crawl like an ant. Horns honked and passengers stared, although some seemed amused.

At first nothing had looked familiar, but as we approached the skyscraper area we recognized Lincoln Park, the Field Museum, and the stores and other business establishments along Michigan Avenue. By now we were in stride with the traffic, but felt relieved we weren't compelled to turn into the labyrinth of thoroughfares in Chicago's Loop, a prospect we had dreaded the day before.

There still was a long way ahead, but we relaxed at last when we crossed the border into Indiana. We now were in the Hoosier State, but not yet in Orphan Annie country. To us, Whiting, Indiana Harbor, and Gary, Indiana were just a continuation of big city Chicago.

At Wanatah I wheeled into a service station.

"We made it," Elliott exulted. He took his hand off the

throttle. "If our good Ford were a horse, I'd feed it an extra bucket of oats."

As for me, I was more grateful for Elliott's role as a throttle jockey, but did feed the Ford a tankful of gas and an extra quart of oil.

— The Log, Sun. Oct. 12, 1924

Chapter III
A Grim Warning

SAFELY THROUGH CHICAGO, we were anxious to be in open country once more. We found northern Indiana delightfully relaxing, and enjoyed talking with its people, detecting traces of the Indiana homespun humor we assumed was more prevalent farther east and south.

We even weren't annoyed when the car's tires picked up a tack a mile beyond Wanatah and a shingle nail outside of Plymouth.

Repairing the punctures hindered our progress, but as Elliott said, "What's the hurry?"

In line with that remark, we took a day off in the Plymouth tourist camp. There we spent Saturday, October 4 rearranging our paraphernalia, repairing the right back tire which flattened during the night, and having the Ford's radius rod welded so the steering apparatus would be more reliable.

In the Plymouth park we met more tourists than in most parks where we had camped so far. Already we had learned that tourists conversed freely, revealing interesting information concerning their varied backgrounds.

A good example was the tall, muscular man in his mid-20s who said he hailed from Oregon. He clenched his fist as he proudly told us he was a boxer.

"I knocked him out in the first round," he said as he described a Thanksgiving Day bout against a favored hometown opponent.

"I was only filling in as a substitute," he said. The boxer expanded his chest, thumping it as he walked a scowling bulldog about the camp. We did not dispute his claim to fame.

Friday morning we made a late start, and were obliged to travel quite slowly. We were on a gravel road, plainly marked Yellowstone Trail, potholed and like a washboard.

I told Elliott I thought a national highway would be paved in this part of the country.

"It's not a highway," Elliott said. "The signs call it a trail."

At least they were honest, I conceded.

Thus far, we had paid reasonable prices for meals when we didn't eat in camp. In Fort Wayne we ate in a restaurant where they were more than reasonable. A pleasant waitress served us a roast beef dinner with apple pie for dessert, all we could eat, and more, for just 25 cents each.

"The food was good," Elliott wrote in his log. "A dollar here must be worth three or four times as much as any place else."

By way of diversion, we estimated the population of Fort Wayne. Elliott's guess was 50,000 people, mine was 35,000. We based our estimates on the appearance of a run-down section of the city. We owed Fort Wayne an apology. Inquiry revealed the city's population was well over 140,000.

"Never judge the size of a city by the street you enter," I wrote in my log.

The YMCA in Van Wert, Ohio, a city of about 10,000 inhabitants, was in our opinion, one of the best we could expect to find anywhere. We refreshed ourselves with a dip in its up-to-date swimming pool. A wealthy citizen had helped finance the Y, we were told.

The cordial welcome we received in the Y enhanced our appreciation for the paid membership cards given us by Secretary Christensen of our hometown YMCA on behalf of contributors to Ashland's annual fund drive. He said the cards would be honored at any YMCA in the country, and this was proving to be true. The cards not only afforded us opportunities to shower and shave, but to swim in pools and exercise in gyms. We laundered our clothes in tourist camps, though, or wherever we conveniently found water.

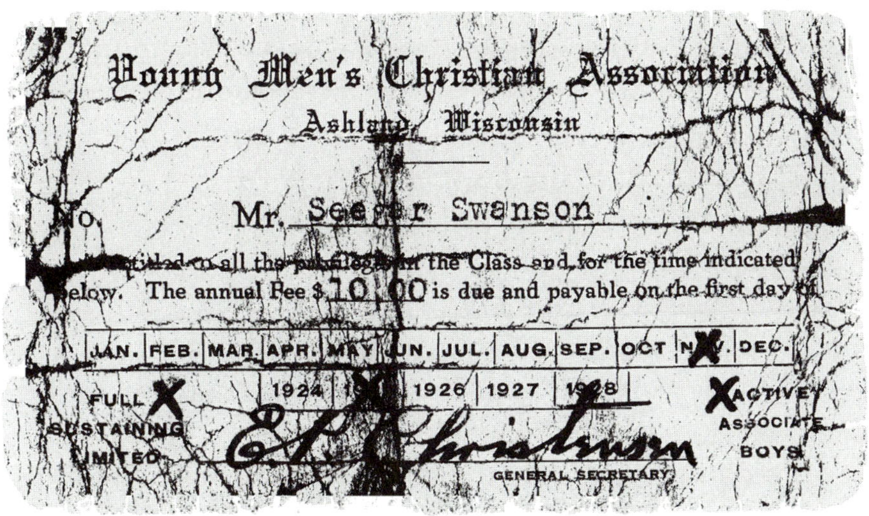

The author's YMCA membership card.

In Van Wert's tourist park we had no choice of campsites. The only vacant spot was near a small tent and a Chevrolet with Illinois license plates. Stepping out of the Ford, we saw two young misses, 19 or 20 years old, obviously trying not to soil their trim blue skirts while prying a flat tire off a front wheel of their Chevrolet. We promptly went to their rescue.

With wavy brown hair and sparking blue eyes, the girls, both about five feet two inches tall, looked like sisters, but said they weren't. They introduced themselves as Cindy and Kathy from Chicago. I couldn't tell one from the other. One of the girls, maybe it was Cindy, concentrated her attention on Elliott, "tall, lean and handsome" she no doubt thought.

The girls told us they were bound for Washington, D.C. to attend the World Series. One girl confided she had someone special playing baseball with the Washington Senators, although both insisted they were loyal fans of the Chicago Cubs.

About 6:30 the next morning the girls woke us as we had requested, in order that we could assist them in starting their car. Their tent was down, and they had only a few more belongings to pack. We pushed the Chevrolet out of the park before the engine ignited. The girls waved at us and shouted, "Thanks," as their car hit the open road.

"I hope they get to the World Series," Elliott said.

I assured him that with their spunk they would.

The scenery along the Lincoln Highway in Ohio fascinated us. The state's numerous farms, many wooded tracts, and gentle rolling slopes reminded us of our own southern Wisconsin. Hour after hour we drove, complacently drinking in the varying landscape and singing to the accompaniment of Elliott's ukulele. Alert for bargains, we stopped often to purchase needed supplies. Bread was nine cents a loaf in

Upper Sandusky, so we bought two.

At Mansfield we caught up with our Chicago lady friends of the previous night, this time in real distress. Two tourists were lining up their car to give them a push to a garage. Elliott, in an aside to me, said, "It's too bad we didn't get here sooner. We could have been the Sir Walter Raleighs."

Naturally, we were curious when we came to Ashland, Ohio. The city had the air of an industrious community. We admired it very much. We wrote home to let folks in our Ashland know their city had a rival both in size and activity.

Hometown pride notwithstanding, we had to admit Ohio's Ashland, with almost twice the 10,000 population of Wisconsin's Ashland, was more impressive. Of course, its residents couldn't view the glorious sunsets of Lake Superior's Chequamegon Bay, nor the lake vessels loaded with coal, iron ore, and general cargoes, but we acknowledged that in other ways they had a justifiable right to claim superiority.

In Ashland, we were puzzled by seeing restaurants almost deserted at what we believed still to be the supper hour. The time was 6:30 P.M., according to my Ingersoll. I hadn't used the "watch that made the dollar famous" for several years, but had resurrected it to mark time on our trip. Glancing up at several clocks, we concluded all were off, an hour ahead. Then a man

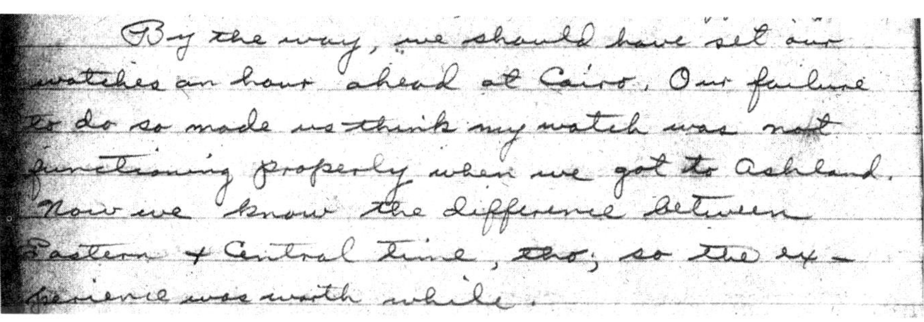

From the Log.

on the street told us we should have pushed my watch an hour forward at Cairo to get in step with Eastern Standard Time.

When we left the Ashland tourist camp the following morning, we set Pittsburgh as our next goal, little comprehending what might lie ahead.

The Sunday traffic was quite heavy, almost a steady stream. Paved roads, miles of them brick, enabled the Ford to glide at top speed, strangely enough without tire trouble or mechanical failures.

With greater frequency we picked our way through cities of noticeable size. To our way of thinking, some of the so-called villages we passed through would have done justice to fair-sized cities where we came from.

At five o'clock we halted about a mile and a half from Unity, and there we camped. Much to our liking, the Midwest was fading from view. We were but a short distance from the Ohio-Pennsylvania border, soon to be crossing into eastern territory.

By this time Elliott had acquired skill in driving the Ford, and was at the wheel the morning of October 6, Pittsburgh bound. Before long, we weren't sure if we would get there.

Long rolling hills were beautiful to look at, but as we rounded a curve about 40 miles from the "Smoky City" we faced a foreboding sign.

Warning to Strangers!
Use Second Gear on This Hill!

We didn't take the warning seriously because we had been in situations like it where milder warnings, in our opinion, would have been more appropriate. Besides, the Ford didn't have a second gear.

As the car moved downward at a moderate pace, we soon

became aware that no ordinary hill dropped below. It was more like a mountain, I thought.

The Ford gradually gained momentum as the hill became steeper. Elliott tapped the pedal of the foot brake to slow down the car. This did little to curb its speed. Then he firmly pressed the brake pedal to the floor, and held it there. About halfway down the hill he exclaimed, "The brakes are shot!"

With growing concern I told him to apply the emergency brake.

Elliott promptly jerked back the brake rod. "It's shot too," he groaned.

There was nothing more to do, it seemed, but to let the Ford continue its descent. It was going too fast to shift into low gear. Elliott jiggled the reverse pedal, and this helped, but we were passing cars proceeding downhill in second gear.

It was fortunate that Elliott's driving tactics on the lengthy hill weren't futile. He avoided disaster by bringing the Ford partially under control. Yet, a turn into the city of Beaver Falls awaited us at the foot of the steep incline. Elliott rounded it successfully, although narrowly dodging collision with an automobile and a streetcar. Steering the car against a curb, he brought it to a jolting stop.

"So this is Beaver Falls," he muttered. "Auto Falls would be a better name for the town."

A tall, rather thin man with a reassuring look offered us encouragement.

"You fellows were lucky," he said.

We had good reason to believe him when he then told us the hill had claimed 19 lives and maimed many more motorists.

He reflected a moment, riveting his attention on our Ford. "Yes, I'd say you were lucky. Last winter I earned $400 hauling wreckage," he said, grimly.

I pumped the brake pedal until I felt the bands take hold, not firmly, but enough to assure us there still was something left of the bands, enough to permit us to continue driving.

At a filling station Elliott inquired how far Bessemer was from Pittsburgh. He wanted to visit a cousin there. Considering the uncertain condition of the Ford's brakes, and the probability of more steep hills, I wondered whether we would get that far. We didn't have to. It turned out there are two Bessemers in Pennsylvania, one, North Bessemer, near Pittsburgh, the other in Lawrence County, just a few miles north of where we were. It was in Lawrence County where Elliott's cousin lived.

Chapter IV
Political Bounce

R ELIEVED BY THE THOUGHT we now wouldn't have to cope with traffic in metropolitan Pittsburgh, we turned north, clinging to the Ohio border. But the gentle slopes of the Buckeye State no longer were with us. Pennsylvania hills, many steep, tested the flimsy brakes of our car.

"Welcome," Elliott's cousin said upon our arrival in Bessemer, population 1,500 or thereabouts. Cordially he extended a hand of greeting. He spoke with a Swedish accent.

Gustaf Frederickson, not as tall, but with penetrating blue-gray eyes like his cousin Elliott, immediately arranged a homelike visit. For two nights we abandoned our bed in the Ford to sleep in a softer and more comfortable one in the home of Mr. and Mrs. Axel Pearson. The middle-aged couple served appetizing Scandinavian meals, all of which we relished.

We were in a settlement of Swedish people, some of whom

had but recently immigrated to the United States, and others who said they had been in Bessemer many years.

They treated us royally. Two parties were given in our honor. We, who were traveling with a little old Ford, didn't understand why, but we enjoyed the attention. Gustaf's friends vied for opportunities to invite us to their homes. No matter what the hour, day or night, they poured coffee, refilling the cups often, and served delicious Swedish pastries. At the gatherings, Elliott's cousin was the life of the party. He played a costly, spanking new accordion, or "dragspel" as he called it, of which he was genuinely proud. Toes tapped and people sang merrily as Gustaf pumped lively American tunes and rollicking Swedish polkas and hambos.

Wherever we went, I tried to be compatible by speaking Swedish. With amused expressions, our new friends let me know I was mixing Swedish with Norwegian, along with words concocted from English. Elliott talked only in English, but we noticed some of his listeners didn't understand what he said. They looked to me for what little help I could offer.

"We have the biggest cement plant in the United States," Gustaf boasted. He invited us to tour the facility, as well as Bessemer's huge cement quarry.

It occurred to us we could obtain jobs here, possibly working with stone crews, but, as Elliott remarked, our systems weren't accustomed to drinking so much coffee, a social obligation were we to remain in this Swedish environment.

Between coffee breaks we worked on the car, tightening loose parts and taking up connecting rods. The folks wanted us to stay longer, but with Maine still far off, the Good Ship Wanderlust lifted anchor October 8 to set sail for the port of Erie, Pennsylvania.

Not content to feed us so generously only during our

pleasant stay, our friends piled fruits, Swedish goodies, canned goods, and coffee into the Ford as they wished us Godspeed on our journey.

Though our cash was dwindling, we knew then we weren't going to starve. Like troubadours, we had, for a brief moment, shared the happy life of these hospitable, down-to-earth Scandinavian-Americans, and now we were gone.

The football season was in high gear at Greenville where we slept two nights near the city ball park, and spent warm daylight hours to remedy knocks, grunts, and jerks emitted by the car. We sauntered over to the nearby gridiron to watch Greenville's football team run through signals for an upcoming game.

It wasn't the right thing to do, but to indicate our interest in football, we donned the gray sweatshirts given us by an athlete of our hometown YMCA. Emblazoned on the front was a bold, red Y, and on the back in black letters was the word Ashland.

A husky young man, his dark eyes quizzical, asked, "Are you guys spying for Youngstown or Ashland?"

The less than cordial tone of his raspy voice was indicative of unfriendly stares from other Greenville fans. We deemed it best to leave, with a feeling that if either Ohio team won the game, we, as spies, would be blamed.

By removing the top of the Ford's engine, we eliminated its knock by scraping off a thick layer of carbon. A persistent piston slap, and a steady growl at the rear of the car convinced us a complete overhaul was overdue. That would be done in Erie, provided we could find jobs. Disappointed, we discovered Erie's employment office had closed for Saturday afternoon. So we obtained no work from that source.

In Erie we joined hundreds of baseball enthusiasts in front

of the city's newspaper building to watch a simulated diamond and a score board give a play by play account of the seventh and deciding World Series game between the New York Giants and the Washington Senators. Spectators jostled for position.

"New York bum," we heard one disgruntled fan grumble contemptuously as a taller man moved in front of him, obstructing his view.

We thought of the two girls we had met in the Indiana tourist park, and along the road in Mansfield, and wondered if they watched the game in Washington. If so, we were sure they were thrilled. The Senators won the world championship in a 12 inning battle, 4-3. As we had hoped, Walter Johnson, American League hurler of the fastest ball in baseball history, was the winning pitcher.

For some, however, fame can be illusive. We soon forgot the name of the National League's losing pitcher. Though he pitched a good game and was worthy of note, we failed to record his identity in our logs.

Minutes after the game, Erie newsboys were on the streets selling newspapers containing the box score and a detailed story of the exciting event. For two cents we bought one.

Uppermost in our minds when we entered New York State was the need to find jobs. They weren't that scarce, after all. We found one on our first try. The foreman of a bridge building crew at Forsythe hired us to begin work Monday, October 12 at a wage of 50 cents per hour.

We camped over the weekend in the ball park in Westfield, several miles away. Lately, tourist parks had become fewer, but for us, grass-covered ball parks served our purpose just as well.

Near our campsite we saw acres of vineyards with purple grapes ready for harvest. They tempted us greatly.

Smiling, her eyes twinkling, an amiable young woman who

said her name was Mrs. Roberts, dropped by with her two small children as Elliott was setting up our camp stove.

"Would you like some grapes?" she asked. She held up several bunches, telling us they were fresh from her family's vines.

Curious about our trip, she lingered awhile to chat. Her children walked around our Ford, scrutinizing it with wide-open eyes. We gathered from Mrs. Roberts' talk that this part of New York State was noted for its grapes, and derived economic benefit from their vines.

We were glad to be sampling some of the fruit. "There are nice people around here," said Elliott after our visitors had left our camp.

On Monday we were dejected about our job outlook. The bridge crew foreman said we would have to wait awhile to begin work.

"There's a gravel shortage," he explained.

We could feel moss growing under our feet, and rather than being bogged down in it, elected to drive on to Buffalo, where we figured there must be better work than shoveling gravel.

Our feelings about Buffalo were mixed. Its prominence as a lake port could not be questioned, and its business section appeared metropolitan in every sense of the word. We wondered, though, why the city had so many rugged brick streets, and why the approach to the main thoroughfare was lined with dingy employment offices, murky doorways, and unkempt lodging houses. Down and out men and women who frequented these places prompted us to continue our own little sociological observations.

Posters urging young men to join the United States Navy drew our attention in front of the Federal Building. We had hardly glanced at them before a recruiting officer was inducing us to enlist. Visions of a sea-faring life flashed before us, but since the country was not faced with military urgency, we had no qualms in casting them aside with thoughts of more thrilling adventures in our land-roving Good Ship Wanderlust.

Later in the afternoon we scouted privately operated employment agencies in search of work. They offered jobs ranging from washing windows to milking cows, but how could we hope to complete a trip around the United States within a year by working for $30 a month?

The last agency posted a call for road workers at Craigsville. Without hesitation we signed up. Worried about advance payment of a fee for the assignment, we told the manager we were nearly broke.

The manager waved his arm, indicating no cause for concern. "The contractor will hold out the fee from your first pay check," he said.

We had become uneasy about the brakes of the Ford. They had little or no holding power, forcing us to bring the car to a complete stop to slow its speed before we let it descend steep hills. Climbing, on the other hand, posed no problem. To show how contrary a Ford could be, our Wanderlust ascended what was known as Buffalo Hill in high gear, a feat we concluded as quite extraordinary. Regarding this achievement, Elliott wrote:

> Compelled to slow down at the foot of the
> mountain we began to climb on high. The
> engine showed remarkable power, and on
> the way to the top we passed three Fords
> laboring on low, and passed a big car that
> had given us the dust at the bottom. We
> enjoyed a good laugh at their expense.

An unusual situation developed as we approached what looked like the top of a cliff. I had to worm the Ford through a crew of road workers before Elliott could jump out to halt the car by bracing himself against the side of the vehicle.

A road contractor and several highway officials seemed amused by our unique way of braking a car. Elliott asked if they thought we could get down the hill safely without brakes.

"Not unless you want to get killed," a supervisor said. "The hill is a mile and a half to the bottom," he pointed out, "and you'll be flying by the time you get there." He warned us of the added danger of colliding with teams of horses working at various levels.

When we told the contractor we were on our way to Craigsville to join a road crew, he offered us jobs with his crew on the very hill we couldn't descend. The pay would be 40 cents an hour. This suited us better than the promised jobs at Craigsville. Here we would have no employment fees deducted.

Told to begin work at the hill the following morning, we were directed to the neighboring home of Mr. and Mrs. Gordon Libby for room and board. The family agreed to feed and house us for $1.15 per day each.

Mrs. Libby served splendid meals. How a housewife could do this and show a profit mystified us. Most of her elaborate spreads were not appreciated by the other boarders, however. Mostly immigrants, they apparently were not accustomed to the fruit, cereal, muffins, and toast Mrs. Libby served for breakfast, nor did they evince delight for the tempting desserts and side dishes she prepared, but they gulped down meat and potatoes.

The boarders likewise struck us as peculiar with regard to their sleeping habits. When Mrs. Libby led us to an upstairs room crowded with cots, we could hardly reach ours because of dense tobacco smoke which evidently had permeated the room since morning. Elliott and I went to the windows, only to find them unyielding. After considerable effort, Elliott succeeded in raising one. We hoped the stale air would give way to fresh air from the outside.

Shortly after supper that first evening, we heard a loud bang upstairs.

"The men don't like the fresh air, boys," Mrs. Libby said. "I'm sorry we must ask you to sleep in the same room with them."

Determined to have ventilation, we went upstairs. Glowering looks warned us to abandon our plans to reopen the window. Willing to put up with almost any kind of inconvenience to obtain funds, we decided to make the best of the situation. The boarders, seated on their cots, continued smoking their corncob pipes and rolling Bull Durham cigarettes.

Thin as usual and still weighing only 130 pounds, Elliott manned a wheelbarrow our first day on the hill. He kept up with the other men and a "pace setter," said to have been hired to keep the road gang working at top speed.

I was delegated to drive a gear shift truck. This would have been fine had I known how to operate a gear shift. The foreman gave me brief instructions, then told me to "get going."

Several times the contractor almost was minus a truck and a driver as I precariously eased the vehicle within an inch or two from the edge of the hillside while dumping gravel to broaden the shoulder of the highway. I shuddered when I saw how far the truck would have plunged had I not braked it in time.

With a sense of relief I turned the truck over to the regular driver when he returned to work the next morning, even though I was directed to a wheelbarrow and told to fall in line with the sand and gravel shoveling crew feeding what Elliott termed "the hungriest cement mixer in the state of New York." I soon understood what a strain the heavy work was for him. My muscles ached, too, although I had experience with manual labor and he did not.

To us, our fellow workers seemed like drudges, performing hard, tiring labor in return for 40 cents an hour. Most of them were immigrants, 40 years or older, apparently with little pride in building a concrete highway for New York taxpayers. Their only interest seemed centered on keeping up with the "pace setter" so they would be sure of their weekly pay.

Word got around that we were from Wisconsin. This generated questions about Senator Robert M. La Follette, who was conducting his "whirlwind campaign" as the Progressive candidate for United States president in the November election. Workers, and supervisors as well, asked about his liberal reform politics, especially with regard to his pro-labor stance.

With no thought of spreading labor unrest or fomenting rebellion against big business, we gave what answers we could about "Fighting Bob," his career as congressman, governor, and U.S. senator. Anyhow, we had nothing against Calvin Coolidge, the Republican presidential candidate. Moreover, we were only 20, too young to vote.

Moments after we began work the morning of our fourth day, a job supervisor called us aside to say our services no longer were needed. He offered no explanation for the dismissal. The timekeeper paid us in cash, $15.60 each for the work we had done.

Surprised, we walked over to the cement mixer to thank the foreman for the interest he had shown us. "Don't feel bad," he said. "You fellows did more than some others." He paused, jerking his thumb toward the cement mixer to signal start up time. "I don't know why you were bounced, but it's not what you do, it's the showing you make."

We didn't comprehend what the foreman meant by "the showing you make," but thought that maybe, from a political standpoint, with La Follette running for president, we were from Wisconsin at the wrong time.

Losing our jobs wasn't a crisis. On the other hand, the Ford posed a serious problem. Without brakes it was a hazard.

As soon as we paid Mrs. Libby $6.90 for three days board and room we used her telephone to call the garage in Varysburg to tow our car down the hill for overhauling.

A mechanic installed new brake bands and repaired the rear axle assembly. He recommended we purchase sturdier bands than the ones we wore out.

"Those bands were like lamp wicks," he said. He showed us the ones he recommended. "They won't burn out, not even on mountains."

The garage bill was $26.79, reasonable for the tow, repairs, and parts, yet a scary dent in our shrinking cash. We took off for Buffalo in search of another job.

Confidence in the Ford restored, we traveled as far as East Aurora before looking for a tourist camp. We asked a man walking on the sidewalk for directions. The man, rather short and quick of step, asked our names and gave his as Mr. Willis. He must have seen dejection written on our faces. To our surprise, he invited us to camp in his back yard.

Mr. Willis crowded into the front seat of the Ford and guided us to his home, an attractive residence on a shady street. We noticed his garage door was open, exposing a large assortment of tools. With strangers camped in his yard, the trusting Mr. Willis put no lock on the door and left it standing open before he and his family retired for the night.

Our second impression of Buffalo was more favorable than the first, perhaps because we kept away from the employment area of the city. We had no intention of again applying for jobs at the agencies there. Also, we were determined to visit famous Niagara Falls.

Another surprise awaited us. We found the waterfalls were not isolated in a wilderness, but were located in a tourist-minded city bearing their name. We spent the night beside a city cemetery.

Before setting out for the falls, we thought it best to shave for the first time in eight days. I placed a round bar of shaving soap in a mug, whipped it into a lather with a shaving brush, and looking into a mirror I had hung on the car, lathered my face. Where had I lost my straightedge razor?

The loss delighted Elliott. We had few differences, but disagreed when it came to shaving. I preferred my old-fashioned razor, which Elliott called a deadly weapon, while he shaved with what I considered a "newfangled" safety razor. Elliott had won the argument. Now I had to use his. It would cost too much to buy a new straightedge razor. But changing to a safety razor, I was about to discover, was almost as difficult as learning to shave with my straightedge. Concerning my experience, Elliott wrote in his log:

> He got shaved all right, but his face was
> smeared with blood and my razor blade
> looked like a hacksaw when he got through.
> I drew first blood on his face trying to show
> him how the safety razor worked. The
> trouble was, I guess, we've been through so
> many close shaves that we got too close this
> time, too.

Elliott shaving with safety razor.

Author cuts himself with "safety" razor.

With a deep feeling of awe, we admired Niagara Falls tumbling more than 160 feet into the gorge below. We were but two of the thousands who already that year had viewed America's world renowned natural wonder.

The days of tightrope walkers and daredevils going over the falls in barrels were no more, but just being at the falls was itself enough. It would have been exciting to walk under the falls at the Cave of the Winds. We were four years too late, however. The cave had been closed to tourists since 1920 after three visitors met death by falling rocks.

Conversing with spectators familiar with the falls, we accumulated background information concerning the scenic marvel. For one thing, we learned the stream forming the falls is the outlet for Lake Erie, and the gorge below leads into Lake Ontario. We learned more. Beneath the stream above the falls is a thick layer of hard limestone, resting on softer rock. Water eroding the softer rock forms the caves under the falls.

We regretted being told Niagara Falls is doomed to extinction. Eventually the falls are destined to retreat toward Lake Erie through continued erosion of the softer rock and the breakup of the upper limestone. But it won't be in the foreseeable future. A comforting thought, as untold centuries must elapse before extinction becomes reality.

Sprayed by mists from the falls, we enjoyed the sensation of their cooling effect. We walked as close to the Cave of the Winds as possible. Looking across the gorge into which the falls spilled, we viewed the Canadian side, realizing we were missing Horseshoe Falls, considerably larger and more spectacular than the American falls.

Too many citizens of Buffalo and Niagara Falls were seeking employment for us, as strangers, to get jobs. We would travel eastward, hopeful something would turn up.

Which way? Elliott studied our road map. "Heh, let's take this road," he said. "It's called the Million Dollar Highway."

The Million Dollar Highway didn't translate into jobs, however.

Before long we were driving through the Niagara fruit belt in the midst of the harvest season. Fruits on sale at numerous roadside stands were so cheap we couldn't resist purchasing some. All the while we applied for jobs. Repeatedly it was the same story:

"We're filled up with help. Try Mr. Jones down the road. He probably needs men."

All day the Joneses discouraged us. Thousands of apple trees waited picking, yet no one required our help.

Evening descended. We would try one more place. It happened to be the F.M. Bradley orchard between Olcott and West Somerset, New York, on "Blue Ontario's Shore."

"Sorry, Mr. Bradley isn't home," a worker said. "Why don't you camp over there?" He pointed to an opening near a large white barn.

We thanked him and said we would.

"You can talk with George in the morning." The worker nodded toward the forest of fruit laden trees. "He needs more men to pick those apples."

— Letter excerpt, Tue. Nov. 18, 1924

Chapter V
Winter Strikes Early

"**G**ET UP, MEN, if you want to go to work." Rousing us at the crack of dawn was George Bradley, tall and broad-shouldered, his welcoming smile assuring us we needn't feel apologetic about being caught sound asleep.

We had found a job to our liking, working for someone whose congeniality was unmistakable. Our first assignment was in the orchard's Jonathan grove where Martin Wendt, supervisor of the Bradley orchard, handed us large canvas bags to strap around our shoulders. These were to be filled with apples, the fruit to be emptied into barrels by pulling a drawstring at the bottom of the bag. Martin, as the other workers called him, was a good-natured man of 35, of medium build, and from all appearances well-qualified for his job.

"Don't pick the drops," he cautioned when we stooped over to pick up the many red apples we saw on the ground. "Just apples off the trees," he said.

We thought this was a squandering of good apples, but changed our minds when Martin said, "one bruised apple can spoil a whole barrel."

Martin also instructed us not to pull apples off the branches, but to tip each apple upward and simultaneously to press a finger against the stem, allowing the apple an easy, gentle separation from the branch. This, Martin said, avoided creating an opening at the top of the apple if the stem pulled out in a yank from the branch, thus causing rot. The trees were loaded with Jonathans. From the first one we filled several dozen bags with apples we could reach from the ground. We used ladders to gather those in the upper branches, where they were equally abundant.

In our eagerness to begin work, we had not eaten breakfast. We felt no compunction about eating Jonathans to make up for this. Neither did we find anything wrong with the fruit on the ground. At first, with accustomed frugality, we ate apples to the core. They were so plentiful, however, we soon did like other workers, took only several bites of the most delicious part and tossed the remainder away.

"They say an apple a day keeps the doctor away," Elliott wrote in his log. "At that rate I ought to be the healthiest guy in the world judging by the amount I've eaten."

Martin said there would be no objection if we parked our Ford inside the big combination barn and garage. Haphazardly we arranged an upstairs area for light house-keeping, utilizing a double cot for comfortable sleeping, a table, benches, and discarded chairs. We were being paid $4 each a day working in the orchard so for 30 cents a meal, felt we could afford to eat in the Wendt home with the other 10 men employed by George Bradley. The crew was housed in a dwelling some distance behind the Bradley home. We visited there evenings to become better acquainted with the men.

Harvesting the Jonathans was completed at the end of our first day. The entire crew then was assigned to a grove of 40-year-old Baldwin apple trees. They were so high we had to use 26-foot ladders to reach the topmost fruit. We had a shaky feeling perched on such a tall ladder against a small limb to reach out for a cluster of Baldwins.

For a week we gathered different varieties of apples in separate areas of the extensive orchard. Then came an unexpected order to pick drops. Martin told us our employer kept a keen eye on the daily cider market. If he thought the price for drops were high enough, he transferred the apple-picking crew from trees to ground.

Under a productive Duchess apple tree I filled 10 bushel baskets. I could only imagine how many more bushels previously had been picked from the branches of that tree. George Bradley was visibly proud of the Duchess trees, which had gained wide acceptance among apple growers throughout the nation.

Whether we collected apples from trees or on the ground, the work never was monotonous. This, we felt, was due partly to the on-going jabber of the men working with us. They were a mixed lot, with all kinds of experiences. Most were glib talkers, inclined to stretch the truth.

For us, the ready wit of an Irish Yankee, Ed Welch, had special appeal. Well into his 60s, with a twinkle in his eyes, thin and scarcely five feet three inches tall, he moved about with the agility of an acrobat. His spontaneous sense of humor enriched his conversation as he twitched the stubby mustache on his upper lip. George Bradley evidently noticed a developing spirit of comradeship. Thereafter he assigned work so

Workers at Bradley orchard. Welch is at left.

our trio was not separated.

Fruit picking was not the only work to be done. There were rutabagas to uproot and leathery leaves to whack off, and one day four of us were delegated to dig potatoes. Jabbing a six-prong fork into the ground to turn over potatoes, we found out, was not as easy as plucking apples off a tree. Our two fellow workers, a Bohemian who never told us his name, and our Irish friend, outdid each other telling tall tales. This helped pass the time.

Ed Welch was philosophical about the chore. "Digging potatoes is a continuous round of pleasure," he said, stopping to pull off a tuber impaled on a tine of his fork. "Up one row, down the next."

Early one morning the whole orchard crew was turned loose in a large cabbage patch, "armed with sharp knives and strong backs," as recorded in my log. Two of the men became hostile toward each other when each claimed he could beat the other cutting the field of cabbages. Finally one of them wagered a hundred dollars he could cut the entire cabbage patch by the end of the day, and set out to win the gamble. He began slashing cabbages with such great speed he worried the other party to the bet, only to give up with exhaustion. He collected his wages during the noon hour and left before the bet could be collected. Even the remainder of the crew could do no more than complete the rest of the patch in two days.

After supper we had an urge to swim. Winding our way through the orchard in a northerly direction we came to Lake Ontario. The evening air was nippy and the water cold. This, however, invigorated us as we ran up and down the beach before dashing into the lake. On Sunday, our day off, we returned for another swim under warmer conditions, what with a sunny sky and a gentle daytime breeze.

We thought of washing our clothes at the beach, but were glad when Mrs. Wendt agreed to do the laundering. She charged us a dollar, blankets included.

The meals Mrs. Wendt served were nourishing, but in true boarding house fashion, some of the men grumbled. For 30 cents a meal they hardly could expect porterhouse steaks, we reasoned. They did have plenty of potatoes, ham and bacon, sausage, bread, and cheese. But one boarder complained the "sow belly," his term for salt pork, was fried "to a frazzle."

Aware of the rumblings, Mrs. Wendt offered to bake peach pies if anyone would pick peaches left on trees after the harvest which had been completed before our arrival at the orchard. The men took her at her word, bringing in nearly a bushel. She gave them their fill of peach pie.

Satisfied we now were earning sufficient money, we drove the Ford to the Frost Bros. garage in Barker for the long-awaited overhaul. Our chief concern was elimination of the oil leak in the cracked crankcase. The leak had become intolerable. Although we had been able to drive much of the way from Wisconsin by adding a quart of oil for each five gallons of gasoline we purchased, the car lately had required two quarts of oil to five gallons of gasoline, with an extra quart poured in now and then for good measure.

For a garage bill of only $52.70 our anxieties were at an end. The Ford had a new crankcase, $11.00; new cylinder head, $6.00; repaired rear spring, $6.50; other minor adjustments, $9.20, all for a labor charge of but $20.00.

Although the Ford was ready for the road, we continued to work for Mr. Bradley. In addition to apples the orchard also had pear trees. The annual New York pheasant hunting season opened while we and Ed Welch worked this part of the orchard. There were birds among the trees, and hunters obtained permission to shoot them. Shots rang out from time to time, reminding us of our grouse and partridge hunting in the fields and woods of Wisconsin.

Wham!

An unusually loud shotgun blast startled us. A pheasant flew up and whirred through branches of the trees. We saw Ed leap off his ladder to wave his fist indignantly at a disappearing hunter.

"Confounded nimrods!" he shouted. "Before you know it, these galoots will think we're pheasants."

Turning to us, he said, "They've got more ammunition than brains." He then climbed up on his ladder to grab angrily at pears.

Considering the proximity of some of the shots, we didn't blame him for his explosive outburst.

It was natural to wonder what happened to the apples we harvested. The answer came on a rainy Thursday when it was too wet to work in the groves. While others loafed around a warm stove in the rooming house, Elliott and I went to Somerset with George Bradley to witness the sorting and packing of apples in a warehouse. The apples had been trucked from various orchards of the Lake Ontario fruit belt. From the warehouse the apples would be shipped in barrels to wholesalers for later distribution to retailers, and ultimately to consumers.

A recurring topic of discussion at the Bradley orchard was the forthcoming November 4 presidential election. As was the case with our road job on the Varysburg hill, it was assumed we knew everything about Senator La Follette, the Progressive candidate from our home state.

Most of the apple-picking crew expressed leanings toward La Follette, but with reservations. Food on the table and assurance of jobs demanded votes for Republican Calvin Coolidge, who already held the office. George Bradley told us this was the general attitude throughout the East. The truth of his political perception was revealed when the votes were counted. A bold front page headline in the newspaper that came to the Wendt home proclaimed:

LA FOLLETTE 13 VOTES

Apparently, we thought, the Wisconsin senator's defeat was greater news than Coolidge's election. Nationwide, La Follette received nearly 5,000,000 votes, a creditable showing, but he carried only his home state with its 13 electoral votes.

The prospect of La Follette winning had, of course, been deemed remote. Yet with three candidates in the race, there had been hope that neither Coolidge nor his opponent on the Democratic ticket, John W. Davis, would poll a majority of the electoral votes. This would have thrown the election into the lap of the House of Representatives, as required by the 12th amendment of the U.S. Constitution.

This, it was reasoned, might win election for La Follette, whose influence in Congress was acknowledged generally. Coolidge, on the other hand, had been given little opportunity to display national leadership. He had been president only 14 months, following the death of President Warren G. Harding in August 1923. Davis, the Democratic nominee, was regarded as relatively unknown.

On November 14 George Bradley paid off his crew. After deducting all expenses to date, we had $102.93 remaining, about the same amount we had at the beginning of our trip. How far would we go this time?

Before we departed, George Bradley told us to load up with apples.

"In case you get hungry," he said.

From the tops of the high Baldwin trees we salvaged a bushel of apples that had been considered out of reach the first time around. From other trees we obtained more favorites, such as the Ben Davis.

With regret we left the Bradley orchard. Working conditions had been ideal, the autumn weather was agreeable, and the Bradley family had shown a friendly interest in our journey. George asked us to write him concerning our progress. The Wendts and the crew also would be missed.

George Bradley in front of his home with it's broad verandas and rail fenced balcony.

Fifty-seven years would elapse before I saw the Bradley place again. With my wife Ruth, our daughter Jean and her husband, Clarence Cross, we sidetracked from a visit at Niagara Falls in October 1981 to search for the orchard. I knew it was east of Olcott, and eventually we came to it.

The expansive Bradley home, with its broad verandas and the rail-fenced balcony on the second floor, was still there, but the Bradleys were gone. We talked with several men in a building west of the dwelling. From them we learned the orchard had changed hands. It now was operated by a company canning baby food, they said.

I explained how Elliott and I had picked apples in the orchard, and asked whether I was looking at the same apple trees.

"No, the old trees have been replanted," one of the men said.

Thinking back about 26-foot ladders and the tall trees from which Elliott and I had gathered our final bushel of apples, I asked about the Baldwins.

"They're the only ones left," the man said. "And those Baldwin trees are still producing."

Had time permitted, it would have been fun to hike through the orchard to relive our experiences, perhaps to the shore of Lake Ontario. But I was glad to see the orchard once more, and that maybe someday I could return.

During our final week on the job Ed Welch repeatedly reminded us he wanted to treat us to a steak dinner before we parted company.

"Even if it takes my last dollar," he emphatically said.

Ed rode with us as we honked good-byes. Soon we were in Lockport where we drove around until Ed was satisfied he had located the best restaurant in town. We all enjoyed sirloin steaks.

We lingered at the table, delaying the farewells. Ed said he would go on to Buffalo.

We shook hands outside the restaurant. "Good-bye, boys,"

Ed said. His voice quavered. "We'll never meet again." Before disappearing down the street, he turned toward us for a final look. "Take care of the office," he said. It was his favorite expression.

The parting was emotional for us, too. Not till now did we fully realize what a deep friendship the three of us had developed while working together at the Bradley orchard. But we were comforted by the thought Ed had a stake from his seasonal job, perhaps enough to pull him through much of the winter, yet like many others in his circumstances, where would he go for his next job? We felt fortunate. Hopefully, we had the Ford to take us to one.

Lockport, with its Erie Canal, reminded us of history we learned in school. We sensed how vital the canal had been since its opening in 1825, but as we watched a barge going through, we were aware the waterway now had a lesser, but nonetheless significant role in the state's economy.

The days were getting shorter, and as we left Lockport during mid-afternoon, the air became colder. With no heater in the car, we put on the side curtains to keep warm.

We got no farther than what looked like an abandoned campground. Actually, it was the site of some old farm buildings which had been torn down but not completely removed. We were near Spenceport. Rather than cook supper in the chilly outdoor air, we placed our camp stove on the front seat of the Ford.

"The stove caved in," Elliott wrote in his log. "Then the thing caught fire and we couldn't put the fire out."

Flames leaped high as gasoline flooded the burner. We feared the fire might reach the gasoline tank under the front seat and touch off an explosion. In desperation, Elliott tore a side curtain off the car and threw out the blazing stove.

"We came through the fire with no casualties except a ripped curtain, a damaged stove, and my eyebrows singed," Elliott wrote.

A steady downpour of rain impeded progress of the Ford the next morning. The windshield was blurred, the car having no wiper. When we reached Rochester, we were in no mood for sightseeing, but did some useless driving after losing our way on the city's streets. We readily saw, however, why Rochester was considered the most beautiful city in the state. Elliott, though, had no praise for the condition of its main street.

The north wind grew colder and the rain turned into sleet as we continued eastward. Spotting a tumbling, open-ended wagon shed in a field to our right, we accepted it as shelter for the night. Jumping around and swinging our arms vigorously, we kept warm enough to cook supper and eat a hearty meal.

We took no chances with the cold. Though we shivered doing so, we put on long woolen underwear, called union suits, before rolling into bed for a night of sound sleep. When we arose the next morning, three inches of snow and a flat front tire greeted us.

Winter had come early, time to head south. At least, that was the thought flitting through our minds. We looked at our map to determine how we could go around big cities like New York and Philadelphia, to get to Florida fast.

"Wait," Elliott said. "If we go to Florida now we'll never get to Maine."

We debated the matter while repairing the flat tire, and by the time I thumped the rubber patch on the inner tube, we agreed on a decision. Regardless of wind, cold, or snow, we would stick to our original plan, touch base in Maine, the first corner state of the U.S.A.

Fortunately, we had drained the radiator the night before. Since there was no pump at hand, we had kept the water in our pail. Despite the precaution of covering it with protective gunny sacks chucked in a corner of the shed, we had to break a layer of ice before pouring the water back into the radiator.

Snow in upper New York nearly sidetracks the tour objective of reaching each corner state.

With snow still coming down and fanned by a brisk cold wind, we didn't wait to prepare breakfast. Contrary to our expectations, the Ford's engine responded immediately when I stepped on the starter. In this respect, we had no cause for complaint. Since the beginning of our trip, the starter had been as reliable as the old-time crank. Five miles down the road we stopped at Cicero Center to thaw out in a garage.

Because there was no place to eat in Cicero Center, we delayed breakfast until we arrived at an inn at Bridgeport, where even steaming coffee and hot cereal failed to revive our frozen spirits. Our apples were frozen too, and although edible, this was no time to eat them. Covered only by canvas gloves, my hands were numb. We spent a dollar for a pair of mittens to be worn by whoever would be driver of the car.

We stopped in several more towns for hot coffee to stimulate ourselves and thus the progress of the Ford. Under ordinary circumstances we would have spent more time in Syracuse viewing its scores of industrial plants and beautiful parks, as well as Syracuse University. We also gave Utica a scant once-over, but long enough to comprehend its importance as a dairy center and a hub of clothing manufacturing.

Significant was the fact we now were traveling through the scenic Mohawk Valley, which helped us recall more history we had studied at school, tales of sturdy American pioneers and Mohawk Indians. Though banks of the Mohawk River were covered with snow, the stream was warm enough to remain open and flowing.

At Amsterdam we entered a city that retained its pleasant atmosphere of colonial days. We looked for a campground, but with the thermometer sinking, we stored the Ford in a garage to prevent freeze-up damage, and for a dollar engaged a room in the city's YMCA.

Surprisingly, the warm bed in our room was not as restful as the bed in the car. The air was stuffy, we thought, and throughout the night we kicked off the blankets. Clearly, we had become too acclimated to sleeping outdoors.

When we left the Bradley orchard we had intended to go to Maine by way of the Adirondack Mountains. Cold and snow made this inadvisable. Reports reached the lowlands that almost a foot of snow had fallen in the mountains, and that vehicular traffic in many areas was at a standstill. Consequently, we redirected our course toward Albany and eastward to the Atlantic Coast. A station attendant, huddling to brace himself against the cold wind as he pumped gas into the Ford, warned us to turn south.

"Maybe you'll get to Maine, but you'll be snowed in," he said. We had the impression he thought the state was next to the North Pole. "Even if you get there, you won't get out until next spring."

That remark, as much as anything, strengthened our resolve. If we became snowbound in Maine, we would find jobs for the winter, we reasoned, logging perhaps, and could resume our journey southward as soon as weather conditions allowed.

Whatever the wintry conditions might be in Maine, the weather in New York State was doing its best to prepare us for them. To keep warm while driving, we covered ourselves with two blankets, and sat on another to keep drafts from coming up through the floor. It was too cold to cook meals comfortably, so we ate in restaurants. One consolation was that generally meals were cheaper than in the Midwest. We stopped frequently for hot coffee and soup. Coffee was five cents a cup, soup a dime. Getting out of bed in the morning was, as Elliott said, "like jumping out of a steam bath into a snowdrift."

As if to add to our difficulties, the car acted up. Tires punctured and mechanical difficulties developed. The only benefit was the warming exercise involved while pumping air into the tires. We arrived at Albany about noon after traveling by way of Schenectady. The commanding row of tall, narrow brick buildings in New York State's capital immediately drew our attention. They clearly were colonial. The structures were taken for granted by residents of Albany with whom we conversed, but to us they were unique. In Amsterdam we already had viewed colonial architecture, but nothing was as distinctive as the brick buildings in Albany.

The design of the state capitol also was that of a by-gone era. Elliott described the capitol as "more like an old castle." We spent more than an hour walking through its corridors.

Albany's hill streets reminded us of Duluth, Minnesota. As we gazed upon the Hudson River, we envisioned a boat carrying us down to New York City where the sting of winter probably had not yet been felt. Nevertheless, we left Albany to continue our journey through the Berkshire Mountains toward Pittsfield, Massachusetts, where we arrived late in the afternoon. We had reached another state.

— The Log, Tues. Nov. 25, 1924

Chapter VI
Jobs Scarce

AS THE FORD climbed the picturesque Berkshire Mountains, clumps of brightly colored leaves still clinging to branches were sufficient to tell us how beautiful the region must have been a week or 10 days ago when it fully was garbed in autumnal splendor. We were sure that New Yorkers who didn't drive as far as the Adirondacks would at least take in the vivid Massachusetts panorama.

The Ford went up the long steep hills perfectly, most of them in high gear, just as it did ever since we encountered the hills of Pennsylvania. Near Pittsfield, however, the lower radiator hose sprang a leak. Elliott obtained a pail of water from a roadside house, enough to get the car to Pittsfield.

Thermometers about the city registered zero and several degrees below. From our knees up we were fairly warm but lacking the protection of overcoats and overshoes, our legs were numbed. We jumped and clicked our heels in midair to get our blood circulating.

Filling stations were charging a dollar per gallon for radiator alcohol.

"If the price stays this high, I hope it gets real cold." The remark wasn't intended for our ears, but we couldn't help overhearing the station operator's chuckling comment over the telephone when we stepped inside to pay our gas bill.

At a dollar a gallon we had no desire to buy radiator alcohol. Since closing time was nearing, we were able to leave the Ford in a downtown garage overnight until a mechanic could replace the leaky radiator hose the next morning. This not only saved us a 75-cent storage charge, but obviated the need to buy radiator alcohol, assuming the cold would moderate once we left the Berkshires.

After booking a room in a Pittsfield hotel for the dollar we saved by not buying alcohol, we purchased two handkerchiefs for a nickel in a store advertising a "slaughter sale," and then spent a relaxing evening in a movie theater. Hoot Gibson starred in *The Rambling Kid from Powder River.* Summer scenes flashing on the screen made us yearn for Arizona.

Although the Berkshire hills still had appeal, we didn't let icicles gather under the Ford's tires. By steady driving we reached the lowlands to the east, and again breathed warmer air, not as warm as in the Ontario fruit belt, but nowhere as bone chilling as in Pittsfield.

We found New England and its people distinctly different. In Springfield we thought there was antiquity combined with modernism in the buildings we observed. The city seemed prosperous.

So it was with other New England cities. From explanations by gasoline station attendants and others we talked with we gathered that manufacturing was the chief source of income. Some cities specialized in cotton, they said, others in shoes and textiles. Work was plentiful, we were told, but was contingent on an understanding of factory conditions. That excluded us in the event we might have to spend the winter up north. Women worked in the plants, too, sometimes outnumbering men.

Inquiry revealed we wouldn't have to drive through Boston's congested streets to reach Maine. We could avoid the city by detouring over a gravel road to Arlington and then get on the Newbury Turnpike. For us, "turnpike" was a new word, New England's version of what we knew as a highway.

Darkness descended, and had it been warmer we probably would have camped. Well-lighted towns we drove through seemed remarkably familiar, yet we had never been in them. It all was vivid, so real. History, as we had studied it, had come to life. We were traveling through territory which definitely reflected an aura of American Revolutionary days.

Lexington brought to my mind Ralph Waldo Emerson's stirring words, "Here once embattled farmers stood," to defeat a British force outnumbering them more than eight to one. Other towns, too, Arlington, Medford, and Malden, recalled for us the momentous events that set the stage for America's independence. Reliving Longfellow's poem, "Paul Revere's Ride," we contrasted his experience on horseback with ours in the Ford. Astride his galloping steed, he couldn't have been confused about finding his way, as evidenced by his timely arrival to sound the alert for the ensuing Battle of Lexington. In our Ford, we were.

Yet, I wasn't quite sure whether Paul Revere had an easy time finding his way because there probably weren't any road signs.

"But maybe there were signs in those days," Elliott said. "The British must have torn them down. That's why there aren't any left now."

He may have been right, because the highways we were on wound in and out and, unlike Wisconsin, lacked signs and road numbers. Seven years earlier, Wisconsin had become the first state to number its roads. Elliott reminded me of our state's boast, "It's easier to find your way on Wisconsin's highways than to lose your way in other states."

While I drove, he jumped out every few minutes to ask directions. A pedestrian added to our confusion.

"Go down this street until you come to the river," he said, pointing straight ahead. After giving us some complicated directions to reach the river bank he added, "Then turn right until you come to a double streetcar track, and then turn left at the first corner, and when you get to Malden Square, ask someone how to go from there."

The route from Malden Square likewise proved complicated. We had dodged Boston to avoid traffic on perplexing streets, but the detour had been just as bewildering. We finally did come to the Newbury Turnpike.

We had noticed the marked change in dialect as we talked with New Englanders. Our attempts to imitate it were miserable. As nearly as we could make out, the people slurred their "rs" and shortened "mouth" to "muth," and did other sleights-of-tongue with the American language.

Near Newburyport Elliott asked an elderly man if we were on the right road to Portsmouth. Like a true midwesterner, Elliott clearly enunciated Portsmouth.

"Neva hea'd of the place." The man bethought himself a moment. "Yuh don't mean Putsmuth?" he asked.

The man's New England accent was so pronounced we had

difficulty understanding the directions he gave. We did, however, pull into a tourist camp after 11 P.M. a few miles south of Portsmouth. We had added another state to our growing list. We were in New Hampshire, and it was much warmer, with no trace of snow. Pines grew by the roadside, and among them we had a restful night's sleep.

In Portsmouth the next morning, as I watched a Ford just like ours coming down the street, the thought flashed through my mind that this was what our car looked like. The approaching touring model was short and narrow, small compared with other makes of cars. Its top was a black fabric, matching the auto's body. The wheels had wooden spokes and two three-inch tires at the front and two three-and-one-half-inch tires at the back, mounted on steel rims. There was no trunk at the rear, nor a spare tire. Two headlights were bracketed between sides of the radiator and the front fenders. The only difference between the two cars was side curtains. We still had ours up, while the other car was completely open.

But it wasn't only the similarity of our vehicles that engrossed my attention. Unbelievably, it was a car wheel rolling alongside the other Ford as the driver casually drove on. The wheel gained momentum, as if pushed by someone rolling a hoop, and spun ahead of the car. We saw the driver's startled look as he suddenly realized the wheel had come off the rear axle of his vehicle. He slammed on the brakes. The last we saw, the driver was running down the street to retrieve his tire after it swerved against a curb and toppled to the ground.

The Yankee dialect of a traffic officer in Portsmouth intrigued us so much we drove around the block to come back for more information. From the outset of our trip, Elliott contended the best source of information was an officer of the law. This had proved to be the case. Never did we encounter one who did not guide us rightly, even if we walked into the middle of a busy intersection to question a policeman directing traffic. Most filling stations gave us good directions, too, but they weren't always reliable. Occasionally an inexperienced attendant merely guessed at the information he imparted. Chambers of Commerce were helpful, too, especially those in smaller communities.

Our first glimpse of the Atlantic Ocean was at York Beach, Maine. The mighty Atlantic awed us with its vast expanse of roaring waves.

We had another first at York Beach, a traffic mishap. A Ford crisscrossing the road brushed against our car, tearing off a grease cup, blowing out the left front tire, and jostling the Ford to the edge of the ditch. The other car kept going, but Elliott jotted down its license number. Indignant, we thought to trace the car's driver, but gave up the idea figuring it wasn't worth the time and effort. Within an hour we repaired the damage and were on our way to Portland.

Trees and the landscape in general were reminiscent of northern Wisconsin. Chickadees emitted *dee-dee-dees,* as if predicting snow. When we drove into Portland, Elliott suggested we mail postal cards to our families and friends to let them know we had arrived at the first corner state exactly two months to the day we began our trip. He also suggested we mail pennants of Maine to be hung in our rooms.

One of the first persons with whom we talked in Portland, a scholarly looking man with ruddy cheeks and graying side whiskers, proudly let us know the city was the birthplace and home of Henry Wadsworth Longfellow.

"You know about him, of course," he said. His assertion led to a lively discussion about America's celebrated poet.

Yes, we were familiar with "The Courtship of Miles

Standish," "The Village Blacksmith," and "The Wreck of the Hesperus."

He asked whether we knew of Longfellow's poem of Hiawatha, the Indian peacemaker of legendary lore.

"We studied that, too," Elliott said. "But do you know about the rivalry Hiawatha caused?"

The man looked at us with amused interest. We told him how areas from Michigan's Tahquamenon Falls to Wisconsin's western end of Lake Superior outdid each other proclaiming themselves "The Land of Hiawatha."

Our friend thought about this a moment. "Why shouldn't they?" he asked. "They are all 'By the shores of Gitche Gumee, By the shining Big-Sea-Water.'"

The way it looked to us, Portland was a thriving city, with a population of possibly 70,000. Parking space was scarce in the busier section of the main street. We drifted into one of the city's buildings during the evening, where we listened to its symphony orchestra rehearse for the next concert. We should have spent more time in Portland to observe its port activities, to view its factories, and to visit its famous lighthouse. But, heeding the chickadees and Longfellow's "sail on," we left late at night to camp at Sacco, Maine.

The next morning I took off the mittens purchased in New York State. Before long we removed our jackets and took down the Ford's side curtains. By the time we reached Boston, moderating temperatures gave hope winter was behind.

Unintentionally we veered from our course, entering Boston by way of a jagged brick street. Without knowing it, we drove in the vicinity of Bunker Hill, but didn't find it until later. We had an impelling urge to be at the historic site. Many a time Elliott and I, as youngsters on our way home from our Ninth Avenue school, had fought imaginary Bunker Hill battles on piles of dirt, one of us on top of the hill fending off the other charging up the mound.

Reasoning that traffic in Boston would be congested, we parked the Ford near the intersection of Washington and Causeway to begin exploration on foot. Aimlessly, we walked toward Haymarket Square, attracted by its name. Wondering how to get to Boston's main street, we approached a man leaning against the wall of a building and asked him for directions.

"Main street?" the man stared at us dubiously. "Never heard of a main street."

Coming to Haymarket Square we understood what the Bostonian meant. We saw no main street. Many thoroughfares jutted from the square.

Elliott asked another man why some Boston streets have twists and turns.

"Why don't cows walk straight?" the man responded. We pondered his question. "They did the surveying," he said. We concluded the streets were cow trails of colonial days.

Our meandering led us to the spot where the Boston Massacre took place prior to the American Revolution. The blotch of red visible on the walkway convinced us Bostonians were determined to preserve identity of the historic massacre location.

Our random tour of the city brought us to Paul Revere's home, the Old State House where colonists proclaimed independence, Faneuil Hall where patriots conducted meetings, and a cemetery where Samuel Adams, Paul Revere, Benjamin Franklin's parents, and other notable persons of the Revolutionary period are buried. We didn't get to the scene of the Boston Tea Party where patriots dumped tea from British ships in protest against an import tax, nor the Old North

ARE HAVING A GREAT TRIP

Elliott Nystrom and Seegar Swanson Who Are on Tour of the United States in a Ford Are Enjoying Themselves.

The two young Ashlanders, Elliott Nystrom and Seegar Swanson, who left September 20 on a tour to the four corners of the United States, have completed the first lap of their journey, according to word received today. They entered the corner state of Maine on November 20, exactly two months to the day since their departure from Ashland.

The boys are enjoying a great variety of experiences in their travels from state to state. Their original nest egg of $100 has long since vanished, but by working on the state roads of New York and by picking fruit on a large farm in the Niagara fruit belt for a period of one month, the treasury has been replenished temporarily. By procuring employment from time to time the young men hope to get completely around the country.

In Evanston, Ill., the police officials invited the travelers to leave their car in a park on the shores of Lake Michigan, but the cold, raw wind that blew off its blue waters dampened their spirits. Accordingly, they parked their Ford on one of the main business streets of the city and slept there for two nights.

The Ford finds many kinds of resting places at night. Sometimes it reposes in tourist camps, other times in back yards, occasionally in baseball parks, and once it spent the night alongside of a cemetery.

Several times there have been narrow escapes from serious accidents. On an exceedingly steep hill in Pennsylvania the brakes of the car burned out, and by the time the machine had glided to the bottom considerable momentum had been gained. At the foot of the steep incline was a sharp right an legturn. The Ford went around that turn on two wheels, missing an approaching street car by inches, and dodging another automobile by a mere fraction of a foot. In order to avoid a plunge in a river ahead it was necessary to bring the Ford to a halt by driving against a curbing.

In western New York, in the Mohawk Valley, and in the Berkshire Hills zero weather was encountered. At Cicero, N. Y., a blinding snow storm arose just as the rear left tire of the Ford blew out. A 3-sided wagon shed offered shelter for the night. While driving the next day it was necessary to stop every twenty miles for hot coffee in order to keep warm.

The New England states proved interesting, especially the colonial atmosphere and the peculiarity in speech. Upon inquiring of native the distance to Portsmouth, the boys received the reply that he knew of no such city as Portsmouth. After a moment, however, he bethought himself and asked if they were referring to "Pawtsmuth."

In Maine when a driver passes another car he steers into the machine he is passing just as he gets to the middle of it. At any rate, that is what one man did to the Ashland youths. Outside of a blow out, the loss of a portion of a front wheel, a damaged fender, and a good shaking in general, no serious loss was suffered. The reckless autoist was in haste, so he failed to stop to see the results of his clever driving.

The sunny south is beckoning to the boys. If snow and cold does not detain them for the winter in Maine,

Ashland Daily Press, *November 24, 1924*

Church where two lanterns were hung in the belfry to start Paul Revere on his midnight ride. Bostonians from whom we sought directions, however, refreshed our memories concerning the historic significance of the tea party and the church.

Hungry after several hours of walking, we entered a restaurant on Huntington Avenue with one purpose in mind. We would order Boston beans, about which we had heard so much. Finding none listed on the menu, we complained to the waiter.

Apologetically he explained we would have a better chance of getting Boston beans if we ate out of town.

Aided by a city map, we reached the Ford about 10 P.M. Though we had parked it on an out-of-the-way street which was practically deserted, everything was intact. Elliott used the map to guide us out of the city. We drove close to the Charles River, and through narrow streets of the wholesale district. That night we camped on a vacant lot in the heart of a small town south of Boston.

About noon the next day we came to Pawtucket, Rhode Island, which impressed us as truly one of the most typical colonial cities. Its streets, patterned after those of Boston, were narrow and difficult to follow. Modern buildings like those which had sprung up in Boston were missing in Pawtucket. From what we observed, the city continued to live in the glory of its colonial past.

Extraordinary in Pawtucket was the opportunity to purchase five gallons of gasoline at 14 cents a gallon, and a quart of oil for 15 cents. We regretted we had but recently filled our tank with gasoline selling at 17 cents a gallon. Had we bought oil, the price would have been 25 cents. Those prices were, on the average, what we had been paying since the beginning of our tour.

More devious roads complicated our drive to Providence, and in the city itself cows must have been as numerous in colonial times as in Boston if the layout of streets were any criterion. The city's aura of colonial days was noticeable, but like Boston, Providence was interspersed with modern buildings. We were sorry to find the state capitol closed.

After entering Connecticut at Pawcatuck, I thought for a moment we were driving backwards to Pawtucket. Elliott's discerning eye detected the resemblance in spelling. We were in Pawcatuck, not Pawtucket.

A billboard served as an excellent windbreak that night as we weathered a gusty deluge of rain. A tall man wearing a raincoat and a rubber hat walked toward us as we were about to leave the next morning.

"You camped in a dangerous place," he said. "There's dynamite stored over there." He pointed to a construction site on the field where we had slept.

In New London we stopped for dinner in a restaurant where we were served by a bustling waitress.

"Do you want soup?" she asked.

"No," Elliott replied, preferring not to add an extra charge.

"It's free," she said.

"Then we'll have soup," Elliott said.

A stubble-bearded man at a corner table overheard the remark about free soup, and in a loud voice demanded, "Hey, waitress, bring me some of that soup! Why didn't you tell me it was free!"

We were drinking the last drops from our coffee cups when the waitress prepared to make out our bill.

"Would you like some pie?" she asked, pausing with pad and pencil before tallying the amount of our bill.

"Apple, if you have it," Elliott said. I chose pumpkin. We thought that dessert, like the soup, would be free. It wasn't.

Cold followed the rain. We dug out our one pair of mittens and wrapped blankets around our legs. Our hope was to reach New Haven in time for the annual football classic between Yale and Harvard. Missing the event by a day, we had to content ourselves by reading a newspaper account of the game which Yale won 19-6.

Had we not read the newspaper, we hardly would have suspected that one of the nation's outstanding games had been played in New Haven so recently, and that the home team had won. There was no sign of celebration and no apparent excitement. Midwest football cities didn't take big victories in stride like that.

As the Ford rambled through Stratford, Bridgeport, and finally Norwalk, we knew we were seeing the last of New England. We were getting close to New York City, aware that a totally different adventure lay before us. At New Rochelle we stopped to map our strategy. We already had successfully driven the Ford over intricate metropolitan streets in several big cities, but we fully expected those of New York to be more difficult. There certainly wouldn't be any tourist camps, and stopping at hotels would be prohibitive as far as our meager finances were concerned. The best procedure, we decided, would be to cross the Hudson River into New Jersey, park the Ford somewhere, and return to New York City to get a close-up look at its wonders.

We hoped it would be possible to get the Ford aboard a ferryboat before we reached the far end of the city. A filling station attendant said this would be impossible.

"Drive to 125th Street and take the Hackensack Ferry," he said. "You won't have any problem getting there. The streets are numbered."

As the attendant said, we didn't have any problem, but drove cautiously nevertheless. Perhaps warning signs had something to do with this. We chuckled as we read, "Fools used to blow out the gas, now they step on it," and "The jaywalker is taking a short cut to the hospital." As we gradually moved into the nation's largest city, we saw that streets were straight and the traffic system so well-organized that a novice could drive a car there with greater ease than even in some of the small cities we had traveled through. We rode part of the way on a street over which ran elevated trains. There some careful driving was necessary, with squeezes that allowed but an inch or so on either side. We would not have hesitated, however, to continue to Broadway, but following instructions, turned toward the Hudson River at 125th Street.

Our Ford was one of the three last vehicles squeezed aboard the ferry. As the boat crossed the Hudson, we had our first opportunity to scan the New York skyline, amazed by buildings taller than trees in Wisconsin, with enough little ones scattered between to resemble saplings growing in the woods.

When the ferry docked at Edgewater, New Jersey, we expected to pay possibly from one to two dollars and a half for the river ride. To our delight, the toll was only 30 cents. At Edgewater we changed our plans. Noting that Richfield Park was nearby, Elliott remembered he had been invited to visit the Paul Nystrom family there. Although the surname was identical, the Nystroms were not related to Elliott. They were friends of his sister Helen, who had taught school in Richfield Park.

We spruced up in the YMCA in Hackensack and left for the Nystrom home. Arriving there early in the evening, we were welcomed warmly. Elliott introduced himself as "the long-delayed voyager" and acquainted the family with his "long-

Nystrom sisters, Mom and a friend of Richfield Park, N.J.

delayed partner." We shook hands with Mr. and Mrs. Nystrom and were delighted to meet their two daughters. Birna, the older, with soft brown eyes and a demure manner, was a contrast to Lucille, fairer and more outgoing.

The Nystroms asked us to relate high points of our trip, and we willingly obliged them. They made us feel so much at home we seriously considered their suggestion we obtain work and delay traveling until warmer weather the coming spring. The Nystroms invited us to sleep in their home, but yielded to our wish to sleep in the Ford, recommending we park it under a tree in their yard.

Partly with the idea of looking for work, we climbed aboard a train for Weehawken the next morning, took a ferry to 42nd Street in New York City, and began a tour of the city on foot.

Purchasing a newspaper, we combed the classified adver-

tising columns for jobs and employment offices. Intent on
obtaining stenographic or bookkeeping positions, we visited
several offices. Clerks were polite, but offered little encouragement after writing our names and other information on application blanks. This didn't disconcert us. We thought the
employment offices demanded too great a percentage of a first
month's salary.

Attracted by a sign in front of an office where no fees were
assessed, we entered and took seats to wait our turn in the
midst of a long line of applicants for jobs. Elliott nudged me,
pointing to a sign indicating a "Stenographic, Bookkeeping
and Clerical Division." There was no rush of men for this type
of work. We were the only ones applying.

"The common labor division is at the next gate," a desk
clerk said as he critically ran his eye up and down the outdoor
clothes we wore.

"We've been traveling, but we're looking for office work,"
Elliott said.

The clerk picked up a printed sheet of paper and ran a
pencil down its margin. "The best I can offer you is a temporary job in the post office. You can fill in as extra typists during
the Christmas rush," he said. "Report tomorrow and I'll give
you a work assignment card. The pay will be 60 cents an hour,
but be sure you show up in office clothes." He again eyed our
outdoor garb, this time with an unmistakable note of
contempt.

We knew our available cash was too meager to buy suits.
Elliott, however, said he had a pair of dress trousers packed in
his suitcase, and with purchase of a jacket, he would be dressed
like a typist. Lacking dress trousers, I expressed willingness to
look for manual labor.

"It's a long time till tomorrow," Elliott said. "Let's see more

Elliott poses with his namesake but unrelated New Jersey girls.

of the city."

We marveled at the countless offices of New York's skyscrapers. Thousands of persons working in them obviously weren't producing any crops or manufactured goods, yet all were making money doing something. Elliott called it paper work, doing things for those who labored elsewhere, be it farming, manufacturing, or conducting business enterprises. It might be insurance, preparing architectural drawings, financing, editing manuscripts, or endless other services. Whatever their excuse for being, the offices were indeed a hub of national and international activity.

We recognized a trip to New York would be incomplete unless we took a ferryboat to the Statue of Liberty. Listening to tunes played by an accordionist, we gazed at New York's teeming harbor as the ferry plowed its way through the water. Against the backdrop of Manhattan's skyscrapers we watched huge ocean vessels navigating into and out of the harbor, and tugs belching smoke. Drawing close to Ellis Island, we were aware of its role in clearing immigrants for life in America after they first had sensed their new freedom by observing the Statue of Liberty. My own parents had experienced this.

Ascending stairs inside the Statue of Liberty was exhilarating. Not all visitors went the entire way up, but we climbed as high as the stairs went. A walk into the hollow of the enormous arm holding its torch aloft would have added to the thrill, but that was not permitted.

As the ferry docked at its Manhattan pier, we lingered to view the ongoing harbor activity, enthralled by our final look at the island on which the Statue of Liberty stood.

By now we were hungry, and drew comment in a cafeteria when we made several trips to the counter for food. New Yorkers, we gathered, were content with coffee and a light snack.

When Elliott proffered a $10 traveler's check for payment of our bill, the cashier handed it back.

"Here we take only money," she said.

"A traveler's check is like money, good anywhere," Elliott said.

The cashier wasn't convinced. She summoned the "boss."

"She's right," he said. "You've got to pay with cash."

We volunteered to get the check cashed elsewhere, but as we started for the door, the "boss" halted us.

"Wait a minute," he said. "I have to hold one of you here for security."

While I was held hostage, Elliott went down the street looking for a bank. When he returned he said a Western Union office had cashed the check.

As the fascination of looking up at skyscrapers diminished, we directed our course to the Bowery. We recognized at once the district's dingy appearance was in sharp contrast with Broadway, and we could see by the dress and behavior of the men and women on its streets they did not have homes on Fifth Avenue. Nevertheless, we thought the area wasn't entirely reprehensible.

We felt the Bowery afforded needed assistance for unfortunates lacking jobs or places to live. A large building had a free employment office, and upstairs were scores of cots placed side by side to be rented at 15 cents to 25 cents a night.

An unshaved man with uncombed hair came toward us in the corridor.

"Are you from Ashland, Wisconsin?" he asked. He had noticed the word "Ashland" on the back of Elliott's sweatshirt. "I was there once, sailing on an ore boat."

Obviously, he had fallen upon harder times, but his recollection of Ashland was music to our ears.

These were the days of the nation's Prohibition
Amendment when it was illegal to manufacture, sell or transport intoxicating beverages. Speakeasies and bootlegging
increasingly were violating this 18th Constitutional
Amendment. So it wasn't strange we should surmise a street
corner orator was giving a temperance lecture. We elbowed
our way through a small group of listeners to hear his message.
His talk, however, wasn't against the use of alcohol. He tore at
his hair, and pounded his fists as he denounced the growing
use of aspirin as the major threat to New Yorkers. He
described aspirin as a menacing drug, but we doubted aspirin
was as much a menace as speakeasies or bootlegging.

By night we wandered as far as the Harlem YMCA where we
booked a room on the eighth floor. Tired from the day's sightseeing, we were confident nothing would awaken us.

That was a delusion. Outside the noise was so disturbing we
looked out the window to see what was going on.

"No wonder it's so stuffy in here," Elliott said when we had
difficulty peering through the haze hanging over the city.
Adding to our discomfort was the shabby mattress on the bed.
Elliott got up to try sleeping on the floor.

When we left early in the morning, we resolved not to
return to the employment office for Elliott's prospective job in
the post office. New York might be all right to work in, but we
preferred fresh air and sleep at night.

With no particular goal in mind, we continued wandering
about the city's streets. The rush for restaurants, cafeterias and
other eating places was so terrific we postponed our lunch until
two o'clock. Such a surging mass of people we never had seen
before. Hemmed in by walls of so many tall structures, what
could they do if a major calamity occurred? When a waiter
served us a hamburger of doubtful vintage, we thought of the

Author poses with Nystrom sisters who escorted Tramps in New York City.

enormous problem of supplying food to the millions of persons working and living in New York.

Bent on averting another night of restless tossing in New York City, we headed for a ferry. We would have preferred to stay long enough to attend a big theater stage show near Times Square, but at $2.50 a seat, felt we couldn't afford the luxury.

We spent Thanksgiving Day with the Nystroms. In true holiday style, Mrs. Nystrom, a motherly woman and an excellent cook, served a traditional Thanksgiving dinner. Radio was in its infancy, so we considered it a rare treat when Mr. Nystrom tuned in the Penn vs. Cornell football game. The broadcast was essentially localized, there being no national hookups. Mr. Nystrom, a soft-spoken educator, intently followed the game to the very end, Penn winning 20-0. To us the broadcast was even more exciting because radio was so new that back home we had listened only to crudely-fashioned crystal sets equipped with earphones.

After the game we enjoyed a long walk with the sisters, and during the evening they entertained with piano music and singing. As students, they were enjoying the holiday vacation. When discussion centered around sights Elliott and I had seen in New York, the girls said there was much more to see. We then asked if they would go to New York with us. With approval of their parents, they accepted the invitation.

It was fun and a new experience for us having two attractive coeds from New Jersey guide us in New York City. Their engaging smiles and eagerness to show us the sights gave promise of a happy day ahead.

The first place we visited was Wall Street. Although we already had briefly passed through it, we were pleased the girls took us to the street again. From them we gained an understanding of how the narrow street actually embraces a whole financial district with its many banks and a myriad of other institutions.

How we had overlooked the old Federal Building on our first Wall Street visit was a mystery. It was there George

Washington was inaugurated in 1789 as the nation's first president, and where Congress held its first session. The old Trinity Church, with its prominent steeple, had more meaning after the girls took us inside. We had a feeling of reverence as we read names and dates on the well-preserved gravestones in the churchyard burial ground. Before we left Wall Street, the girls led us into the stock exchange to witness the spirited and, at moments, hectic buying and selling of stocks.

We had an encompassing view of New York City after a smoothly operating elevator took us to the top of the 60-story Woolworth Building, the world's tallest skyscraper. We had heard somewhere along our trip we would have butterflies in our stomachs if we rode the elevator. To the contrary, the ride was delightful. As we looked over the city from the 60th floor, we realized the futility of covering all of New York in a few short days, especially on foot.

We asked the girls where they would like to have lunch.

"Let's eat in the Automat," Lucille suggested.

Elliott and I had never heard of an Automat. It was a novel experience to put nickels in a slot, open small compartment doors, and withdraw whatever we wanted to eat. Chicken pie was the unanimous choice for lunch. For each pie we inserted six nickels in the chicken pie compartment. We ate more than enough of rolls and dessert just to put in nickels to watch the system work.

The afternoon flew by all too quickly as we covered considerable ground. We took a subway to the Bronx Zoo, for which we paid a fare of five cents each. Actually, going to the zoo was a pretext for Elliott and me to experience a ride on the underground railway. Passengers made a rush for the doors when the subway came to a sudden halt. I almost didn't get aboard. The door closed in on me just as I squeezed in.

We also visited the New York Museum, went through the Pennsylvania Railway Station, and had our first ride on escalators in Macy's and Gimbel's department stores. At Times Square we bought copies of the *Superior Telegram* and the *Duluth News-Tribune* at five cents per copy. From them we gleaned bits of back-home news.

Throughout the day Elliott and I were aware what a melting pot New York City really is. The girls paid no attention to peculiarities of speech, but we realized New Yorkers had a dialect of their own when we heard "foist" for "first," "woik" for "work" and other differences in pronunciation. "Ither" for "either" and "nither" for "neither" sounded to us like affectations, but no, they rolled off New Yorker tongues like everyday language.

When we at last returned to the Nystrom home, Elliott and I had the feeling we had seen more of New York City this one day than on the two days we had been there on our own. Besides, the day had been more romantic. In Richfield Park, we went to a movie with the girls to see *Potash and Perlmutter in the Moving Picture Business.* We topped off the evening with sundaes in an ice cream parlor.

Resolved to leave for the south, we ate a late breakfast served by Mrs. Nystrom the next morning, and then bade her good-bye when she left to spend the day in New York City. The Ford had a flat tire, the only one since Portland, but somehow it was late afternoon before we finished repairing it. The girls, of course, had something to do with our procrastination. By late afternoon Mrs. Nystrom returned from New York City to find us still in Richfield Park. We maintained there was need to start traveling at once. The Nystroms, however, prevailed upon us to wait until the following morning, promising to waken us at seven o'clock for an early start.

The weather had turned colder the last two nights, and the ground was covered with snow. We left, nevertheless, on a note of optimism. Quoting a billboard sign we had seen in New York City, Elliott called out, "It's June in Miami," as the Ford pulled out of the Nystrom yard.

— The Log, Thu. Dec. 4, 1924

Chapter VII
Funds Hit Bottom

THE BEGINNING of our southward journey was principally through cities like Newark, Elizabeth, and Princeton. Since it was Sunday morning, university students at Princeton apparently were "sleeping in." There was little sign of activity as we drove around to gain a better insight of the educational institution we had heard so much about.

A big truck crawling slowly ahead of us in northern Pennsylvania led me to slow down the Ford. The snail's pace of both vehicles seemed endless, and the truck driver made no effort to turn off for me to pass. Seeing no traffic coming toward us, I steered into the outer lane to get by the truck.

A short distance beyond we were waved to a halt by a lean, rabbit-like man who hopped onto the road displaying the badge of a town officer.

"I have to take you to the justice of the peace," he said.

Getting into the Ford, he directed us to a house a half-mile down the highway. In the living room we saw several men lounging around a stove, smoking and talking, giving the room an atmosphere of bachelor quarters.

In a wooden swivel chair behind an oak table, the justice heard the charge, "recklessly passing a truck near a curve."

The justice, a sympathetic middle-aged man, seemed more interested in our trip than in conducting a judicial trial. He listened attentively when we told him we were working our way around the United States, and were so low in cash we were looking for jobs to get us to Florida for the winter.

"You won't find jobs around here," he said.

For a moment the justice pondered. I wondered, would it be a fine, or 10 days in jail?

Tapping a hand-carved gavel on the table top, the justice pushed back his chair and said, "Boys, I like the idea of working your way around the country. I'll let you go with a warning. If you were from Pennsylvania I'd fine you $15 and costs."

As we gratefully left the room, we saw the town officer grab a chair to sit beside the stove. We thought maybe he had arrested us just to get in from the cold.

A broad paved highway separated by a beautiful boulevard impressed us as we neared Philadelphia. We knew William Penn had ideally platted the city when it was founded, but here was evidence his dream had been extended way beyond his model plan.

Much as we desired to explore the nation's third largest city, our eagerness to reach Florida before our cash ran out was more impelling. We did want to see Independence Hall, though, and in our search for it, fortunately stumbled upon other major attractions, such as gorgeous parks, the towering

First edition of Rand McNally road atlas was published in 1924 and used by the Tramps. Courtesy of Newberry Library, Chicago, Illinois.

city hall capped with a statue of William Penn, the Art Museum, and varied historic buildings.

Unfamiliar with one-way streets, I drove our Ford the wrong way on one of them. Though we were in the "city of brotherly love," drivers apparently resented a car coming at them. As if in protest, they swerved their vehicles toward us, compelling me to dodge away from them. A pedestrian who saw our plight motioned the Ford toward the curb, directing me to drive back the way we had come. Another pedestrian suggested we turn off to the right at the intersection just ahead. Acting upon this advice we soon were out of our predicament.

We recognized Independence Hall immediately. Once more, something we had read or heard about, all of a sudden popped out as reality. We were at the center of Revolutionary activity, standing before the building where the Declaration of Independence was signed on July 4, 1776, and where America's famous Liberty Bell was preserved. Other historic events came to mind. The U.S. Constitution had been signed in Philadelphia, and there in 1775 George Washington had been appointed commander in chief of the colonial forces.

Snow and darkness overtook us as we reluctantly left the Quaker City. With the traffic quite heavy, and the taillight of the Ford broken, we dared not risk travel at night for fear of arrest. Parking in a vacant lot near Chester, we planned to retire without supper because our larder was empty. But we didn't go to bed hungry. We discovered a bag of goodies and a box of chocolates the Nystrom girls had packed in the car without our knowledge.

The route as traveled in this chapter is highlighted on this map taken from Official Automobile Road Maps of the United States published by Rand McNally & Company in 1924 and used by Tramps. Courtesy of Newberry Library, Chicago, Illinois. (opposite)

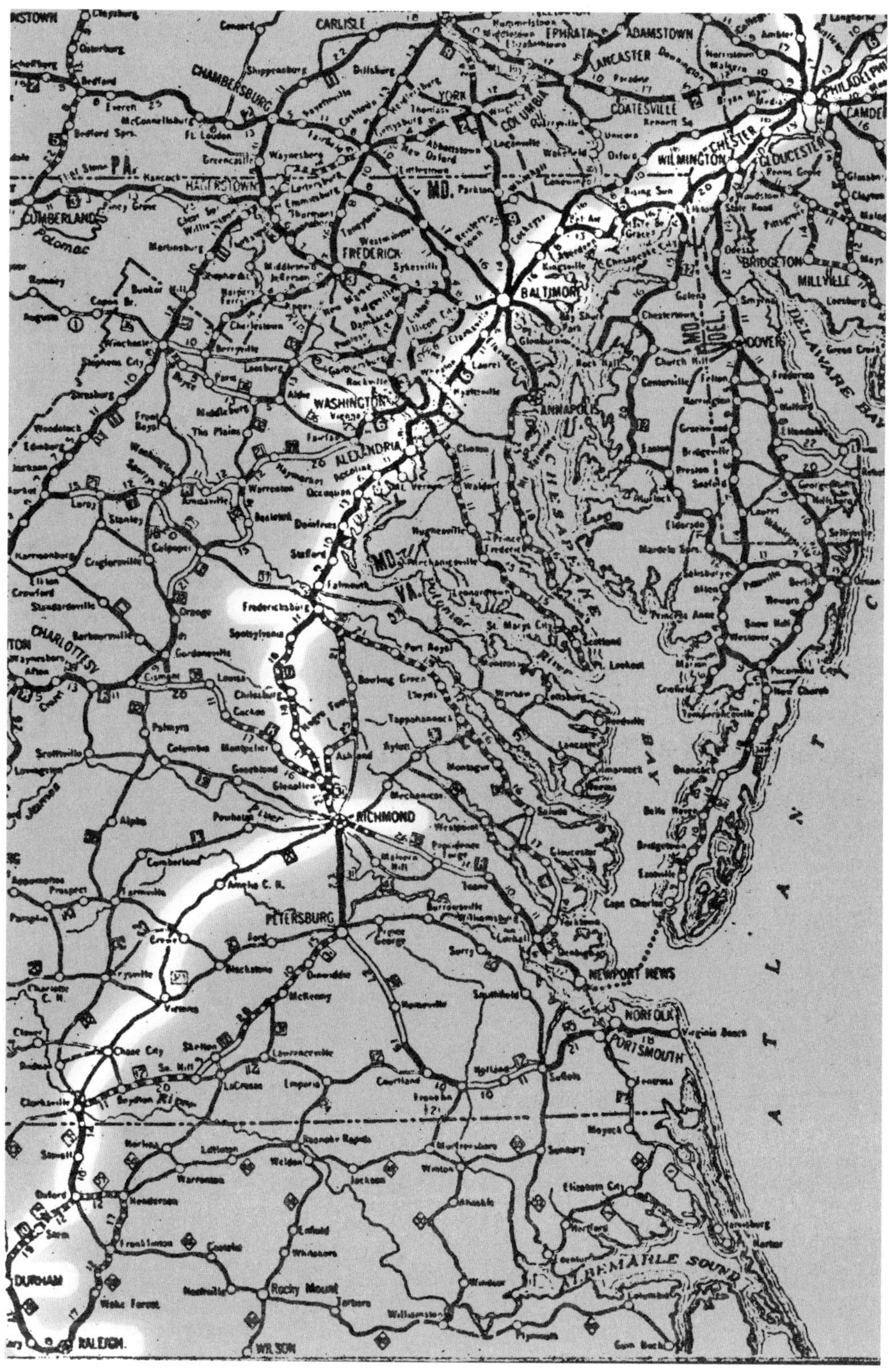

Up to this time we had crossed many bridges in the various states, but not until we were in the vicinity of Havre de Grace, Maryland, did we have to pay toll. Here they assessed 65 cents to cross over a northern inlet of Chesapeake Bay. We thought this was a needless drain on our cash reserve, but as Elliott said, "it beats paddling."

In snowy Wilmington, one of the few places where we stopped in Delaware, a storekeeper drolly remarked it was warm in Virginia. We thought he might be right when we noted the large red leaves still clinging to oaks along the highway in Maryland, giving the effect of an extended autumn. Birds flitting among tree branches added to this effect.

Baltimore with its population of over 800,000 deserved more attention, but we hurried through it. We took time, however, to note its splendid harbor, large department stores, historic monuments, and attractive parks. We were aware that somewhere nearby Francis Scott Key wrote "The Star-Spangled Banner."

After setting up camp in a wooded tract on the fringe of Washington, D.C., we hiked into the city to gain a nighttime view of the nation's Capitol, the dome of which was lighted elegantly. Streets were comparatively empty so we had an excellent opportunity to observe leisurely other buildings and attractions.

Guides escorted us through the Capitol the next day, for which we paid 25 cents each. We watched an artist apply new colors to designs and paintings, which the guide said was exacting work requiring great skill.

Our timing for being in the nation's Capitol was good, we thought. We watched Congress convene for its short term, and felt privileged to hear the reading of President Coolidge's message.

Hiking down Pennsylvania Avenue to get a close-up view of the White House, we then looked at other government buildings. South of the White House we came to the Washington Monument by the Potomac River.

The opportunity to ascend the more than 550-foot marble memorial, highest in the world, was enticing. An elevator was available inside, but we chose to climb the stairs. Someone told us there were about 900 steps, and we believed this when we finally reached eight windows 500 feet above ground. From the windows we had a spectacular bird's-eye view of the city. We admired Washington's imposing buildings, its magnificent parks, its streets bordered with trees, and, of course, Capitol Hill.

Disdaining descent by elevator, we went down by foot. This, we found, required cautious effort. But having both climbed and descended the stairway added to the thrill of our visit at the Washington Monument.

Equally unforgettable was the Lincoln Memorial. Dedicated on the banks of the Potomac River in 1922, only two years before we stood in front of it, the white marble temple reflected its newness. Within the monument we stood in awed silence before the huge statue of Abraham Lincoln. It portrayed him in concerned thought while seated in a big chair, his arms resting on its sides. In our minds, Daniel Chester French indeed had created a realistic statue of the Great Emancipator.

Poor roads confronted us after we crossed the Potomac River to enter Virginia. Signs told us we were near Mount Vernon, the home of George Washington, but we did not go there. This we regretted when tourists later told us of their pleasant experiences on Washington's plantation.

Although Virginia's frost had killed their greenness, leaves still draped oak branches, and pines grew in abundance. The air was warm and gentle, giving us spring fever. We were in Dixieland, and we sensed an atmosphere of change. For one thing, we felt more like camping, as if freed from researching historical sites and big cities. The out-of-doors again was beckoning, just as it had done at the outset of our trip.

Some of the change was minor, but significant nevertheless. There was the matter of buying butter. Never had we purchased less than a pound at a time. Yet in Virginia we bought "sticks" weighing a quarter of a pound. Now that we were getting into warmer weather, that obviously was an advantage. Expecting to see large cotton and tobacco plantations, in northern Virginia we saw small farms instead. We were told owners of large acreages divided them into the smaller farms to be tilled largely by Negroes.

When we camped for the night at Fredericksburg we were in the midst of five other touring parties. For the first time in weeks we joined fellow travelers around a cozy fire. Also, we resumed the practice of preparing outdoor meals over our camp stove.

The tourists said they were going to Florida to get jobs for the winter. Among them were a baker, a carpenter, and a bricklayer. Optimistic about employment opportunities, they assured us the prospect for unskilled work also was good.

"Go down the East Coast, boys," the carpenter said. "If nothing else, you can pick oranges. The pay is good."

This all sounded encouraging, but there was one drawback. Elliott had counted our money, and knew we didn't have enough to get to Florida.

There also was discussion about being camped on historic ground. Fredericksburg, we learned, was the boyhood home of George Washington, and in this valley of the Rappahannock

River, Confederate soldiers under command of General Robert E. Lee had soundly defeated an attacking force of the Union Army in one of the fiercest battles of the Civil War.

Fredericksburg had another distinction. Dogs barked at night in all parts of the city. In no other community had we heard so many.

In glowing terms our fellow tourists spoke of their hometowns as perfect places to live. We wondered, though, if back home they wrote letters to the editor or complained to councilmen about poor streets and high taxes.

Nearing the city of Richmond the following day we contributed our mite toward payment of another bridge with a 10 cents toll. Arriving at Bryan Park, Richmond's tourist camp, we parked in the best facility we had seen since leaving Wisconsin. A log cabin was equipped with hot and cold water, shower baths, a fireplace, and other camping luxuries.

The elderly man camped next to us surprisingly asked if we wanted a job. He showed us a device for making silvery plaques embellished with black numbers. The plaques, he said, not only were ornamental, but they distinctly displayed a house number when mounted over a doorway. He offered us a 20 percent commission for orders we booked.

Elliott objected to selling house numbers door to door, but I thought it was worth a try. So while he scouted Richmond employment offices, I undertook salesmanship. Though I covered much of the city's residential area, I sold nothing.

In contrast to the tourists in Fredericksburg, we concluded those in the Richmond camp were a pessimistic lot. There was no work in Florida, they said, and the "whole South is no place for a northerner looking for a job," simply because there wasn't even enough work for people living in the South. Members of a family from Olean, New York were returning to their home.

Another said they would travel north as far as Maryland, hoping something would turn up.

Rain in Richmond made our search for employment unpleasant. We filed applications for work varying from stenography to street cleaning, and unsuccessfully tried a direct approach by applying at stores, offices, and factories.

A recruiting officer sought to enlist us in the army for three years. We told him, however, that we were looking for jobs.

"All right," he said, "but I'll bet you won't find any. If you don't, keep the army in mind."

The next day, renewing his effort to enlist us, the recruiter volunteered to sell our Ford as an added inducement. Elliott told him the car was worth at least $150.

"What?" the officer exclaimed. "You'll be lucky to get $25."

With that we left, determined to continue our quest for jobs.

When a young man accosted us to sell his new overcoat for $3, we thought the recruiter may have been right about the going price of our Ford. The overcoat with its fur collar was a bargain, we knew, but $3 was as much beyond our means as $40. We even declined to buy a needle threader for a dime, notwithstanding future need for one. If we ever got around to patching clothes, we, no doubt, would spend half the time poking thread through the eye of a needle.

After the fruitless search for work, we boarded a streetcar to return to the tourist park. It was so crowded, passengers stood tightly squeezed against each other, ignoring vacant seats for three or four people on a bench occupied by two Negro women. We thought it prudent to stand with the other passengers.

Giving up on Richmond as an opportunity for jobs, we drove the next day as far as South Hill, to be encouraged by

two carpenters who pitched their tent next to our car. They
said they were Florida-bound where they knew carpenter jobs
were plentiful, and that if we pretended to know something
about the trade we could get jobs as carpenters' helpers. They
gave us a few instructions, telling us how to handle lumber, tear
down scaffolds, supply carpenters with nails, and perform
other duties incidental to the trade. We thanked them, hoping
to make use of the instructions.

Because Sunday was a poor day to seek employment, we
rode southward. The air was so warm we traveled in shirt
sleeves. That evening while we heated a can of beans for
supper, a tired-looking hiker stopped by.

"Take my advice. Don't go to Florida," he said. "The best I
could make there was a dollar a day. Then they soaked me 40
cents for an egg sandwich and 15 cents for a cup of coffee."

Appreciative when we offered him supper, he gave us
further insight concerning his views about Florida. He
described it as a poverty state for those who couldn't afford
high prices, and a pleasure ground for the rich who could
afford to pay them.

"Why don't you ride freight trains?" Elliott asked when he
said he didn't get many rides while hitchhiking.

"That's all right up North," the man replied, "but ridin' the
rails in the South is as bad as stealin' chickens. They put you in
the pen for a long stretch."

Elliott suggested a winter in jail would mean free lodging
for a man out of work.

"No, it don't," our visitor responded. "They put you to
work on roads, and you work hard for nothin', an' you can't
break away because prison guards carry big rifles. They shoot
first and ask questions after."

Before reaching Durham, North Carolina, we heard about a

$2 million project for a new dam requiring a thousand laborers. The superintendent was a Mr. Gooch, we were told, so we looked him up. He asked where we were from, and when we said Wisconsin, he started to walk away.

"Don't need any men," he said.

We gave him the benefit of the doubt. The superintendent wasn't biased against us as northerners. This was a project intended for jobless southern workers.

Walking upriver two miles, we applied for jobs at a sawmill. A fairly large crew was turning out lumber at a rapid rate. There were no jobs for us, however.

About to cross a narrow footbridge over a rippling stream, we stopped when we saw a Negro coming toward us. Although he was more than halfway across, he turned around to walk off the bridge on the opposite side. We waved to him, beckoning him to cross the span, but he waited for us to cross first. We asked him why he had backed off the bridge. "White gentlemen is fi'st," he said.

In Durham, North Carolina, we noticed a variety of manufacturing enterprises, textile, fertilizer, lumber, and flour, but each was outnumbered by tobacco manufacturing plants. An old-timer, puffing a pipe, told us Durham became famous as a tobacco center after the Civil War. He said its tobacco products were especially favored by Union soldiers.

"We make more smoke here in a day than Pittsburgh does in a week," he said, proudly.

The old-timer also pointed in the direction of Durham's Duke University, and delighted in telling us about the many millions of dollars recently given to what was originally Trinity College by James Duke, a wealthy tobacco manufacturer. These grants resulted in the renaming of the institution and its expansion to university status. He seemed equally proud of the

University of North Carolina, the oldest state university in the country, located only 10 miles from Durham.

We made no effort to seek jobs in the tobacco plants, although we were told prospects were better there. After futilely applying for work at a hotel construction site, we departed for Raleigh. Our cash had diminished to $12.50, and of that we spent $2.00 for an inner tube.

A downpour of rain led us to camp in a field near an abandoned farm house. Here we found what we thought could have been the inspiration for the familiar song, "The Old Oaken Bucket." Hanging above a well was a bucket, solid oak with several hoops wrapped around its staves. A thick layer of moss enveloped the bucket. We lowered it into the well and brought up enough water to cook a pot of coffee.

Our stay in Raleigh was brief. We quickly toured the state capitol and sized up the city's spinning mills and several other manufacturing plants, and then applied for work in Raleigh's free employment office. A clerk said no jobs were available, even for "our own people." Only Negroes were hired for a paving project down the street, he said.

That night we stopped at Southern Pines which Elliott called a "mid-winter summer resort." There was a touch of the tropical at the place, beautifully surrounded with green vegetation. Prices were higher, though. A grocer charged us 20 cents for a stick of butter and 20 cents for a loaf of bread, inflated almost 100 percent.

The southern warmth suddenly turned to a wintry chill as we continued our journey the next morning. It was December 10. Therefore, the change probably was seasonal, although so far south we hardly expected again to wear the mittens which served us so well up north, nor to require blankets to keep warm while driving.

Roads became poor as we crossed into South Carolina. With our low cash balance, we naturally grumbled when we paid 50 cents toll to drive across an antiquated wooden bridge south of Camden. As if this weren't enough, gasoline at Camden jumped to 19 cents a gallon. We had been paying 18 cents, so we bought only two gallons.

And then, arriving in Columbia, we faced a real crisis. Grimly, Elliott counted our cash.

"It's shrunk to $6.20," he said.

— The Log, Fri. Dec. 19, 1924

Chapter VIII
Bread and Beans

QUITE CONCERNED, we drove the Ford two miles south of Columbia and camped in the woods to think matters through. Much as we detested appealing back home for financial aid, we reasoned there was no alternative. Then I remembered a letter I had received from my cousin Nels Olson, while we worked at the Bradley orchard in New York State. He was employed by the Ford Motor Company in Iron Mountain, Michigan, and wrote:

"If you ever need money, let me know."

Let him know we did. I immediately wrote Nels a letter explaining our predicament and requested a loan of $25. This, I said, would get us to Florida to find work.

Early the next morning, December 11, we mailed the letter in the Columbia post office, hoping for a favorable response before our money ran out.

Elliott calculated rapidly.

"It's bread and beans from here on," he said. He grinned resignedly.

As if preparing for a siege, we stocked up with bread and beans. We noted, however, that prices for a few other staples compared favorably with beans at 9 cents a can and bread at 10 cents a loaf. So to lend a bit of variety to our restricted daily menu we bought tomato and chicken soups at 10 cents a can, pancake flour at 10 cents a carton, coffee rolls at a cent apiece, evaporated milk at 10 cents a can, and crackers at five cents a box. We still had a few Baldwin apples from the Bradley orchard, but couldn't resist buying three oranges for a nickel.

Elliott noted that gasoline had dropped a cent, prompting us to fill the Ford's tank.

It was a strange feeling, broke in South Carolina, food for a few days, and an anxious wait for a $25 loan from faraway Michigan.

We chose a grassy and sparsely-wooded site two miles south of Columbia for our anticipated wait of six or more days. Although not officially designated as a tourist park, the area served that purpose, attracting campers like us.

Five dirt highways converged in the vicinity we had selected to park the Ford. Across the road was a wide-open spot that attracted peddlers, horse traders, and vendors who made house-to-house calls in Columbia. The itinerants, we observed, had a distinct knack for trading, or "swapping" as they called it. We visited with them, especially around bonfires at night.

Among the first to arrive were two middle-aged men with a wagonload of old stoves. They had the look of midwesterners. So we were not surprised when they introduced themselves as stove repairers from St. Paul, Minnesota.

"Got a stove that needs fixin'?" one of the men asked.

Elliott pointed at our Ford across the road. "We can't haul a kitchen range in that," he said, "just a portable gas stove."

"You could use a good cook stove," the man insisted. He led us to the rear of the wagon piled with stoves and lifted out a rusty box model we judged came from a junk yard. "We'll swap this dandy wood burner for your camp stove," he said. "Wood is free, so that'll save you buying gas," he said glibly.

We weren't convinced.

A horse and mule trader named Wilson established headquarters the next day in the area vacated by the stove men. With him were his wife and young son. Wilson drove wooden stakes into the ground to tether a half-dozen skinny bedraggled mules and horses. His whiskered face lit up when we walked over to talk with him.

Neither Elliott nor I was impressed as we surveyed the animals staked nearby. We watched Wilson feed them a small amount of oats and a bit of hay procured from the wagon. Bluntly, Elliott asked, "How can you sell mules and horses like these?"

Wilson showed no resentment. "Don't always get cash for 'em," he said. "Mostly I swap 'em for better ones."

"But who would trade a good horse or mule for these?" Elliott asked. "They've got heaves."

"I'll get rid of the heaves easy enough," Wilson said. "I'll feed 'em wet hay."

That evening a glowing bonfire lured us back to the horse trader's camp. Elliott brought his ukulele, and as he strummed and sang, the rest of us joined in. Reacting to the cheery fireside mood, Wilson became talkative, revealing what he said were secrets of the horse trading business.

"You make a 12-year-old horse 6 years younger by filing grooves in its teeth," he said. "The buyers always look at the teeth," he added, "and if the teeth look sharp, that cuts down on the years." He lifted his hand to stress a point. "It always works," he said.

I felt a nudge from Elliott. "This is only a yarn," he whispered. "This guy never would go to all that trouble to sell a horse."

The next morning we had an opportunity to observe Wilson conduct his enterprise. We saw a young man, about 25 years old, pull into the camp with a buggy-like contraption drawn by a single horse. Tall, his rumpled brown hair uncombed, he alighted from the vehicle. For a moment he said nothing, then advanced shiftlessly toward Wilson. His bent for dickering soon was apparent.

"Got a good saddle horse to swap?" the young man asked. His hand cupped his chin.

Wilson responded quickly. "You bet I have," he said. "And she's got a pedigree a mile long."

"But I'm not sure if I want a saddle horse." The young man hesitated. "Have you got a good loggin' team? I need one for a skiddin' job."

Wilson was unabashed. Straight-faced he said, "Sure have. Those two horses over there pull together like twins, strong enough to drag a house."

Again the young man pondered. "Got a speedy racehorse?" he asked.

"Race horse? Why man, I've got a horse that can outrun anything in the Kentucky Derby."

The young man seemed dubious. "Maybe a race horse costs too much. Got a mountain mule?"

"You bet I have," Wilson replied. "Got one that's a never-stop climber. She's a little lean right now, but that's because I

Ashland Daily Press, *December 27, 1924. (opposite)*

'Ford Tramps' Tempted To Swap Car For Mules

Seegar Swanson, former stenographer for the Chamber of Commerce, and Elliott Nystrom, also of Ashland, now in the midst of a one year tramp of the United States in their Frod "Wanderlust", are experiencing adventures to fill many volumes.

In a letter to the Chamber today, Swanson says that they are playing a ukelele in the moonlight in South Carolina, and wondering how much longer their last thirty cents will last, and whether they will ever reach Florida.

His letter follows:

Columbia, S. C.

"It's June in Miami" but it's July at Columbia. The sun is so hot that the last quarter of a pound of butter we have left has melted into oblivion. Twi-light comes at six o'clock. Bright shining stars and a mellow moon permit us to sit on the ground at night, singing and playing a ukelele. The mosquitoes are gone, so are most of the flies. Columbia would be paradise, if we had some money.

For five days the good ship "Wanderlust" has anchored in a wooded spot on the outskirts of South Carolina's capital, while its pilots have been searching vainly for work. The worthy vessel is eager to move on to Florida, but gasoline and oil demand priceless shekels, and these are lacking.

Did you ever get stranded 3,000 miles from home with only thirty cents in your pocket? That's the situation we are up against right now. Yet we don't propose to starve, even though climatic conditions are ideal. Our larder contains two cans of beans, two loaves of bread, a can of soup, and a half dozen crackers. That will tide us over a couple days if we control our appetites. Than we have thirty cents. With proper manipulation of the treasury, we can live another three days. By fasting, life should not fade away for still an additional five days. All in all, the wandering knights are good for at least ten days. Next time you hear from us, we will be in Florida. We'll find a way, don't you fear.

A party of horse traders made us a tempting offer the other night. They suggested that we trade our Ford for a team of mules and a big wagon. As an extra inducement they offered to throw in a spare horse, so that if one of the mules died, we would still have a team. Of course, we would see more of the country driving a team of mules, but we see enough of it driving a Ford.

It was just our luck that a patent medicine vender went bankrupt a couple days before he met us. Otherwise we might have obtained a job performing before the public in the smaller towns, while the quack was advertising his cure all medicine.

Today we watched the horse traders I mentioned above dope a couple of mules so that their heaves would not be so apparent to prospective purchasers. They made a twelve year old horse six years younger by filing grooves in its teeth. We see many schemes devised to deceive innocent buyers.

The south is wooded, and is a decided contrast to the east. There one city after another bobbed up wherever we went. Driving through cities, however, is invaluable experience, and highly educational. In Washington President Coolidge's annual message to Congress was being delivered in the Senate while we were there.

Some day I am going to ask you to write me a letter. We sometimes wonder what's stirring in "the old home town."

With due precision I shall cease. Merry Christmas and Happy New Year.

Sincerely yours,
Seegar Swanson.
With Elliott Nystrum

don't feed her much. Mules get livelier if they don't overeat."

The young man glanced questionably at Wilson. "To tell the truth," he said, "I've got my eyes peeled for a bobtailed mule."

"Here are two of the niftiest bobtailed mules this side of 'Arkansaw,'" Wilson countered, "dirt cheap."

Elliott smiled at me as the relentless haggling continued. We wondered who would prevail. We knew Wilson's stock comprised but four scrawny horses and two mules. Yet he professed to have an unlimited supply, while his prospective buyer seemed to want something the trader didn't have.

The upshot of the dickering was the buyer driving away with a bobtailed mule, and Wilson collecting what the buyer termed a roan horse, together with "a chicken and a dollar to boot."

"How do you know the horse he traded you is a roan?" Elliott asked.

"Makes no difference to me," Wilson said. He shrugged his shoulders. "I got the chicken and the dollar. I can swap his horse tomorrow."

The following day we accepted Wilson's invitation to partake of the chicken. He had boiled it into a stew.

Wilson nibbled on a wing. "It's hard tellin' where that fellow lifted this chicken," he said. "Anyhow he picked a tender bird."

Elliott and I agreed the chicken stew was tolerable, considering we were restricting ourselves to two meals a day to stretch our groceries. We didn't trouble, however, to ask for Wilson's recipe.

The five-cornered intersection near our camp was an ideal place to "flag a ride," we noticed. Hitchhikers bound for Florida occasionally stopped by to ask us for a lift in the Ford. A few hikers were en route north rather than south. Plainly, they had not prospered in Florida. Hungry, several dropped by at mealtime. Though our own status was precarious, we felt obliged to share what little we had.

The sheriff stopped by, too. He tipped his hat politely. "Just checking," he said.

Satisfied we were campers, he chatted a bit, and then crossed the road to talk with the horse trader. Finding nothing suspicious during his inspection of Wilson's layout, he drove off.

We experienced delightful South Carolina weather during our wait for the hoped-for letter from Michigan. We enjoyed warm sunny days fanned by gentle southern breezes. Cool nights, some dropping to 35 or 40 degrees, assured us of sound sleep under the warm blankets of the Ford's cozy "folding bed." With the shortest day of the year approaching, we felt no

Elliott, broke and waiting for the mail.

urge to "roll out" before the late rising sun.

We frequently saw mules driven past our camp, and soon became familiar with commands of the drivers, "Come up, mule." We also saw Negro women stroll on various roads, carrying large baskets on their heads without aid of their hands.

Elliott walked to town twice to check for mail and to buy a few groceries, and I did likewise. With time at our disposal, we probed the Ford to make certain it still was in good running order. The connecting rods required tightening, and as was customary for Ford owners, we scraped off carbon under the cylinder head. We were glad none of this called for any cash outlay, although we did have to spend a dime to replace a pan gasket.

To keep from getting restless we hiked each day, exploring the countryside, devoid of summer's greenery, but alive with birds and small animals. We failed, however, in our search for opossum. A small lake nearby held promise as a possible source for food, but we heeded a "No Fishing" sign. Enthusiastic about baseball, we frequently played catch by our camp with the ball and gloves we brought along from home.

A huge truck pulling in next to the horse trader's domain interrupted our game during our third day in camp. Arousing our curiosity was the word "GEN-TONKA" painted in bold letters on both sides of a high and extremely wide house-like structure mounted on the frame of the truck.

We allowed the driver sufficient time to set up before strolling over to get acquainted and to ascertain what GEN-TONKA was all about.

"No, we're not from Gen-Tonka," hastily explained the driver, lean and sprightly, with black hair and kinky sideburns that twirled behind his ears. We sized him up as a go-getter, a middle-aged man with a good sense of humor and propensities of a huckster. He introduced himself as Jeff Ainsworth, and presented his wife Eldora, much younger and comely with rounded cheeks and upbraided chestnut hair. She blushed.

"I get around," Jeff continued. He asked that we call him Jeff. "We were traveling with a circus until it went bust. Now I sell medicine, Gen-Tonka."

Jeff pointed to one of the signs on his truck. "You must have heard about GEN-TONKA."

As if trying to sell us some, he began a lengthy spiel. We surmised it was the one he would pitch from the tailgate of his truck before a crowd of gullible listeners.

"Gen-Tonka's a sure cure for everything, headaches, backaches, lumbago, and rheumatism," he said. He held aloft a bottle labeled Gen-Tonka, waving it from side to side. "Guaranteed to cure toothaches, blood poisoning, corns, swollen joints, coughs, colds, earaches—"

Jeff thrust a bottle at us. "It sells for a dollar," he said. "You can have it for 50 cents."

"Sorry, we're broke," Elliott said. "That must be powerful stuff. Where do you get it?"

"From an old hermit in the Blue Ridge Mountains. It's a secret formula." Sober-faced, Jeff didn't twitch an eyelash. "He mixes roots, leaves, and grass with swamp water, and sells it to me in a keg. I bottle it and call it Gen-Tonka."

As we turned to leave, Jeff invited us to come back for an evening visit. A huge bonfire crackled near the Gen-Tonka truck when we returned. Before long the horse trader's family and several newly-arrived campers joined us. The fireside mood was convivial. Conversation flowed freely, with continuous interruptions, but Elliott and I focused attention on Jeff.

"I'll be going into town tomorrow to tune pianos," he said.

"Tune pianos?" Elliott directed a glance of incredulity at Jeff.

"If no one wants pianos tuned, I'll sharpen lawn mowers, or maybe try my hand at filing saws," Jeff continued. "I'm a chimney sweep, too, but I suppose it's too warm around here for sooty chimneys."

What a versatile entrepreneur! I thought. He seemed able to procure plenty of jobs, but, lacking his skills, we could find none.

No one suspected why we were camping so long at the crossroads, nor why we walked to town so often. Returning to the Ford at a rather late hour after the evening's campfire visit, we realized five days now had elapsed since we mailed my letter to my cousin Nels. The following afternoon, as Elliott started

Author killing time, waiting for financial relief from his cousin.

for town, we thought there possibly might be a response waiting in the post office. We were disappointed, however, when he found none. Nonetheless, we weren't overly concerned. Our larder still contained a can of beans and a loaf of bread.

No doubt a letter would have arrived by the time I reached the post office the next afternoon, I thought, but again we were disappointed. Now things really were becoming serious. Our cash balance had dwindled to 30 cents.

On the eighth day, December 19, Elliott and I both hiked to the post office. I breathed a sigh of relief when the general delivery clerk handed me an envelope postmarked Iron Mountain, Michigan. In it was Nels's money order for $25.

"Wish I could send you more," he wrote, "but I can't draw on my pay at Ford's plant and this happens to be all I have at hand."

We were truly grateful.

But we rejoiced too soon. Another postal clerk said he couldn't cash the money order without identification by some responsible person, preferably someone from Columbia. Adding to our frustration was his reluctance to acknowledge our plight. We dug into our pockets for letters and other possible means of identification, but not until we produced our YMCA membership cards did he finally yield.

"Florida, here we come," exulted Elliott as we gleefully strode out of the post office clutching five crisp five-dollar bills.

Around Jeff's bonfire that evening we broke the news we would leave camp early the next morning. What started out as the usual nightly get-together developed into a hearty going away party featuring Jeff's mulligan stew. As the festivities progressed, some weird proposals evolved. The party began with animated discussions, and then all spontaneously joined in singing "Oh! Susanna," "On Top of Ol' Smoky," and "On the Trail of the Lonesome Pine" to the accompaniment of Elliott's ukulele. His bass voice carried the tunes for a somewhat discordant mixture of tenors, baritones, sopranos and my off-key falsetto.

In keeping with the individuals assembled, the party eventually became a swapfest. Wilson, the wily horse trader, led off by offering to exchange his wagon and a team of mules for our Ford.

"You fellows get around the country so fast you miss the scenery," he said. Wilson suggested we could feed the mules for free along the grassy roads. "Think of the gas money you'll save," he said.

Elliott objected. "What makes you think we're missing the scenery?" he asked. "The Ford travels only 25 miles an hour. In Florida hay for the mules will cost more than gas for the car."

Jeff broke into the dickering. "What'll you swap for these shoes?" he asked. He dangled a brand new pair before eyes of the campers.

"What's the cash price?" Elliott asked.

"Five dollars," Jeff replied.

"Too much," Elliott said.

"Try 'em," Jeff persisted.

Having caught some of the swapping fever ourselves, Elliott and I did as Jeff suggested. "They don't fit," Elliott said.

Jeff instantly lowered the price to $2.50. "You can get the shoes stretched," he said.

Apparently noting his feet were smaller than ours, Wilson offered to swap a horse for the shoes if Jeff paid "$20 to boot."

"Can't do that," Jeff said. "Tell you what. I'll swap the shoes and $10 to boot for your tent and a team of mules."

As we expected, nothing came of all the haggling.

Turning his attention to Elliott, Jeff said, "I'll sell you my Gen-Tonka for a hundred dollars," he said. "You and your partner can earn traveling expenses selling it." He painted a rosy picture of Elliott drawing crowds with his ukulele, and me acting as pitchman.

Elliott disagreed with the idea of a traveling medicine show even though Jeff reduced his price to $25.

Jeff shifted his attack. "What'll you swap for these ukulele strings?" he asked. He swished eight of them before Elliott's eyes.

"How about a double-bitted ax?" Elliott asked.

"It's a deal," Jeff said. He shook hands with Elliott to clinch the transaction.

Much as I felt we might have need of the ax, I was glad that Elliott now had a reserve supply of ukulele strings.

It was midnight before the party ended. A soothing rain the next morning had such a lulling effect we stayed in bed later than we planned. Not until noon were we ready to depart. Though happy to be on the move again, I felt rather sad. We had grown sentimental about our temporary campsite and the friendly folks who invited us to share their bonfires and adaptive way of life.

The horse trader came over to say good-bye. "Better stay awhile longer," he said. "Have another dinner with us. Sure as taxes someone's goin' to offer me a chicken on a trade-in."

Hands waved and Jeff's horn honked as we drove away to Columbia for groceries before heading south for Florida. We were reminded of the neighborly send-off in Ashland, only this time the Ford didn't balk.

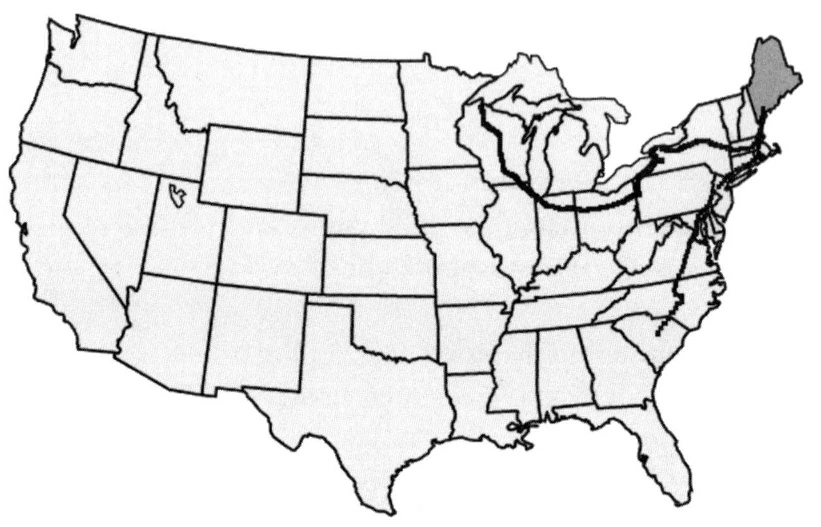

Chapter IX
A Wintry Reception

IN HIGH SPIRITS, we took time to tour the elegant state capitol in Columbia before turning the wheels of the Ford in a southwesterly direction. The capitol gave us an acute awareness of the Confederacy. As we recalled from days of high school history, guns fired in South Carolina sparked the Civil War in the time of slavery. We suspected that wounds of that bitter conflict still were scarred. We hadn't known the stately capitol was one of few buildings left standing in Columbia after Union soldiers set fire to the city.

We thought Columbia, population of about 55,000, was a beautiful city, heightened by its wide streets, public parks and appealing residential area. Especially impressive was the University of South Carolina. A tourist folder boasted the city's cotton mills ranked first in the state.

With the late-autumn day advancing, we took to the road.

The tourist folder indicated we were driving in "the middle country." The Ford rolled smoothly over the hilly road down the center of South Carolina. Farms were proof this was an agricultural area, a land of cotton as well as peanuts and sweet potatoes.

The agricultural area continued into Georgia. Here we learned crops were even more extensive because Georgia's fertile soil is varied, so much so the state claimed it could raise just about anything grown in any other state of the nation. Sensitive about their inability to raise sub-tropical fruits profitably, native residents stood "tall as a Georgia pine" extolling their celebrated Georgia peaches, pecans and, of course, peanuts.

Nevertheless, we saw evidence of a seamy side. Georgia had its low-income tenant farmers, sharecroppers who tilled the soil with crude implements. These farmers, called "Georgia Crackers" by some, contributed their bit to Georgia's flagging economy, in a state where the average teacher's salary was less than $600 a year.

In Augusta, population 60,000, we mistook the county courthouse for Georgia's state capitol. We should have known the capital city is Atlanta.

We learned other significant facts, too. Eli Whitney set in motion his first cotton gin in the Augusta area. Also, President Woodrow Wilson's boyhood home was there for us to see. And in Augusta oranges still were six for a dime.

Supper simmered on our stove as we arranged camp in the tourist park near a carnival in Millen. We plainly heard the haunting organ music of the merry-go-round and the clamor of the midway. A young carnival worker came over to chat.

"Hear it's goin' to get cold tonight," he said gloomily.

"How cold?" Elliott asked.

"Ten above, maybe colder," the worker replied. He huddled, as if shivering in the anticipated cold.

Elliott reached into the Ford for our pail. "Better drain the radiator," he said.

After supper we joined the Saturday night throng on the midway. Times were tough, but it was apparent people weren't pinching cash now that a carnival was in town. We, however, weren't there to ride the ferris wheel nor to win Kewpie dolls, but to consider joining the show. Twenty-five dollars might not be enough to get us to Florida, we thought.

We changed our minds about a carnival job, though, when we woke the next morning to see several inches of snow on the ground.

The carnival was moving out. We ate breakfast beside a bonfire the clean-up crew built to burn trash, and watched Negro boys comb the grounds for coins.

"Little money found," I wrote in my log. "Not much to lose in the South."

Bundled up for a cold drive, we expected to make slow progress that day over roads reputed to be the worst in the South. Poor roads, oddly enough, didn't hamper headway as much as a romantic couple in the car ahead.

We were on a rutted, six-mile detour bordered by swamps, and the highway was so narrow we couldn't pass. Paying no heed to honking cars coming up from behind, a youth leaned over his girl friend seated in front of the steering wheel, ostensibly teaching her to drive. In the process the couple found occasion to spoon. By the time the detour ended, the couple still spooned while drivers honked indignantly as they zoomed by.

It was the first day of winter, Sunday, December 21, according to the calendar we saw hanging on the wall inside a filling station.

"As if we didn't know," Elliott quipped, alluding to our all-day drive through chilling cold after early morning snow. He drew up his jacket collar; his lips quivered.

Confronted by the tottering Lane's Bridge, which spanned the Allama River after hovering over a lengthy swampland, we were annoyed by the $1.25 toll required to cross it. Farther south in Folkston, another 50 cents for crossing St. Mary's River further dented our meager purse.

In Waycross we slept behind the Methodist church. We wondered what the neighbors thought of the aromatic whiffs of coffee brewing on our camp stove.

The highway improved after we left Waycross, but we were slowed by another six-mile detour, narrow and sandy.

Understandably, we were pleased to hit concrete pavement when the Ford at last left the "Empire State of the South," to cross the border into Florida, where it was supposed to be June but wasn't. This hardly was the welcome we expected. If anything, the Florida weather was colder than the freezing temperatures of Georgia. Unseasonable, we hoped, but frigid nevertheless.

"Coldest spell we've had in years," loyal Floridians apologized.

Our cash balance also was all but frozen, less than $14. There was one consolation, however. We had, in spite of adversity, reached the second corner state, half the goal of our trip around the country.

Before entering Jacksonville, which we knew was one of Florida's major cities, we camped free of charge in a large grove, together with dozens of other travelers, many of them "tin can tourists" like us. Next to our camp was a band of gypsies, colorful in their distinctive garb. We watched them move freely along the footpaths, disturbed by no one, and remembered how police, presumably on complaint of concerned citizens, ordered gypsies out of our hometown as they arrived in their caravans each summer in Ashland.

Curious about our Ford, three warmly-dressed men, parked in a spot near ours, sauntered over to talk. We were unhinging the front seat and unrolling blankets for our night's sleep. The men, in their late 40s, said they were from Middletown, New York, and planned to spend the winter in Florida. They became interested when we told them of our need to find jobs. We didn't learn their names, but the one we came to know as Mr. Frostman suggested we follow them down the coast.

In Jacksonville the next morning we lost track of our newly found friends. The city, with its population of 125,000, gave us a feeling it was a promising place for work, what with its lumber and other commercial activity. It was the same old story, though. "Sorry, no jobs."

The 35-mile drive to St. Augustine over a choppy road did little to relieve our growing anxiety. Our gloomy outlook changed, however, when our New York friends unexpectedly hailed us at the city's arched entrance gate. They told us not to worry about jobs.

"The real estate boom is still on in Florida," Frostman said. He assured us there would be "plenty of work farther south. We know because we worked there last winter."

Frostman advised we travel to the Indian River country, halfway down the East Coast. "You're bound to find some kind of work, at least a job picking oranges," he said.

Our friends recommended we first spend the day exploring St. Augustine. "It's the oldest city in the U.S.," Frostman said. "Start with the Spanish fort, then tour the old city."

At the outset we recognized that Fort Marion emphasized

St. Augustine's antiquity. We envisioned Spanish artillerymen manning their posts at strategic outlooks along the sturdy stone walls. Though constructed by Spaniards in 1565, the fort plainly was well-preserved, seemingly as impregnable as it was nearly four centuries ago.

Ponce de Leon, of course, didn't find the "fountain of perpetual youth" when he landed on St. Augustine's shore in 1512, but we discerned the seeds of antiquity he sowed in St. Augustine as we toured the old residential and business districts of the city.

Typical of historic places we visited was the "Oldest House" on St. Francis Street, which, we were told, was testimony of the

As advertised in 1924. It's 75 years older in 1999.

changing life and structure of the house through the eras of Spanish and British control, and in later years, the United States.

Unique was the extremely narrow business street in old St. Augustine, a street far more narrow than any we had seen in colonial cities of New England. We repelled the temptation to buy souvenirs as we inched our way through a crowd of tourists that were sightseeing concurrently. Beckoning shoppers were the stores lined up closely on both sides of the thoroughfare.

More and more historic sites loomed ahead, but in sharp contrast to this part of St. Augustine were the many pretentious residences scattered about the city, and the large modern hotels, winter homes for northern visitors. The abundance of palm trees gave us a strange new feeling.

The Good Ship Wanderlust passed beneath another arched gateway when we left St. Augustine. We regarded our brief visit in the singularly enchanting city as richly rewarding.

Wild boars scampering through underbrush of the low, flat, and sandy surfaces of this barren part of Florida drew our attention. We imagined that these boars, a strange sight to us, either were abandoned by early settlers leaving the area in disgust, or had escaped from their hog houses.

Whether sportsmen here engaged in wild boar hunting, as in foreign countries, we did not know, but we surmised Florida's wild boars might be a source of meat for families eking out an existence in what appeared to us to be an impoverished area.

So far there had been no inducement to step on the Ford's accelerator while we slowly progressed over Florida's highways. True, there was that bit of concrete leading into Jacksonville, but this had given way to rougher surfaces. Now we were on a highway paved with brick. With some of the bricks cracked, others sticking up here and there, and a few missing entirely, we were having a rumbling ride in the Ford.

All about us was evidence of a subtropical climate, palms, palmettos, and species of tropical birds we had never seen. Yet it seemed so out of place, considering how cold it was.

All this, to our pleasant surprise, came to an abrupt end.

The temperature suddenly zipped from cold to hot. I jammed the brakes. Immediately we shed our winter clothes, woolen jackets, long johns, and flannel shirts. What a relief to don cotton shirts and roll up the sleeves way above the elbows! It was as though a line had been drawn across the road. Behind the Ford it still was cold, in front the temperature was warm and soothing.

Elliott appropriately described the sudden change in weather. "It's balmy!" he exclaimed.

As if adding frosting to the cake, a small orange grove loaded with ripening fruit caught our eye across the road. The magnificent sight, utterly new to us, enhanced the thrill of being in Florida, a land so vastly different.

"Let's really enjoy this balmy weather," Elliott said. He jerked side curtains off the Ford, and I did the same. In short order the car was on the move again, breathing freely.

Soon we were in Daytona, and later in Titusville, both reflecting Florida's boom. Obviously, the pride of Daytona was its unobstructed, solidly-packed, sandy beach stretching 35 miles along the coast, ideal for its celebrated automobile racing.

The owner of an orange grove gave us permission that evening to camp on his property. He indicated a spot where he already had granted three other men permission to camp. As luck would have it, the three men were our friends from New York. Their greeting was as enthusiastic as ours. Almost in unison they exulted over the warmer weather.

We eyed one of the trio who had gone us one better by stripping to the waist.

"I came south for sunshine," he said, "and now that I'm here, by George, I'm going to collect." He patted his chest and flexed the biceps of his muscular arms.

The campsite became indelibly stamped on our minds for two reasons. First, the owner had allowed us to pick oranges from his trees, something we never had done before, and second, we had our first taste of a new kind of water.

"Want some spring water?" one of the New Yorkers asked. He had been looking around while his companions prepared their supper. "There's an artesian well over there," he said.

We followed him over. "It smells like rotten eggs," Elliott said. He held his nose.

"It's sulfur water," our friend said. "Try it." He handed Elliott a dipper he took off a post.

One gulp was enough. "It's the last time I'll drink this kind of water," Elliott said. I echoed his remark.

"Don't be too sure about that," our friend cautioned.

Elliott strumming ukulele on Florida beach.

"Florida is full of it."

Back at our campsite, the other two New Yorkers chuckled over our reaction to sulfur water. "Coffee kills the taste," one of them assured us.

We weren't convinced after drinking coffee we brewed with sulfur water for our supper.

"Make your coffee stronger," we were advised. "That will make it drinkable."

Before leaving the next morning, the New Yorkers asked how we were faring.

We told them we had been unsuccessful in applying for jobs, but did not tell them how precariously low our cash was, scarcely more than five dollars.

"You'll soon find work," they reassured us. "Maybe we can help."

It was Christmas Eve when we found ourselves halfway down the coast. Now was a time to be merry, not dejected. Our spirits brightened, though, when we sighted the three New Yorkers parked by a building adjoining a vacant corner lot in the business district of Cocoa. The city looked prosperous. Tourist literature described it as "the home of the world-famous Indian River Orange, the sweetest orange produced in the world."

The five of us slept that night in the vacant lot. Having learned how low our cash really was, the New Yorkers tried to cheer us early Christmas morning, saying they would help in our search for employment.

"This is Christmas Day," Frostman said, "not a good time to apply for a job." He suggested we cruise around Cocoa to size up the situation.

All around we saw fancy new homes going up, even new buildings in the commercial district. The warm summery day, with palms and other tropical greenery growing everywhere, hardly created a Christmas atmosphere. Firecrackers set off by youngsters reminded us of the Fourth of July. We looked in vain for a Christmas tree. Here and there porches were decorated with Yuletide trimmings, but palms draped with tinsel were a far cry from northern balsams with Christmas candles.

"Let's go fishing," one of our friends suddenly said. His

Sampling oranges on Christmas day.

remark seemed incongruous, yet it made sense. Men and boys with fishpoles were heading for the long, wooden bridge connecting Cocoa with Merritt Island.

We joined them. Our friends loaned us fishing gear, and with artificial lures we lined up with the Cocoa anglers to try our luck over the railing of the bridge.

From Cocoa fishermen we learned that fish caught could be sold at the city's fishery for five cents a pound, but not blowfish. Trout were at a premium, fetching 18 cents a pound, they said. Encouraged by this as a possible source of much-needed revenue, Elliott and I hoped to land trout. Instead, we settled for a couple sheepshead and a half-dozen blowfish.

The New Yorkers weren't having much luck, either. The tallest of the trio pulled up his line, and turning toward us asked, "Would you like to see what's on the island?"

Elliott looked at me, and when I nodded, he said, "Let's go."

Had we walked to Merritt Island, quite a way off, the bridge toll would have been five cents apiece, but since we drove, the Ford also was assessed a nickel.

On the island we were impressed by beautiful homes, most with ripe oranges hanging on trees in their yards. We accepted invitations to sample the fruit.

The New Yorkers led the way down to the Indian River shoreline. Soon we met a lean and loose-jointed man, a middle-aged person whose deeply-tanned complexion revealed much exposure to ocean breezes and Florida sunshine. He said his name was Bob Simpson.

While Simpson was observing details of our Ford, the New Yorkers told him of our urgent need to find some kind of work.

"H'mm," Simpson mused. "I'm a fisherman. Maybe I would catch more fish if I had some help." He reflected a moment, then looked toward us. "How would you like to work for me?" he asked. "I set out nets at night, and drag them in about sunup. The work is hard, but with you two as helpers I could set out more nets and bring in more fish. I sell them to the fishery in Cocoa."

We mulled his proposition, but were dubious whether there would be enough money earned to split among the three of us. Our misgivings sank lower when Simpson said, "Some nights you'll make money, other nights you won't. Depends on your luck. The fish come in schools. I catch different kinds of fish and have to sort them out for the fishery."

"We can't be choosers," Elliott said to me.

"We'll take the job and start tonight," he told Simpson.

Tramps pose with New York camping friends.

Smooth asphalt pavement on road to Sunset Groves.

The New Yorkers obviously were pleased. They suggested we celebrate by frying the fish we had caught from the bridge.

"Let me shoot some ducks to go with your fish," Simpson interrupted. Without waiting for a response he darted into his house and emerged with a double-barreled shotgun.

Assuming he soon would return with ducks, we held off cleaning fish. We had seen thousands of ducks on the Indian River, easy targets for a man with a gun. Like tourists, these ducks had flown south for the winter.

Chagrined, Simpson returned empty-handed. "No luck," he said. He leaned his shotgun against a palm.

He winked. "The wind was so strong it almost blew the shots back into my face," he said. We gathered it was a hunter's version of "the big one that got away."

Directing his eyes toward Elliott and me, Simpson drawled, "I was thinking it over. You boys are too light for sea fishing, so I found you an easier job. Would you like to pick oranges?"

"Pick oranges? Of course we would," Elliott said. "But where?"

"At Sunset Groves. Mr. Lockett, he's the superintendent, said he'd hire you. You'll like working for him."

There was no point in delaying. We shook hands with our New York friends, thanking them for having led us to jobs we so urgently needed. We bade them good-bye, and after thanking Simpson, set off for Sunset Groves.

Following Simpson's directions, we traveled north several miles on a smooth asphalt pavement skirting the Indian River. We stopped when we reached the square, white house described by Simpson. We couldn't mistake it. Surrounded by orange trees laden with ripening fruit, we were at Sunset Groves.

We drew up at the front of the big frame house to be met

by Mr. Lockett. I wondered why he wore high leather boots on such a warm day. Attracted by the travel-worn Ford, he scanned it with interest. His broad smile made us feel at ease. Plain-spoken, he hired us on the spot after briefly outlining the nature of our work. The pay would be $2.50 for a nine-hour day, with Saturday afternoons off, with pay. We would be working for the Blue Goose Packing Company.

— The Log, Fri. Feb. 8, 1924

Chapter X
Island Moonrise

AMUSED that we would sleep in the Ford—"flivver," he called it—Lockett led us to a nearby pair of grapefruit trees nestled in an orange grove.

"Camp here," he suggested. "Help yourself to the fruit."

With water at hand, the site was perfect.

Lockett asked whether we had experience picking oranges. Not oranges, we explained, but apples in New York State.

"Picking oranges is different," Lockett said. He moved toward an orange tree to show how it was done. "You don't pull them off, and you don't pick up oranges that have fallen on the ground. You snip each orange from its stem with a clipper. That keeps the orange sealed." He handed each of us a clipper. We noted that unlike scissors, they had springs for easy operation.

Eying the enormous grapefruit almost touching the hood of

the Ford, we took advantage of Lockett's offer as we prepared supper. I had never eaten a grapefruit, but Elliott had. He plucked two off a tree, cut them in half, and with his knife deftly freed the juicy pulp from the rinds and connecting tissues. He sprinkled sugar over each half. We ate the grape-fruit for dessert, relishing each spoonful.

"We'll put two more on the running board tonight," Elliott said, explaining how this would give the juice time to dilute the sugar. "They'll be delicious for breakfast," he said.

Later on we sometimes parked the Ford by orange trees, so close we could reach out to pluck an orange if we chose to eat one.

It was 10 o'clock the next morning before we began picking fruit. The late start was caused by heavy dew slowly evaporating under the morning sun. Although this generally was a nightly occurrence, we were told the dew was beneficial, supplying needed moisture during periods of scant rain.

Working with us was a small crew of native Floridians and several Negroes. All were exceedingly friendly, and curious about two northerners who chose to join southerners to harvest Florida oranges, and to sleep at night in a "rattle-trap" Ford. We took a special liking to several members of a family named Monroe.

Elliott and I greatly enjoyed climbing up and down ladders, unloading oranges from our picking bags as soon as they were filled. The sight of so many oranges dazzled us. The apple-harvesting experience we gained in New York State proved a blessing, so much so we could almost keep pace with the Negroes and the Monroes.

Contented with their work, the Negroes sang or hummed. They seemed to improvise, often melancholically and sometimes in a spiritual sense, although such lyrics as "my heart's in the jail house now" sounded more like the blues.

Oranges looked so tempting that Elliott and I peeled a couple and pulled apart juicy slices to eat. One of the Monroe boys surprised us when he dashed over, raising his arm as if to halt traffic.

"That's not the way to do it," he said.

Jabbing an orange with his jackknife, he twisted the blade beneath the rind to form an opening, and lifting the orange, he squeezed juice into his mouth. Then he tossed away the rind and picked up another orange from the ground to repeat the process. We thought this was a wasteful procedure, even if oranges were so abundant. It was time saving, though.

We found a simpler solution to peeling oranges, however, when we came upon two trees bearing fruit similar to oranges, but smaller. From the Monroes we learned the trees bore tangerines. The rinds hung loosely around the fruit and were removed easily. The tasty tangerines were another new treat for us.

One afternoon Lockett assigned us to hoe weeds and tall

Monroe children who taught tramps local orange eating practices.

grass around trees in a remote part of the grove. As he handed me a hoe, I saw he still wore knee-length leather boots.

Whacking down tall grass rooted in the sandy soil proved more arduous than picking oranges, but I was glad for a change of pace. With my hoe raised high for a downward swing, I was startled to see a six-foot black snake standing on its tail, ominously waggling fangs in my direction. Frightened, I dropped the hoe and ran. I was relieved that the snake did not pursue me.

I knew I should retrieve the hoe to resume work, and eventually did so, but very cautiously. The snake had vanished, but fearing there might be more, I poked the grass carefully before wielding the hoe. I was told later the snake was non-poisonous, but it could have been a "rattler." I now suspected why Lockett wore high leather boots.

Whether stimulated by the citrus fruits we ate, or because of nine-hour days working in the orchard, we grew increasingly hungry, yet did not seem to gain weight. Lockett showed surprise when we requested his truck driver to buy us 10 loaves of bread plus a supply of groceries when he was in Cocoa. He showed greater surprise three days later when we asked the driver to buy 10 more loaves. He was astounded at week's end when we went to Cocoa and returned with 20 additional loaves costing $1.92. We also purchased what became by far the longest entry in our expense book:

> Pie $.10, two pounds of wieners $.50, one
> and one-half pounds of hamburger $.30,
> two pounds of butter $1.10, four cans of
> soup $.45, three cans of beans $.33, one can
> of syrup $.19, two cans of milk $.22,
> pancake flour $.10, cookies $.20, one peck
> of potatoes $.60, one pound of coffee $.56,

oatmeal $.12, one dozen eggs $.65, one pound of bacon $.42, two packages of noodles $.18, two boxes of crackers $.12, one can of sauerkraut $.14, one can of corn $.19

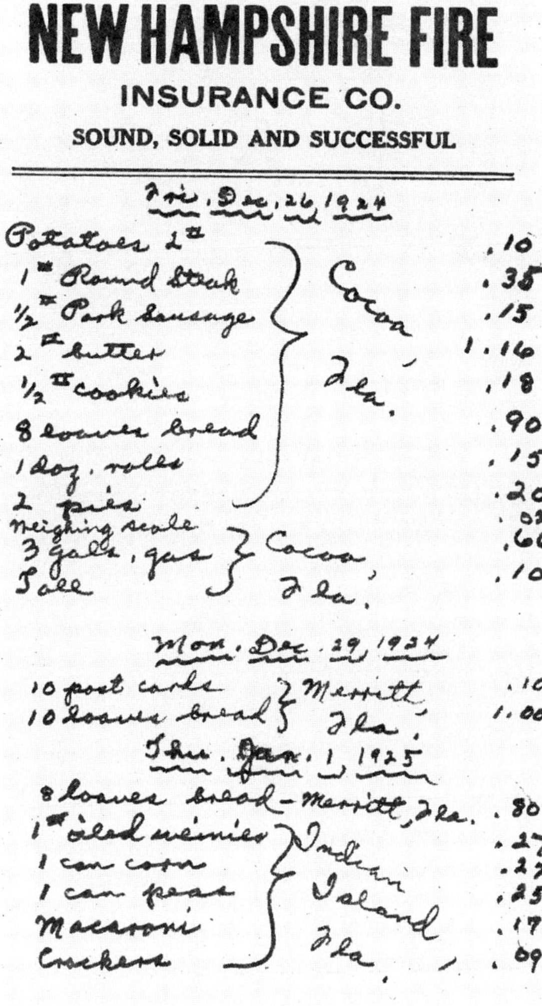

Page from Expense Book.

"I ought to start a bakery," wryly quipped Lockett.

"Ah couldn't eat all dat food even if'n it waz possum," one of the Negroes said.

Tranquility of the orange grove was disrupted one morning when several men, glowering, scurried among the trees, and questioned members of our crew. They said they were on a manhunt for a "nigger" who allegedly struck a white man, an islander for whom he worked. We learned the search had spread to other parts of the island, and there was talk of a

Monroe and author do some clowning.

lynching. For days the hunt continued, and other Negroes on
the island were victims of ill-feeling because they were believed
to be aiding their unfortunate fellow man. Tension mounted
until a rowboat was reported missing. The searchers then
abandoned the manhunt, concluding the runaway Negro had
stolen the boat and rowed safely to the Florida mainland
during the night. As far as we knew, no one questioned
whether the islander may have provoked the worker's attack.

In our minds, the campsite Lockett had recommended was
ideal, except for mosquitoes. At first they were few in number,
but during warmer nights they became pesky. We solved the
problem by purchasing four square yards of mosquito netting.
It was cheap enough, 50 cents.

On moonlit nights we enjoyed strolling among the orange
trees, blissfully aware of the orchard's serenity, and speculated

whether the man in the moon had anything to do with it. Little did we realize then that 44 years later three American astronauts, Neil Armstrong, Edwin E. Aldrin, Jr., and Michael Collins would fly to the moon in a space ship, Apollo XI, and that on July 20, 1969, Armstrong and Aldrin actually would walk on the moon for over two hours while Collins would remain in lunar orbit. Nor could we foresee that the momentous flight would be launched from Merritt Island, just five miles more or less from the spot where our Ford obliviously was parked by two grapefruit trees in Sunset Grove.

A slump in the orange market after we had worked three weeks ended our employment. Lockett said we could return after a two-week layoff. We hated to leave, and apparently the

Members of Monroe family.

Bananas grow upwards.

Monroes shared our feeling. They invited us to a farewell
dinner in their home.

In their modest unpainted dwelling we felt that the
Monroes had gone all out to serve a sumptuous full-course
pork roast dinner. At the table was their eldest son who had
returned home for a visit. He had left Florida to seek better
opportunity "up north," and had made good. He wound up as
chauffeur for a well-to-do family in New York, and drove one of
his employer's expensive cars to make the trip home. The
family naturally showed great pride in his achievement.

We went on a hike during the afternoon with several of the
Monroes, who guided us to an isolated area where bananas
grew wild. Not only was this our first sight of banana plants,
but also the revelation that bananas pointed upward on their
stalks, not downward as we always had seen them in stores—
upside down, so to speak, one stalk to each plant. The
Monroes demonstrated how they would chop down banana

plants when the fruit became ripe, provided someone else didn't beat them to it.

With the Monroes we discussed the uncertainty of our plans. We said we had a little money saved to resume our trip, but that we preferred to remain in Florida for the rest of the winter. The chauffeur son suggested we look for construction jobs in Cocoa, and volunteered to help us find work.

In Cocoa the next morning we were surprised when he asked us to remain in our Ford while he applied for jobs for the three of us with the Speidell Contracting Company. He came back with the welcome news we had been hired and should report for work at noon. We did so, but our friend had left us. We reasoned that as an older and experienced-looking person, and as a southerner, he had included himself as a job applicant in case we, as youths, would be rejected, rambling about as we were in an old Ford bearing northern license plates. Confirming this suspicion was the foreman who hesitated before letting us begin work.

"Where's your partner?" he asked. His query was abrupt.

Our evasive answer finally satisfied him.

Pay for an eight-hour day would be $3, a boost of 50 cents over the nine-hour day at Sunset Grove. We knew from experience on the New York road job the work would be harder than in the orange grove, but we didn't let that deter us because the increased pay meant accelerated accumulation of money for our travel fund.

Elliott's first duty was to feed sand and cement into the iron jaws of a hungry cement mixer, while I was delegated to push a "Georgia buggy," which meant nothing more than wheeling an oversized wheelbarrow filled with concrete pouring from the cement mixer Elliott fed.

Tired when quitting time at last arrived, we reconnoitered

for a place to camp. We selected a vacant lot in the area known as Carlton Terrace, a couple miles north of Cocoa. Here we ate meals and slept undisturbed for two nights.

"This is great, no camp fee," Elliott said elatedly.

While we prepared supper the third day, a stranger approached.

"Sorry, boys, but you can't camp here. This $10,000 lot belongs to the governor, and he won't like having you park on it with that antique you're driving around the country."

We left right away and soon settled in the R.E. Fish tourist camp a half-mile south of the governor's lot. Here the fee was only one dollar per week. It included a table for preparing meals, the drinking water was more tolerable than the sulfurous water in Sunset Grove, and we were next to the little general store in which the Fish family lived. Florida's Dixie Highway ran beside us, along the west bank of the mile-or-so-wide Indian River. Best of all, we were camped in another orange grove.

For a week Elliott and I endured shifting from one construction job to another, working for different bosses of varying temperaments. Then Speidell assigned us to Carlton Terrace. He had a contract there for a booming housing development project. As things turned out, we would work for only one boss, Halsey Huele. A Florida resident for a dozen or more years, it so happened he once lived in Superior, Wisconsin, just 65 miles west of our hometown, Ashland.

In Carlton Terrace streets and sidewalks already had been laid out, with concrete curbs and posts for street lights. Six houses had been erected, but as yet were unoccupied. Huele's job was to lay out and construct foundations for scores of additional residences.

Tall and slender, Huele impressed us as genial and skilled

in his trade as a mason. He kept us busy, but found time to indulge in friendly discussions about our common interest, the Lake Superior country of northern Wisconsin.

"Of course," he grinned when we recounted the annual basketball games at Ashland High School in which Superior Central always managed to defeat Ashland in the contests, generally by just a single point or two, 16-14 or such, with a desperate last-second shot from the middle of the court.

Promoted from cement sack lifters and wheelbarrow pushers to the more satisfying jobs of laying forms for sidewalks, excavating trenches for foundation walls, and helping mix and pour concrete, we found our work less boring.

Interrupting the routine one morning was a truck driver delivering a load of cement. A wiry youth, his gray eyes flashing and his red hair bristling, he excitedly related his experience with a speeding motorist, "mad because I didn't turn off to let him pass."

"The motorist drove into the ditch," the young driver said, "and demanded to know my name. I told him it might be Calvin Coolidge or Johnny Witherspoon."

Our crew laughed, waiting for the truck driver to continue. "Old stick-in-the-mud got so mad he said he'd bring me to court for crowding him into the ditch. He got madder when I said I'd tell the judge he was speeding. He said I couldn't prove it, but he cooled down when I told him I was going exactly 30 miles an hour, and if he tried to pass my truck he'd have to go more than 30 miles an hour, and that would be speeding."

We were not sure what a judge would rule in such a trial, but considered it probable the case against Calvin Coolidge alias Johnny Witherspoon would be dismissed.

Huele taught us much about laying foundations for houses,

Tourist hides in orange tree near tramp's Merritt Island campsite.

stressing the need for making concrete walls perfectly square on top. But it remained for Joe, a young Negro worker, light in weight and slight of stature, to show us how to grub out a large palmetto root. Assigned to the task, Elliott and I had struggled with picks, shovels, and axes, perspiring freely but accomplishing little or nothing. Huele told Joe to take over.

The Negro's casual approach to the job contrasted sharply with our feverish though futile effort. He went about his task so slowly and deliberately he appeared to be loafing. He wasn't, however. Before long the three of us lifted out the palmetto root Joe had so methodically pried loose.

At our campsite in the orange grove we spent many pleasant evenings. In front of the little store we often chatted with Bob Fish's father, well into his sixties. Elliott called him an "armchair philosopher." The cognomen was apt enough. Seated in an old wooden chair, his knuckled hands firmly gripping the curved side supports, he speculated about any subject coming to mind. Frequently he discussed Florida's expanding economic growth, fervently contending the flourishing prosperity was no "boom-and-bust" as many were predicting.

"As sure as God made green apples, the bubble won't bust," he said. His reference to God and green apples prefixed most of his philosophical remarks, as if to affirm them.

We had only to walk a few steps across the Dixie Highway to spend pleasantly warm evenings among the palms on the west bank of the Indian River. Moon beams flickered across the water and the palms were outlined along the shore. Now and then young couples rowed up and down the stream, and once we heard singing to the accompaniment of a banjo. We sat for what seemed like hours, dreaming the time away in those delightful subtropical surroundings while Elliott strummed his ukulele, attracting tourists from Bob Fish's camp. Motorists tooted their horns as they drove by. The campers joined in singing old-time tunes, "Oh Dem Golden Slippers," "In the Evening by the Moonlight," and "Polly Wolly Doodle."

The mood became nostalgic as Elliott, with his deep bass voice, sang bits from Dvorak's New World Symphony, "goin' home, goin' home." When he struck up "Dixie" the mood livened with intensity, even though the tourists generally were northerners. Of course, I chirped along, as usual.

One evening Elliott covered his pocket comb with a piece of paper and hummed on it, imitating a saxophone. Soon rumors went around that he was a real saxophone player of some accomplishment. This would not have been of any consequence, I figured, had not the rumor reached an orchestra leader. Urgently in need of a saxophone player, he waited an entire afternoon for us to return from work so he could engage Elliott to play for the season's gala social event, a ball at one of

Elliott's music entertains tourists.

the leading hotels in the vicinity.

"Oh!" was all he could manage to say when Elliott pulled his "saxophone" from his pocket and demonstrated his virtuosity.

Up the highway was another orange grove to which Elliott and I often retreated. A sulfur spring in the center of the grove created a pool in which we took a nighttime dip. We inhaled the fragrant scent of orange blossoms, reminiscent of the trailing arbutus growing wild in our Chequamegon Bay region back home. Unlike the orange blossoms, the arbutus regrettably was becoming increasingly rare because of excessive picking.

Ignoring protests that we had no money to spare, real estate agents called evenings at our campsite, persisting in efforts to sell lots. Some offered installment plans. A Richard Brown was aggressive to the point of being pushy. Nattily dressed in white trousers and a matching open-collar shirt, Brown trumped up any number of reasons for us to buy lots "while they're still cheap."

One evening he described to us what he called "a real bargain." He offered a "good lot for just $1,000." Brown said it was located at the upper end of Carlton Terrace, "just a little bit out of line with the rest of the subdivision." That meant "it's not restricted," he added. Glowingly he pictured ways in which we could use the lot. "Unrestricted means you can pitch a tent on it, if you want, and no one can make you tear it down. Or you can put up a gas station and have a prosperous business."

Failing to convince us, Brown offered another inducement. "There are six orange trees on the lot," he said. "Think of all the oranges you can pick, and sell."

His jaw dropped noticeably when Elliott said, "Six orange trees! What good are they if we have to chop them down to make room for a gas station?"

"Well, buy it for investment, then," Brown fired back. "Downstate they're selling lots in swamps. What's the difference what kind of land it is if you can sell it in six months for double your money?"

We still were unconvinced. Disconcerted, Brown started the engine of his car. "You'll be sorry," he said loudly as he drove off into the night.

On Sundays we swam in the Atlantic Ocean at Cocoa Beach, its water warmed by the Gulf Stream. We donned swimsuits in the public bathhouse. Sometimes we drove the Ford up the beach to get away from the crowd. This almost had dire conse-

Tramps take Sunday swim.

quences.

I had parked the Ford on the sandy beach. The tide was going out, and as we dashed out for a swim in the retreating waves, a middle-aged man with a commanding voice waved his arms and called us back. He pointed toward the Ford.

"Better move it," he warned.

We saw the car gradually sinking in the moist sand left behind by the outgoing tide. Already mired to the rims the car's wheels stuck firmly in the clutching sand, then yielded slowly as Elliott and the friendly stranger pushed the Ford and I alternately stepped on its low and reverse bands.

With the car parked safely on hard dry sand, we thanked our benefactor who said he was Bill Sommers of Hoboken, New Jersey. Immensely relieved, we raced out to splash in the receding tide.

For more than two weeks we had been annoyed by intensely itching scabs. They formed mostly around our ankles and waistlines, as though preferring areas hemmed in by shoe tops and leather belts. Bob Fish told us chiggers were to blame.

They were in the sandy soil, he said, and attached themselves to our skin.

"It helps to cover the scabs with rags soaked in kerosene," he said.

The prospect of walking around with kerosene rags had no appeal, so we tolerated the itching. To our amazement, and joy, the scabs gradually disappeared. We eventually felt no more itching.

We rationalized that aside from the recreational benefit of swimming at Cocoa Beach, the salty water of the Atlantic Ocean had effected a cure for our chigger bites. Or that

Tramps on Atlantic Ocean beach.

Tourist friends enjoy ukulele music.

possibly the sulfur in the orange grove pool in which we bathed had brought about the healing.

We made several trips to the beach with the Barretts of Columbus, Ohio. Professor Barrett, a researcher at Ohio State University, had set up camp near ours. With him were his wife and two sons. They seemed intrigued by our Ford, especially the boys, and listened with absorbed interest as we related experiences of our trip. We were equally curious about theirs. Enjoyable was the mess of fish the Barretts gave us. Professor Barrett had carefully cleaned and scaled each fish.

Heavy-set and broad-shouldered, Professor Barrett easily

could have obtained a job with one of Speidell's cement mixing crews, we thought. He, however, said he was "on leave to research spiders." In Ohio he had discovered nine new species, he said, "but I hope to find many more in Florida."

We cheerfully accepted the family's invitation to go swimming at Cocoa Beach. When Professor Barrett suddenly stopped his car after we crossed the Banana River toll bridge, we had our first opportunity to see him at work. He walked to the edge of a swamp, and disregarding the mosquitoes on his arm, grasped a tiny insect with a pair of tweezers. Holding up the tweezers for us to see, he said, "might be a new species."

He carefully deposited his find in a small bottle, labeled it, and said he would examine the spider under a microscope after he returned to Ohio. Responding to a question by Elliott, Professor Barrett desisted from his search for more spiders long enough to explain that he recognized the insect he just had bottled was a spider because of its "various distinguishing characteristics," the nature of which he told us, but which whizzed through my mind faster than the cars zipping by on the highway.

Resuming his search, Professor Barrett found and bottled several more spiders before giving up his quest.

"Let's go swimming," he abruptly said.

Though Elliott and I at first wondered why a man as large as Professor Barrett would pursue creatures as small as spiders, we now felt he was a man truly dedicated to his research, and by no means the "butterfly chasing" scientist we often had seen depicted on the movie screen. Rather, he was practical, down-to-earth, spoke to us about car motors, fishing tackle, and mechanical devices in common use. His range of practical knowledge seemed so comprehensive we sensed an enormous lack in ours.

As the days rolled by we increasingly enjoyed Florida's warm summery weather. We had no inclination to be back home contending with a cold and snowy winter. We kept in touch, though, writing letters to family and friends.

I wrote one of my letters to Oscar King, the Ashland Chamber of Commerce secretary. He promptly answered, proudly relating progress being made in Ashland. He said:

> We have an aeroplane school in Ashland now, and one plane makes regular daily trips. Eleven or twelve fellows have signed a note to secure a radio broadcasting station, and we've hired Theodore Steinmetz of Wisconsin's 32nd Army Division, who has formed the world's largest boys' band. Then again, we have a symphony orchestra and an adult North Woods band under the direction of Steinmetz. How's that for big town stuff? Boy, the 'Old Town' surely is getting metropolitan.

We agreed. "Nothing exciting like that happened when we were in Ashland," Elliott remarked.

King said he gave my letter to John B. Chapple, city editor of the *Ashland Daily Press.* John, a friendly and jovial young newsman whom I had come to know from his daily visit at the Chamber office, gave the letter front-page space with a three-column headline:

Florida Governor Has Our "Ford
Tramps" Move On; Oranges Fine!

The lead for his story quoting the letter was:

> Stranded in the Carolinas with but 30
> cents when last heard from, Seegar Swanson
> and Elliott Nystrom, Ashland boys who are
> on a nation-wide `Ford tramp' have finally
> reached Florida.
>
> Parked in an orange grove where they
> can pick their dessert after every meal
> without getting out of the car, they are
> having a superb time, and are making plans
> to pull up stakes and hit for California soon.
>
> Even the Florida governor took notice
> of them—by ordering them to quit camping
> on his private lot.

The "power of the Press" soon became apparent. Dozens of letters poured in, including one from Bill Lynch, who wrote, "Wonder if your Ford still has four wheels?"

Gratefully received were numerous boxes of homemade cakes, cookies, candies, and preserves. Two of our former high school teachers, Harriet Rymer and Gladys Bahr, sent us stuffed dates and candy.

One letter came from Spokane, Washington. Claude Monteith, a high school classmate, wrote that he learned of our trip when he removed the January 29 edition of the *Ashland Daily Press* wrapped around a canary cage his mother sent him.

Paul Anderson, serving aboard the U.S. naval vessel *Pennsylvania* on the Pacific Ocean, wished us luck in sunny Florida, but said, "I prefer a place where there is cold weather during the winter. Someday I'll be back in the great north woods, and expect to see you there."

Chapple's front-page story evidently influenced many of those who wrote letters to us. His designation of us as "Ford Tramps" stuck, although we also later were referred to as "Ford

Florida Governor Has Our "Ford Tramps" Move On; Oranges Fine!

Stranded in the Carolinas with but thirty cents when last heard from, Seegar Swanson and Elliott Nystrom, Ashland boys who are on a nation-wide "Ford tramp" have finally reached Florida.

Parked in an orange grove where they can pick their dessert after every meal without getting out of the car, they are having a superb time, and are making plans to pull up stakes and hit for California soon.

Even the Florida governor took notice of them—by ordering them to quit camping on his private lot.

A letter of Swanson to the Chamber of Commerce, says:

Cocoa, Fla.,
Gen. Delivery,
Jan. 1925

"The wandering knights are all settled for the winter. When we learned from you in your recent letter that the thermometer has been hovering near the 30 below mark we determined without the least hesitancy to make our home in the land where the sun shines warmly, and where the balmy breezes are inviting. That place is no other than Cocoa, Florida

Yes, our financial status is on a finer basis than it was back in Columbia, S. C., where our money dwindled to a mere thirty cents. Being without funds is embarrassing and somewhat inconvenient. Just at the time when a nickle looked as large as a pumpkin to us we had a chance to buy a new overcoat for three dollars. Worse yet, a gentleman offered to sell us a device for threading needles for the apear-ently insignificant sum of ten cents. An affair of that kind is something that we need very much, but when ten cents represented one-third of our available capital, we deemed it inadvisable to invest in a needle threader. Somehow the science of threading a needle is baffling. The thread always seems larger than the hole in the needle. It took thirty-five minutes to sew a small three-cornered tear in my shirt tail other day. Seventeen minutes of the time was spent in threading the needle, while the remainder was required to sew the aperture. When I found later that I had sewed the shirt onto my B. V. D's, I knew for certain that I wasn't "cut out" for a tailor.

For two weeks Elliott and I were picking oranges and grapefruit on an island near Cocoa. A slump in the market resulted in a temporary lay-off, so we sought work in Cocoa, and succeeded in finding it. At present I am pushing a "Georgia buggy," which is nothing more than wheling concrete in an over-sized wheelbarrow, while Elliott is feeding sand and cement into the iron jaws of a hungry mixer. The work pays three dollars for eight hours, with no provision for a bonus or a pension. A pension wouldn't interest us, though, for as soon as our stake approaches $200 we will leave our jobs and drive to California. That ought to be about April 1.

Continued on page 8)

FLORIDA GOV. HAS OUR "FORD TRAMPS" MOVE ON; ORANGES FINE

(Continued from page 1)

The good old ship "Wanderlust' is still our house and home. It is now parked in an orange grove, so as soon as our meals have been prepared and eaten, we need but pluck our dessert from the trees near at hand. For awhile we lived in the exclusive residential section at Carleton Terrace. Of course, it made little or no difference that the houses on the terrace are still in the process of construction, and consequently unoccupied. The fact remained that we were living in a restricted suburb of Cocoa. It so happened that we chose as a camping place a lot belonging to the Governor of Florida. Evidently the governor wasn't overly fond of having his $10,000 lot disfigured by a time and travel-worn Ford, because a summons was issued requesting us to find a new home. So that's why we are now living in an orange grove.

Out of Jacksonville, Florida, we were driving along at a fair rate of speed one day, when a car ahead of us suddenly stopped. A man with his face completely masked jumped out of it and confronted us with a double barreled shot gun. Presumably he wanted our money, but he didn't get it. We stepped on the gas and shot by him at a terrific pace, nearly knocking him over as we did so. The would-be bandit was undoubtedly dumbfounded by our action, for he failed to shoot. If any more highwaymen attempt to detain us in the future, we will do the same thing over again, even if it becomes necessary to equip our Ford with steel side curtains and hard rubber tires.

The North Woods Band certainly should prove a wonderful asset to the city of Ashland. We have mentioned to a number of people that our city boasts of a band that is far beyond the ordinary, and they all are impressed by the unique idea of the players wearing the native garb of Northern Wisconsin woodsmen. The "world's greatest boys' band" is another thing that attracts attention as soon as we mention it.

Our address is: General Delivery, Cocoa, Fla. News from home is ever welcome.

Sincerely your friend,
Seegar Swanson.

Ashland Daily Press, *January 29, 1925*

Bums" by the *Milwaukee Journal* and the *Superior Telegram.*

Our friends, it appeared, identified themselves with the Ford, alluding to it as "Flivver," "Tin Lizzie," "Perkol 8" and "Roving Blunderbuss." Christy, the YMCA secretary, concluded his letter by writing, "always glad to hear from you and the Henry."

We were moved and encouraged by the last paragraph in Oscar King's letter. He said, "I imagine that the joint treasury is in much better shape now. If not, let us know and we will see if something can be done."

February neared its end, and so did our stay in Cocoa. Attracting our attention were reports that pay was higher farther south. Bricklayers and plasterers, we were told, earned $9 a day in Cocoa, whereas in Melbourne, just 20 miles to the south, the pay was $12 a day. As common laborers we could expect higher wages, too, but not that much.

Not that we were dissatisfied with our jobs in Cocoa. The weather had been nearly perfect. We lost only one day of pay in January due to rain. It rained twice in February, but at night. The days were hot sometimes, but generally were fine for working. We shivered and had to bundle up with warmer clothing, however, when for two days temperatures dropped to the freezing mark. Floridians, lacking our experience with cold weather, suffered more.

Each week we spent but eight to nine dollars for groceries, thanks to the goodies from home, and a few more dollars for gasoline and incidentals. And in Cocoa we no longer faced the problem of keeping eggs fresh. Instead of buying them by the dozen, we now could purchase two at a time at a trifling cost of seven or eight cents, depending upon market conditions.

We had come to regard Cocoa as a rapidly growing little city, its streets paved and its business district brilliantly lighted by a whiteway. Its residential area was expanding, too, with beautiful modern homes.

In Cocoa's new bank building we had accumulated a deposit of $160, regretting somewhat to withdraw it when we finally decided to break camp.

On Saturday, March 7 we departed. In the Ford were oranges and grapefruit given us at Sunset Grove. Added to these citrus fruits were kumquats, a delicious small fruit we first saw growing on a tree in the backyard of a home in Cocoa where we helped lay a sidewalk.

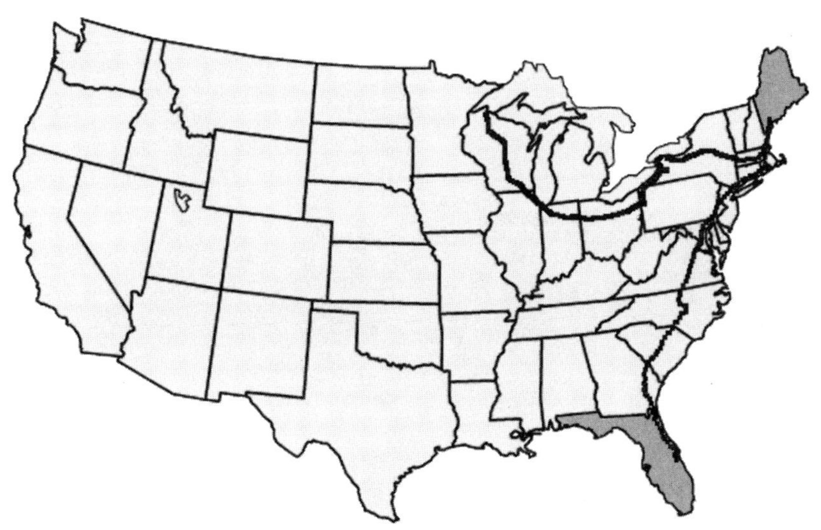

Chapter XI
Life on Hogan's Alley

IN COCOA the majestic Indian River had cast its spell upon us. Now that once more we were traveling on the Dixie Highway, we were glad the river still would be with us as the road wound south.

In Rockledge, contiguous with Cocoa, we drove about its elegant streets, realizing at once it primarily was a resort and residential community, with orange groves all about. Even the luxurious dwellings had orange trees in their yards.

"I don't see any Fords parked here," Elliott said as we stopped to view Rockledge's new Indian River Hotel, constructed at a cost of $300,000. Neither did we see any by the older Oaks Hotel, nor on the streets.

Our Ford, however, could hold its hood high, decked as it was with a flashy new 1925 Florida license plate. It replaced the dingy-looking Minnesota plates which expired at the end of

1925 REGISTRATION CARD.—The accompanying number plate has been registered and assigned to the addressee named hereon to be used on a motor vehicle of make and weight indicated for the year ending December 31, 1925.

Appn. No. **238224** Tag No. **C113806** Tax $ **8.00** *

Name **Ford** Type **Tour** Use **private**

Weight **1600** lbs. Capacity lbs. Pas.

Engine No. **3259413** Tires **pneu** Date acquired **1924**

County **Brevard** Res. or Town **Res** T. C. No.

F L A

Seegar Swanson
Gen Del
Cocoa
FLORIDA

1 9 2 5

Ernest Amos, Comptroller of Florida. *(Over)

Forced to renew their automobile registration in Florida.

1924. Florida required only one, to be fastened on the rear of the car.

We had expected difficulty when we applied by mail for license renewal, knowing we were negligent by not obtaining Wisconsin plates after buying the Ford in Minnesota. Florida obviously didn't care about that as long as we paid $8 for a Florida license, plus $1 for a title and 50 cents for its issuance.

With Elliott at the controls, we inhaled balmy air and drank in magnificent scenery as he purposefully slowed the Ford. Subtropical trees, bushes, and plants were everywhere. Huge oaks draped with Spanish moss were a new and fascinating sight for us. Vast orange groves lent added charm to the scenery.

Melbourne, slightly larger than Cocoa, looked like a promising place to seek work. With its population of possibly

Construction crew at Flatiron building. (opposite) Tramps are on roof. (inset)

FLATIRON BLDG.
KIBBE & CLARK
BUILDERS
STORES & OFFICES
FOR RENT
EGERT & LUX
CHURCH BLDG.
ING HERE

eight or nine thousand, the city showed signs of much activity. New houses were being built, and its business district was enlarging. Elliott drove the Ford to the Midway Tourist Camp in the heart of town, where we parked for the night.

Landing jobs in Melbourne was easy. The trouble was they lasted only a day, so we had to waste a day looking for another. Anxious to get something permanent, we talked with workers spending the winter in the tourist camp.

"I'm a carpenter at the Flatiron Building," one of the men said. "You can get steady jobs there."

Acting upon his suggestion, we applied at the Flatiron Building early the next morning, and were happy to be hired. As common laborers we would be paid $3.50 for an eight-hour day, 50 cents more than at Cocoa. Our employers were Kibbe & Clark Builders.

The Flatiron Building, to be three stories high, was designed to make good use of a triangular area between two streets converging at an apex. The first floor had, in the rough, neared completion, and the framework for the second and third floors was under construction. Already a sign was up advertising "Stores and Offices for Rent. Apply at Egbert & Lux, Church Building." About 25 men were employed, mostly carpenters and masons.

Elliott and I dreaded looking down from high places. The second floor wasn't all that high. Nevertheless, when we toted heavy planks over narrow boards laid loosely over beams on the second floor, we had nervous feelings. On my first trip up I carried but one plank, a 23-inch one, long and heavy.

"Next time carry two planks," a foreman sternly directed.

Lugging two planks didn't ease my apprehension of falling from a dizzy height. Fortunately, there were other jobs to

Flatiron building in 1999. (opposite)

FLATIRON BUILDING

perform on the second floor, somewhat easier, and as the day wore on we gradually became accustomed to height. By the time we carried planks to the third floor all fear of looking down to the street level faded away.

Work at the Flatiron Building was more strenuous than in Cocoa, we agreed. Welcome were days when we transferred to jobs in other parts of the Melbourne area. Long drives to the Atlantic coastline to load a truck with sand pleased us. It was fun shoveling sand onto the truck, and we could relax completely during the rides to and from the beach.

The day I mixed mortar for a bricklayer in Magnolia Gardens was so gratifying I hiked back that night to gain even more appreciation by strolling past the dwellings and their scented yards. If only somehow I could retain this leisurely walk, I thought, visualizing friends up north huddling in winter togs while here in Magnolia Gardens I wandered at night in shirt sleeves.

Assured of steady work we decided to remain in the Midway Tourist Camp. The fee was one dollar per week, the same as in Cocoa. The registration clerk assigned us a spacious lot near the far end of Hogan's Alley.

The camp, we thought, was a veritable village populated by about 250 tourists living in tents or shelters built on the frames of their trucks. One man slept in a hammock. Campsites were lined up in orderly fashion along pathways laid out as streets and avenues. Automobiles of different makes, including Fords but no ritzy limousines, were parked all around. At the park entrance several small shops and a general store catered to the wants of campers. Laundry facilities also were available. A branch post office handled incoming and outgoing mail, and sold stamps, cards, and money orders.

We boiled strong coffee for our meals because the water was

so sulfurous. The sulfur, however, didn't interfere with enjoyment of a swimming pool formed by a spring. Youngsters spent hours in the pool, and so did we.

At night a dance pavilion attracted us. Campers reveled nightly until a late hour. The cost was five cents per dance, two cents for the "hard times" dance. Elliott joined in for a dance or two, but I just looked on because I hadn't learned how. A small but talented campers' orchestra played old-fashioned schottisches and sprightly polkas, and an occasional up-to-the-minute "Naughty Waltz," or a haunting "Meet Me Tonight in Dreamland."

Campers often stopped by our Ford on Hogan's Alley for friendly conversation. They spoke of interesting trips made in the Melbourne area, showing souvenirs they gathered.

One man and his wife, however, spent only one night on Hogan's Alley. Describing himself as a sausage grinder by trade, he told us they were on their way back to New York after an unsuccessful attempt to make a living while spending the winter in Florida.

"They don't eat enough sausage here to keep a sausage grinder in business," he explained. "We're goin' home where people like high-class weenies and baloney." He remained silent a moment, then said he knew construction work was available in Florida, "but I know I can't handle a wheelbarrow like a sausage machine."

The short, mild-mannered man who slept in the hammock offered us oysters in the shell. His name was Hal. He said he spent the afternoon collecting them. Talkative, he impressed us as more or less a drifter who happened to land in Melbourne. We listened as he gave pointers on how to cope with problems of traveling.

"If you ever run low on gas and there isn't a gas station

near, try this," he said by way of helpful advice. He walked to our Ford and lifted the front seat cushion to expose the gas tank. "Put a tire valve in this small hole on the cover of your tank and pump air into the tank with your tire pump," he said. "That'll get you to a gas station."

Before he left, Hal showed us how to remove the oysters from the shells he gave us, and told us his recipe for an oyster stew. The next day Elliott liked the stew we prepared, but I didn't. This gave rise to the observation by Elliott that except for this occasion we generally agreed on everything. This was true, I reflected. There was no arguing, no bickering. We indeed were compatible.

Elliott, however, corrected himself. "Not always," he said. "I can't understand why you put butter on sweet rolls, and you don't understand why I spend a nickel for an ice cream cone."

We attended the Methodist church near the Flatiron Building one Sunday morning. Lacking dress-up clothes, we felt somewhat out of place, but were inspired by the service. We saw that a foreman of our construction job was in church, too. From then on he became more cordial on the job, often asking us questions about our trip.

With so many new things to see and do in Florida, Elliott and I devoted little time to reading. Once in awhile, though, we picked up tourist literature, and sometimes read it.

Having seen so many cars on the road, we hadn't been aware that Florida's numerous railroads also brought thousands of visitors to the state. Judging by the folder I read, the railroads did their utmost to promote this travel, and to speed it up. Drawing my attention were such enticing appellations as "The Dixie Flyer," "The Dixie Express," "The Dixie Limited," "The Seminole Limited," "New York to Cocoa, Florida," "The Royal Palm," "The Ponce de Leon," and so on. Definitely, not

Methodist Church.

all Florida's travel was by automobile.

Days lengthened as April drew nearer, and with the sun's rays becoming noticeably warmer, Elliott and I grew increasingly restless.

"Time to move on," Elliott said.

Accordingly, we quit our jobs during the first week of April, left the Midway Tourist Camp, bought a $25 money order to repay our loan from my cousin Nels Olson, and withdrew our savings from the Melbourne bank. This we did in the form of traveler's checks. The bank cashier shook hands with us, and with a grin said, "Good luck, boys, and come back to Melbourne some day."

Neither the banker nor I foresaw that 55 years would elapse

before I accepted the invitation. Together with my wife, Ruth, our youngest daughter, Jean, her husband, Clarence Cross, and their son and daughter David and Mary Jean, we drove to Melbourne while en route to their condominium in Naples, for the express purpose of visiting the city where Elliott and I had, in our small way, helped erect the Flatiron Building.

I wondered whether it still would be there, and if so, how it looked after its construction had been finished. Melbourne had grown so much, its population now about 12,000, that I couldn't spot the structure. Asking a pedestrian whether he could direct us to it, he surprised me when he responded, "the Flatiron Building? Everyone in town knows where it is. Drive straight ahead and you'll come to it."

As we continued along the street I suddenly recognized the church Elliott and I had attended, and then the Flatiron Building came plainly into view. Recollections surging through my mind momentarily stunned me. Now shops and stores occupied the ground floor and I surmised that offices filled the upper two. Tropical shrubbery and trees planted in the apex formed a beautiful landscape.

From the friendly barber in Wagg's Barber Shop, I learned that some of the men who worked at the Flatiron Building still lived in town, and often dropped in at the barber shop for a shave or haircut, now and then reminiscing about the days when the Flatiron Building was constructed.

When I asked the barber whether the Midway Tourist Camp still existed, he nodded. "Sure," he said. "It's where it always was." He pointed in the direction of the park. "It's different now, no tourists camping there."

We readily found the campground and looked around. The stores were gone and neat little houses had replaced the tents and trucks. I looked for the lot where our Ford had been parked along Hogan's Alley. A small house stood there now, occupied by its owner or a tenant. The dance pavilion had become a community center.

Hoping to locate the original site where Elliott and I had camped in an orange grove, we drove to Cocoa. That city, like Melbourne, had grown substantially. The old Dixie Highway, now superseded by a modern freeway, was easy to follow. It was the same as we had known it, still hugging the Indian River. So many new homes had sprung up I had difficulty locating the site of Bob Fish's store and campground, thinking they no doubt also had succumbed to housing development. Several times I thought I recalled where the store stood, but couldn't be sure. Suddenly we came to a small orange grove.

Three raccoons, strikingly apparent with their black-masked cheeks and black-ringed tails, emerged from roadside bushes. I peered over and beyond them, and remembered there had been only one orange grove so close to the Indian River when Elliott and I camped there. The store was gone, but I felt sure I now could show my family the exact spot where the Ford had been parked beside it.

Oranges were ripening, although the orchard seemed neglected. At both ends exquisite new homes extended along the old Dixie Highway. Wondering why this cluster of orange trees hadn't become part of the residential expansion, I inquired at an adjoining house. There I learned an heir of the Fish family now owned the property. He lived "up north," and steadfastly refused offers as high as $100,000 for sale of the riverside frontage.

Back in Cocoa, another pleasant surprise awaited me. A modern concrete bridge had been built across the river to Merritt Island, but a section of the old bridge was left standing for use by fishermen and boaters. We walked to the end of the old span. I had a feeling that was just about the spot where Elliott and I had fished with three New Yorkers on Christmas Day so long ago.

In search of Sunset Grove, where Elliott and I had picked oranges, we crossed the new bridge to Merritt Island. We had trouble finding the orchard because the river road leading to it had been gobbled up by a residential area. After futilely driving on several other roads we were about to give up, concluding Sunset Grove no longer existed. I was glad, though, to spot a roadside sign, "Sunset Grove." As soon as we reached a familiar white, two-story frame house, I knew I was back at the place where Elliott and I first went to work in Florida.

Mrs. David Prather, who responded to my knock on the door, granted us permission to drive through the large orchard, and to "pick yourselves some oranges."

She listened with keen interest as I recalled events of 55 years ago. When I asked if the grapefruit trees still were growing where our Ford had been parked, she said, "They're right over there."

She led us to them, not far from the house. "They're the only two grapefruit trees we've ever had," she said.

I told her about our first taste of tangerines.

"You'll find the tangerine trees when you drive over there," she said, pointing toward the middle of the grove. "There were never more than two of them."

The question naturally flashed through my mind, should Elliott and I have eaten so many grapefruit and tangerines from only four trees? Nevertheless, I sampled some more tangerines when we located the two trees.

As we drove slowly through the orchard, we saw row upon row of orange trees, waiting to be picked. I marveled that these same trees so heavily loaded with oranges in 1925, now were equally laden with fruit.

Nothing had changed, I thought, except that up the island a way, three astronauts successfully had launched man's first flight to the moon, two of them landing on it.

<blockquote>
Hit extremely large bump & practically knocked off rear right fender. Said fender has been suffering from automotive dropsy for some time. Decided to take it off before it fell off on its own accord. Thought steering apparatus "kawumpus" when hit sand trying to pass big truck.

— The Log, Wed. Apr. 15, 1925
</blockquote>

Chapter XII
The Faltering Ford

WITH A STAKE of $250 in traveler's checks and a few dollars in small change we naturally were exuberant when we left Melbourne at 9 A.M. Sunday, April 5 to resume our journey around the U.S.A. We were California-bound, but first we would visit Miami, hoping the Ford and our nest egg eventually would get us to the Pacific Coast. We soon had misgivings about the Ford, however. It creaked, rumbled, and rattled as we drove it over a rough 10-mile detour. When the steering wheel gave us trouble before we left Melbourne, we had purchased a new radius rod, hoping it would remedy that flaw. To make matters worse, Florida's dew had begun to rust the fenders, and other signs of deterioration were manifest. To replace the Ford now would deplete our funds.

"I wonder how far we'll get before it falls apart?" Elliott asked dourly.

Continuing south, we went through a number of fair-sized towns. These, we observed, had a head start over a multitude of new housing areas being laid out with streets, sidewalks, and lights. We wondered how many thousands of dollars were tied up in these speculative ventures, and whether the tracts ever would become residential districts.

Elliott remarked that the promoters "know how to choose fancy names for their projects." We saw names of this kind posted on signs announcing public auctions of lots, with free band concerts and prizes. Some signs urged viewers to contact real estate agents in nearby towns, with the privilege of picking oranges and grapefruit free of charge.

The farther south we traveled the more evident became the inflationary effects of tourism. In a Fort Lauderdale restaurant a skimpy sandwich and a cup of weak coffee cost us 45 cents each. It was just an appetizer as far as we were concerned. We satisfied the pangs of hunger by purchasing bananas and doughnuts in a store down the street, but again the cost was inflated.

Knowing we would have to retrace our travel through this part of Florida, we accelerated the Ford toward Miami after spending a night in Fort Lauderdale's excellent tourist camp.

With its population of maybe 100,000 or so, Miami seemed bent on becoming the metropolis of Florida. Traffic crowded its streets, and wherever we turned brisk construction was evident.

Traffic congestion on one street caused us an embarrassing predicament. I was driving, and as we approached an intersection, a traffic officer blew his whistle and signaled me to get across to line up at the rear of a long string of automobiles. Noting we might hinder cross traffic if the Ford jutted back into the intersection, I misinterpreted the officer's signal, thinking he meant for me to go to the left of the string of cars and to travel down the street to form a second line. Stalled motorists scowled and honked horns while we serenely passed by. When we reached the end of the traffic line, a distance of four blocks, a traffic officer defiantly stepped toward our car.

"And where do you think you're going?" he thundered.

I stared at him blankly.

"Back up and take your turn at the end of the line," the officer shouted.

Sheepishly, I bore down on the reverse pedal. The Ford was too conspicuous for such a plight, I thought. We sensed chuckles of "heh, heh," as our car slowly wormed its way backwards. Choosing not to line up at the rear, I scooted up the side street.

Changing our course, we drove willy-nilly about the city, noticing that dozens of real estate offices dotted the streets. Walking into a clothing store, we had a nostalgic visit with a salesman who gave us a back-home feeling when he said he sold caps and hats to Lew Anderson, a leading clothier in Ashland.

After having imbibed so much of Florida's sulfur, we eagerly drank several glasses of distilled water offered free at a filling station at the edge of Coral Gables, Miami's suburb, so luxurious with its homes and elegant landscaping.

We wandered about Coconut Grove and the Deering Estate, winding up at Miami Beach, which Elliott described as "marvelous." Winter guests concentrated in several new tall hotels. More hotels were on the drawing-board, we learned, because Miami's attraction as a noted resort center was increasing at such a rapid rate. We entered one of the hotel lobbies, but knew we were out of place among the affluent guests milling about the corridors.

When it started to rain, we left Miami. At last we really were California-bound. First, though, we had to travel several hundred miles more to get out of Florida.

We began by retracing the route we had journeyed to reach Miami. That night the Ford rested in a free tourist camp in Hollywood. So much new construction was under way we had the impression Hollywood was endeavoring to establish itself as a mushrooming city rivaling Miami.

Departing from Hollywood, we again relished the exhilarating ocean drive. At Palm Beach we drove around for a critical view of the fabulous city we had read so much about in Sunday newspaper supplements. We witnessed ruins of the recent Breaker's Hotel fire, and in the swank residential area eyed the extravagant homes that only the wealthy could afford.

Ruins of Breaker's Hotel fire.

At the beach we stepped out of the Ford in our blue, loose-fitting, one-piece bathing suits to swim in the Atlantic Ocean with a crowd of "the nation's 400."

After crossing a bridge to West Palm Beach we looked for a tourist camp. The drinking water there was almost as good as the distilled water of the Coral Gables filling station. Before retiring, we attended a free band concert in Seminole Park.

We joined the crowd in applauding the novel way in which the band made its exit for the intermission. A sudden blare of discordant notes filled the air, and one by one each player left the bandstand as if disgusted with the bandmaster. A man in a police uniform clamped handcuffs on one "unruly" player. The snare drummer withdrew after a vicious rap on his drum, and finally the bass drummer banged his big instrument with a thunderous roar. The bandmaster then tossed his baton high in the air, and was the last to storm off. Amidst enthusiastic applause, the entire band came back to perform the remainder of its lively program.

Elliott hoped to visit his cousin Algot Lindstrom, formerly of Ashland, but now residing in St. Petersburg. To do this, we had intended to reach the western part of Florida by way of a northern highway out of Orlando. This meant we would duplicate many more miles we previously had traveled down the East Coast. It therefore pleased us to learn in West Palm Beach that a more southern route had just opened for travel. For a toll of two dollars we could drive 50 miles over the new concrete Connor's Highway to Okeechobee, to link with other roads leading to the West Coast.

We were familiar with toll bridges, but this was the first toll road we had encountered. We thought a two-dollar fee a bit high, considering all other highways had been free. But when the paved highway took us over swampy terrain along the northern border of the Everglades we concluded Florida had come up with a novel way to finance and speed up construction of such a desirable highway, one which had lacked top priority.

As Elliott said, "it's a short cut, and cheaper."

About 10 miles east of Okeechobee we stopped when the Ford acted up again, hitting on three cylinders. Across the pavement we saw a motorist filling two gunny sacks with black soil he dug out of the swamp. License plates on his car indicated he was from Iowa. He looked up as we curiously watched him dig and bag the soil.

"I collect dirt whenever I go on a trip," he said. He dug a shovelful for us to see. "This is some of the richest I've found."

"What do you do with the dirt?" Elliott asked.

"When I get home with it I'll plant flowers. My neighbor brags his flowers come up earliest and best. I'll show him."

While we tinkered with the Ford, we were thankful to be parked on the shoulder of a concrete highway. The swamp where the motorist dug seemed a likely haven for alligators and poisonous snakes.

At noon we stopped opposite the small post office in Okeechobee, hiked up and down the business block, and viewed Lake Okeechobee, headwater of the Florida Everglades. A postal clerk told us the lake was only 10 or 12 feet deep, but was at least 40 miles long and 25 miles wide. Remote in the Everglades, he said, Seminole Indians had retreated to continue living primitively.

Westward from Okeechobee the Ford plowed through a dozen miles of sandy highway, rutted to the hub caps. Not until we neared Sebring did the road improve.

The layout of Sebring's streets immediately caught our attention. It reminded us of the capitol area in Madison,

Elliott envies one of Florida's favorite sports.

Wisconsin. A circular park formed the hub of the business district, with streets running out from it like spokes in a wheel.

Driving closer to Florida's west coast we found ourselves in an area of alluring inland lakes. Nestled among low sandy hills, the lakes gave us a feeling we were back in northern Wisconsin, enjoying lakes in the sand barrens close to our homes. We got out of the Ford to walk along the shorelines, noting tropical growth had given way to scenery more like Wisconsin than Florida.

We devoted little attention to most towns we drove through. In Bartow, however, we remained long enough for another first time experience. Here we drank water at a fountain after stepping on a foot pedal similar to the accelerator of our Ford. Streets in Lakeland were busy, and in Plant City gas had dropped to 27 cents a gallon, 4 cents lower than we had paid in Sebring. Eggs, on the other hand, held steady, two for 8 cents or four for 14 cents. We later passed filling stations pumping gas at 23 cents a gallon, a price in line with the 25 cents we usually paid on the East Coast.

Getting closer to Tampa we saw groves of citrus fruits, glad again to be in a land of oranges. Fruit was so abundant it was easy to comprehend why Tampa had become a distribution center for west coast fruit. We made but a cursory survey of the city, intending to return after our forthcoming visit with Elliott's cousin in St. Petersburg. The 85 cents toll to cross the five-mile Gandy Bridge we deemed worthwhile. Spanning Tampa Bay, it was regarded as the world's longest auto bridge. Soon we were in St. Petersburg, arriving in time for supper in a downtown restaurant.

Early in the evening we called on the Algot Lindstroms. They warmly welcomed us. After an exchange of greetings, they took us on a long drive in their Dodge Roadster.

Obviously proud of St. Petersburg, they showed us many points of interest, as far out as Pasadena Park.

"As you've probably heard, we're called the Sunshine City," Algot said. "We see the sun here every day, except maybe three or four." He said we ought to consider St. Petersburg as a future home.

Invited to spend as many days as we wished in their ideal one-story home, we told the Lindstroms we had better sleep in the Ford. Mrs. Lindstrom, however, insisted we sleep in a bed for a change. We acquiesced. It was our first night in an indoor bedroom since that uncomfortable experience in New York City in the Harlem YMCA.

After a hearty breakfast, and amid protests by Algot and his wife, we were on the move again. Before leaving St. Petersburg, though, we followed Algot's suggestion that we ask for tourist pamphlets at the Chamber of Commerce. While walking out of the Chamber offices with a stack of maps and folders, I halted in front of a desk when I saw a desk sign, "Jack O'Connor, Director of Public Relations."

Could this be the same Jack O'Connor of Superior, Wisconsin, who now and then dropped in at the Chamber of Commerce office in Ashland?

The secretary at the desk said, "Mr. O'Connor is out, but will be back shortly."

We waited. When he appeared I knew he indeed was the man I had known as a representative of the University of Wisconsin Extension Division. His medium build, penetrating blue eyes, and engaging smile walked out at me, his features completely distinct from the thousands of persons we had seen on our trip. He was as different as night and day.

O'Connor recognized me, too. He asked for news about Ashland, but promoter and salesman that he was, hastened to speak glowingly about St. Petersburg.

"The city is growing fast," he said. "It won't be long before we have 40,000 people here." O'Connor paused, then related some of his own experiences as a Chamber of Commerce executive. "My new work is exciting," he said. "I bought a house as soon as I came here, and before I could move into it, I sold it because someone else wanted to buy it from me at a much higher price. That's the way it is in St. Petersburg."

When we shook hands and bade him good-bye, he said, "Have a good trip, but remember to come back to St. Petersburg."

For the second time we had the thrill of crossing the Gandy Bridge as we drove back to Tampa for a closer look at the city. As nearly as we could estimate, Tampa appeared almost three times the size of St. Petersburg, its population possibly 90,000. We window-shopped, attracted mainly by curio stores. Among souvenir items they offered stuffed baby alligators at $2 and alligator teeth at 75 cents each. We couldn't resist sending stuffed alligators home to our families.

A sign hanging in front of one of the smaller shops caught our attention. It read, "A. Guinand, Watch Repairing."

"That must be the Guinand who had a jewelry store in Ashland," Elliott said. He pointed toward the shop door.

We entered and instantly recognized Mr. Guinand, intently scrutinizing the inner workings of a watch through a one-eye magnifying glass jewelers use. The Guinands had lived within two blocks of my home, and their son Percy was one of our high school classmates.

Delighted when we introduced ourselves, Mr. Guinand said, "It's good to see someone from Ashland. What's new there?"

We did our best to bring him up-to-date.

"You must spend the night at our home," Mr. Guinand

interrupted.

He closed his shop and, with his car, led us to his house.

Mrs. Guinand, cheerful and motherly, was as eager as her husband to hear news concerning Ashland, and of the adventures of our trip. Proud of their son Percy, the Guinands told of the progress he was making at the University of Florida in Gainesville studying to become a doctor.

Mrs. Guinand served a delicious home-cooked supper, and after a long evening of animated reminiscing in the living room, we retired for another blissful night's sleep in a comfortable bed.

While Mrs. Guinand set the table for breakfast, she asked whether we ever were afraid to sleep outdoors in the Ford in so many strange places.

"We haven't thought about that," Elliott said.

Mrs. Guinand gave us a freshly-baked coffee cake when we were ready to depart. She and her husband urged us to visit their son in Gainesville. We needed no urging for that. They waved as the Ford pulled away. We understood fully we would be roughing it again, but having been with friends like the Lindstroms and Guinands, we were thankful to have had a homey respite from our traveling.

Although Florida's lush growth of subtropical vegetation continued north of Tampa, the roadside became sparser the farther north we journeyed. As we approached Gainesville, it became apparent we then were in a productive agricultural area.

Driving by a fraternity house in Gainesville, we sighted Percy Guinand reading a book on the front porch. He looked up, and with a smile of surprised recognition, greeted us warmly. For the remainder of the day the three of us talked about old times. We relived high school days in Ashland, dwelling largely on sports. We told Percy the school's basketball team was having an excellent season, judging by letters and newspaper clippings we had received, but had to struggle to defeat Hurley 10-9.

Percy accompanied us to the Gainesville tourist park to watch us set up camp. We built a fire, and under blinking stars talked until almost midnight.

Befitting the joyous day, Easter Sunday dawned pleasantly on April 12, bright and sunny. Rested by a good night's sleep, Elliott and I got out our baseball gloves to play catch, and pitched two games of horseshoes, a popular pastime in Florida tourist camps. Elliott won the first game and I the second.

Back at the university during the afternoon, Percy guided us on a tour of the campus. He showed us classrooms and laboratories where he studied for his medical degree, and introduced us to fellow students as we walked about the school grounds. We said good-bye at his fraternity house.

On Monday the countryside became even less tropical as the Ford navigated farther north. Though we had seen many new forms of wildlife in Florida, including such heretofore unfamiliar birds as egrets, pelicans, pileated woodpeckers, and mockingbirds, we were unprepared for what we saw next. Three wild goats unexpectedly dashed across the front of the Ford. I nearly hit the last one which hesitated before making a determined sprint to catch up with the other two.

The goats, of course, weren't at fault when the roof of the Ford collapsed just as they crossed the road. Adding insult to injury, the car again hit on three cylinders.

"She's really falling apart," Elliott moaned.

We quickly cleaned spark plug No. 1 to get the engine running smoothly, and braced the car top temporarily. The Ford soon was on its way again, "but for how long?" Elliott asked.

In Lake City we decided it was time to map the route to follow westward. Acting upon advice the Chamber of Commerce gave us, we chose the northerly route by way of Thomasville, Georgia, and Montgomery, Alabama. Purposely we would stay clear of New Orleans to avoid paying tolls to cross numerous bodies of water along the Gulf Coast.

At a Piggly Wiggly store in Lake City we bought groceries. We had noticed during our travels, particularly in the South, that both Piggly Wiggly and A & P stores were prominently in business. Called "chain stores," they marked a new and growing trend in meat and grocery merchandising. They competed with long-established, independently-owned local stores. The A & P stores spurred patronage by featuring tea and 8 O'Clock coffee at lower prices. Back in Jacksonville we had paid 20 cents for a half-pound of A & P coffee, compared with 30 cents in other stores.

Reaching Thomasville without incident, we camped in the city park because a fee was required in the tourist park outside of town. An evening stroll about the city led to a pleasant experience. At the YMCA Elliott read the sign on the door: "J. F. L'Hommedieu, General Secretary."

"I remember him," Elliott exclaimed. "He was the Y secretary in Ashland."

Entering the building, we soon talked with the secretary, the same J. F. L'Hommedieu Elliott had known. He invited us to have breakfast in his home, an invitation we gladly accepted.

Discussion around the family breakfast table centered mainly on Ashland. L'Hommedieu glowingly recalled fishing trips in northern Wisconsin, trips familiar to us. Of interest to me was the fact that a daughter had attended Northland College when the family lived in Ashland.

When Elliott commented about the colorful roses blooming

Elliott with fallen fender in Alabama.

in the yard, L'Hommedieu said, "Thomasville is famous for its roses. It's called the City of Roses."

Before leaving Thomasville we gave further attention to the city, especially its residential streets and avenues. We wanted to see more of its roses.

On our trip we had learned that "life doesn't always come up roses," but in our view, Thomasville belied the saying. As in the L'Hommedieu yard, rose bushes profusely were in bloom throughout the city, their blossoms permeating the air with sweet fragrance.

In Thomasville we were well into Georgia, where spring had burst forth. Having left the year-round subtropical surroundings of Florida, we now were in the midst of flowers and deciduous trees awakened from their winter dormancy. To us, the feel of Georgia's spring was as buoyantly delightful as our reaction to the balmy atmosphere we had suddenly encountered four months ago on the east coast of Florida.

While we patched a tire shortly after leaving Thomasville, a man in his early fifties got off his bicycle and cheerfully offered assistance. He didn't tell us his name, but talked amiably, more eloquently substantiating our opinion of springtime in Georgia.

"Spring doesn't just wake up after a winter nap in Georgia," he said, "it springs to life. You see it in the plants and bushes. Around here, you smell it in the flowers."

The freshness of spring continued as the Ford moved toward Columbus. The car now behaved well, perhaps due to better roads.

Not that we were racing the clock in a mad rush for California, but in Albany I noted by my Ingersoll it was two o'clock, but one o'clock on town clocks. Obviously, my watch was an hour fast because it was on Eastern Time, and in Albany folks slowed down to Central Time. We should have remem-

Author examines dislodged fender.

bered. The same thing happened in Ohio, but in reverse.

Having been so long in low, flat country, it was with relief we cruised over hilly slopes as we neared Columbus at the western edge of Georgia. We parked the Ford in the free tourist camp a mile or so out of the city, and walked into town for the evening. After a shower in the YMCA we ran to a fire to see a garage go up in flames.

We derived so much benefit from that evening's exercise we wisely resolved to make more frequent stops with the Ford, to walk around more, keep physically fit by stretching our legs, and to limber up our joints.

Alabama hailed us with a poor road, in sharp contrast with those we had just traveled over in Georgia.

"Something is going to come of this," Elliott said as the Ford jolted over the rugged highway. He was right.

We heard a dull thud, followed by a rattling noise. To our dismay, the car's rear right fender had come loose. It dangled precariously, held in place by a single bolt. We saw no way of reattaching the fender to the body of the Ford. So Elliott freed it from the bolt and tossed it into the car.

A few miles beyond, a tire blew out. While we replaced it with our spare, Elliott noticed three leaves of the rear spring were broken, one of them shifted out of line. Another mile down the road the roof sagged, and finally the Ford threw in the towel by hitting on two cylinders.

"Guess we'll have to junk her," Elliott said. "Wouldn't Bill Lynch laugh at this!"

We mulled over the crisis. To discard the Ford posed the problem of buying another car and finding jobs before we would have enough funds to continue our trip. Having no desire to give up the car in which we had begun our U.S. tour, we decided to have its present difficulties remedied, and to have a mechanic appraise its overall condition.

Not until we reached Montgomery, the capital of Alabama, did we find a Ford garage we thought could fasten the fender back onto the car. There we had the broken spring repaired, the sagging top firmly braced, and a new tire purchased.

"There's no telling when your car will break down," the garage foreman said. "Right now I can only say it's in fair condition. The battery is good, the carburetor works, and there's nothing wrong with the brakes." He kicked a rear wheel. "Of course, you'll have to tighten the connecting rods now and then, and keep an eye open for any loose parts."

Although the appraisal wasn't altogether encouraging, we decided to keep the Ford, even if we weren't sure whether it could get us to two more corner states and back to Wisconsin. We gladly paid the $9.65 the garage charged for the repairs and $8.00 for a new tire. We didn't buy an inner tube because the old one could be patched. Since the garage had been unable to refasten the fender, we left it for the junk heap, wondering what it would be like to travel in a three-fendered Ford.

— Letter excerpt, Mon. Apr. 20, 1925

Chapter XIII
Bootlegger Suspects

WHILE THE FORD was being repaired we spent several hours walking about Montgomery. As was the case in other places, we had no intention of making an in-depth study of the city, but made observations and picked up whatever information we could.

We viewed the high bluff of the Alabama River that gives the city its unique backdrop. Evidence that Montgomery with its 50 or 60,000 inhabitants was a busy shipping point were the vessels docked along the Alabama River and the railway freight cars that rolled by. What amused us was Montgomery's recognition as a center for mules. We learned the city also was known for its cotton and lumber enterprises, and that agricultural products marketed in Montgomery included peanuts and sweet potatoes.

A tour through the state capitol added to our limited

knowledge of Civil War history. There we learned Montgomery had been the first capital of the Confederacy. We scanned the portraits of Civil War heroes and other leaders who had distinguished roles in Alabama's growth. Outside was the huge monument dedicated to the memory of the conflict that had pitted North against South.

We became aware there still was a poll tax in Alabama, effectively denying Negroes the right to vote. We didn't understand why.

Making no effort to find a tourist camp, we slept that night by a creek five miles west of Montgomery. Finding no water fit to drink, we boiled no coffee for breakfast, so ate dry bread and a couple of rolls. The next morning we passed through Selma, observing the Alabama River there was muddy.

Two miles west of Demopolis we paid 50 cents toll to cross a narrow stream. Not over a bridge, though. No one had bothered to build one. Instead, we had to maneuver the Ford onto a fair-sized raft. A middle-aged man, whose stubby beard accentuated chubby red cheeks, casually guided the raft to the opposite shore.

"No need for a motor," he said. We reasoned that the current, guided by an underwater cable, propelled the raft.

"What a money-maker," Elliott said as I drove the Ford ashore. How simple it would be to build a bridge, I thought.

For awhile we feared it would be necessary to hire a team of mules to pull the Ford over the hump of the hill on the far side of the stream. Halfway up, the Ford stalled. With a bit of coaxing it went a few feet farther. We waited for the engine to cool, then tried again. Fortunately, the Wanderlust had enough power to take us slowly over the top.

Thirsty when we arrived at Livingston, we couldn't down the water available at a gas station.

"There's better water at the courthouse," the attendant said.

The courthouse water tasted salty. At a garage we thought we were back in Florida. The water wasn't sulfurous, but had a taste we considered just as obnoxious.

On the whole, however, we felt Alabama was a delightful state to tour, especially now that it was spring. The hills and trees were magnificent. True, Alabama's muddy streams didn't seem like a haven for fish, yet we saw several catches made by anglers when we stopped to camp. We wondered how fish could see the bait.

The part of Alabama we were in, though, woefully lacked good roads. Besides, the highways were difficult to follow. They needed signs to guide a motorist. The roads wound hither and yon, and too often were rough and bumpy.

Baffled when we came to a fork in the highway, Elliott braked the Ford. We saw no sign indicating which prong to follow.

When Elliott sang, "You take the high road, I'll take the low," I smiled. He kept time tapping fingers on the steering wheel.

I chose the "high road." Elliott stepped on the gas peddle, and in accordance with my choice, steered the Ford to the left.

"I guess we took the wrong road," Elliott said moments later. The car seemed lost winding beside and through cotton fields and patches destined to grow watermelons. It went so close to front doors of several weather-beaten houses we saw their occupants inside.

This hardly resembled a highway designed for tourist travel, I thought. We were reassured, however, when the "high road" and the "low road" eventually came together again to form a single highway.

The merged thoroughfare led to Bonita, Mississippi, where

we camped by a filling station after a hot day's drive. We had added another state to our credit. Either we had reached "the Bayou State," or "the Magnolia State," depending upon which Mississippi appellation we preferred.

In Mississippi the highway improved immediately. A well-maintained gravel surface and a stretch of concrete pavement accounted for the changed condition. The Ford behaved accordingly.

In Jackson a Hudson car drew up to a curb. For another of the few times on our trip we had the electrifying experience of seeing someone we recognized instantaneously, an individual who stood out from thousands of strangers we had seen, none of whom resembled anyone we knew. We shook hands with George Betz who had operated the former Northern Office Supply Company in Ashland. He was as surprised to recognize us as we were to see him. He said he intended to engage in business in Jackson. For fully 20 minutes we reminisced at the curb.

We enlarged our growing knowledge of the Civil War by visiting the state capitol in Jackson. We did not know that Jefferson Davis, president of the South's Confederacy, served as a United States senator from Mississippi, but vaguely were aware that much of Mississippi was ravaged by its conflict with the North.

We judged Jackson to be a city of nearly 50,000. We had a favorable reaction to the beauty of its public buildings vying with the stateliness of the capitol. Industrially, the city obviously relied substantially upon cotton and timber, and possessed railroads to transport its products. Half, if not more, of Jackson's inhabitants were Negroes, we guessed.

The night of April 17 we spent at the edge of monuments and observation towers perpetuating memories of the historic battlefield where General Ulysses S. Grant captured Vicksburg. Now it was a peaceful site, abounding with the verdancy of spring. The tinkling of cowbells broke the evening silence. Birds flitted about, settling down for the night. Through my mind ran the Civil War song, "Tenting Tonight on the Old Campground." I had a distinct feeling of loneliness. I felt homesick.

Before beginning a tour of the extensive battleground the next morning, we talked with an elderly man we soon took to be a dyed-in-the-wool southerner. With his distinct southern drawl he recalled events of the Vicksburg siege.

"That was 60 years ago," he said. "Vicksburg hung on for months. If it hadn't been for Grant, things would have been different."

His steel-gray eyes looked the Ford over from crank to taillight, surprised we slept in it.

"Odd," he said, "maybe on the very spot where Yankees had a tent."

We thought he might resent us as northerners when we told him we weren't from Florida, as our rear license plate may have indicated, but from Wisconsin. He, however, asked whether we had seen the Wisconsin monument.

"Don't miss it," he said. He turned, pointing off in the distance.

Many monuments decked the landscape, so it took awhile to single out Wisconsin's. We lingered there because on top of the marker we saw a replica of Old Abe, the bald eagle that served as a mascot for Wisconsin soldiers during the Civil War.

For us, the replica of Old Abe was a special attraction. We remembered that Colonel John Hill, a Civil War veteran from our home city, was a caretaker for the eagle during his service with the Union troops. From his Lincoln birthday talks in our

Ninth Avenue grade school, we had learned how Old Abe remained unscathed when carried into the thick of battle, encouraging Wisconsin soldiers to fight on.

We also knew from Colonel Hill's speeches that Old Abe had been caught by a woodsman on northern Wisconsin's Chippewa River, and later had been adopted as a mascot by soldiers of Eau Claire. I recalled how Colonel Hill injected humor into his talks. We laughed when he drolly said there was money to be made after the war by selling chicken feathers to persons seeking souvenir plumage from Old Abe.

The Ford glided over excellent gravel roads as it cruised through the memorial park. To gain a better view, we ascended several observation towers. Illinois, we thought, was honored by more monuments than most other states.

Over hilly terrain we drove into Vicksburg to buy postal cards to mail home, and to assimilate what information we could about the city which had recovered so admirably from its siege. Among other things, we gleaned that this vital Mississippi River port, with its population of approximately 20,000, had lumber mills humming with their saws, and being in the thick of cotton plantations, produced cottonseed oil and cotton goods.

A store clerk, observing we were strangers, courteously advised us to visit the burying ground of Civil War soldiers. Thus we viewed the beautifully terraced National Cemetery, a reverential site with 17,000 Union servicemen buried there, heroes of the siege of Vicksburg.

Driving to the eastern bank of the Mississippi River, we gazed in awe at the wide expanse of the "Father of Waters."

"It's going to take more than a raft to get the Ford across this," Elliott said.

And an extra dollar in toll, we found out, when we boarded

Ford and tramps cross Mississippi River.

a ferry that landed us and the Ford in Louisiana. We reckoned the toll reasonable, however. The raft in Alabama with its toll of 50 cents, had about 100 feet to navigate, the ferry had more than a mile.

As in Mississippi, we had the choice of two nicknames for Louisiana, the "Pelican State," or the "Creole State." The sobriquet might just as well have been the "Oil State," as we soon discovered. Hundreds of wells yielded countless barrels of oil, and a dozen or more refineries processed the petroleum the wells produced.

In the tourist park in Monroe, our first stop, natural gas was so abundant it was available to campers without charge. This gave our camp stove a rest.

Although it was early afternoon and we could have negotiated a few more miles, we thought the commodious Monroe camp a suitable place to scrape off carbon from the Ford's engine. We didn't anticipate trouble removing the top of the engine, but spark plug No. 3 had been malfunctioning and refused to come off. Elliott suggested we soak the base of the plug with oil overnight, and wait until morning before again attempting to loosen it for removal.

That evening we went into town to attend a movie, *When a Man's a Man*, by Harold Bell Wright.

About eight o'clock the following morning we were disappointed when the spark plug still held firm in spite of the soaking with oil. An Ohio tourist came over from the neighboring camp.

"You're using the wrong tool," he said. He noticed that Elliott struggled futilely with a small wrench. He went back to his car, returning with a hammer, a chisel, and a larger wrench. He positioned the chisel, gave it several raps with the hammer and twisted the wrench. Finally the spark plug yielded. Once again we benefited by help from a fellow tourist.

We hiked a mile to a garage to buy a new spark plug costing 65 cents. The price seemed high, yet we didn't grumble, knowing the Ford wouldn't go any place with a nonfunctioning piston.

It was late in the afternoon before we finished scraping the carbon. We pondered. "Let's spend another night here," Elliott said.

Lured by the smacking sound of baseball bats, we strolled to a nearby ball park to watch the last three innings of a 12 to 11 contest. After the game we went back to camp for our baseball gloves. The local ball players let us join in their practice session. This pleased us much. It was wishful thinking, but we gladly would have become members of their team.

Quite a few newly-arrived tourists pitched tents in the campground while we played ball. That evening campers gathered at a huge picnic table. It reminded us of similar get-togethers we had spent with tourists heading for Florida. We joined in singing "Just a Song at Twilight," and such other familiar tunes as "My Wild Irish Rose," and "In Apple Blossom Time." There was the customary swapping of tales, of course, some of which we thought highly imaginative.

Running low on gasoline the next morning, we stopped at an out-of-town filling station where we became concerned when a tall and rangy man we took to be a sheriff or a federal marshal strode resolutely toward the Ford. He sternly eyed the rear wheel, conspicuous by its lack of a fender.

"Do you suppose it's against the law not to have four fenders?" Elliott asked me. Maybe in Louisiana, I responded.

"Looking for bootleggers," the man said, flashing a silvery badge. "Your car looks suspicious. I'm going to search the flivver for hooch."

With grim determination, the officer pawed through our blankets and the other belongings in the car.

"Open your suitcases," he commanded. He thumped the side of the holster containing his large-handled six-shooter.

He then ordered us to lift up the front and back seat cushions, and walked around the back of the Ford to see if it had a trunk attached, which it didn't. Having found no bootleg whiskey after all his searching, he grumpily flicked his arm, waving us on.

"As I said, your car looks mighty suspicious," he grumbled. "I was sure you fellows were rumrunners, and I'm still not sure you aren't."

As we drove away Elliott looked at me. "I think he meant you," he said.

In Shreveport we wandered about the second largest city in Louisiana. It's population, we thought, was likely about 75,000. In the midst of the state's oil and natural gas resources, augmented by cotton and lumber, it flourished with industrial activity. We paid 20-$1/2$ cents a gallon for gasoline, the lower price influenced, no doubt, by the city's refinery.

Before leaving Shreveport, Elliott, for some reason not immediately apparent to me, led me into a dime store to buy a packet of white chalk. He explained the purpose of the chalk while we traveled on good, mostly graveled roads. The land surface from the Mississippi River and beyond Monroe was quite flat, but now we were in a rather hilly region.

The sun lowered as we crossed the border into Texas, the "Lone Star State," largest in the U.S.A. We veered off the highway to camp a mile east of Marshall. After a supper of tomato soup and ham and cheese sandwiches, Elliott unwrapped the white chalk he purchased in Shreveport, and together we carried out his plan.

Swanson and Nystrom, our "Ford Tramps," Halted in Louisiana As Rum Agents; Now in Los Angeles

"WE ARE NOT BOOTLEGGERS."

Aided by this sign plastered conspicuously on their car, Seegar Swanson and Elliot Nystrom, Ashland's "Ford Tramps," succeeded in convincing Louisiana authorities that they were not dealing in illicit liquor.

The two Ashland young men have visited many of the southern states and are now in California.

A letter from Swanson says:

Los Angeles, Calif.,
May 11, 1925.

Hearken ye to this tale of unparalleled adventure, devoid of fiction, and breathing the roving spirit of the "vanguards of civilization," piloting the good sloop "Wanderlust."

Since the fore part of April we have rolled ponderously over the face of the American continent in our 1919 Ford, from Florida to California.

Back in Alabama lies our rear right fender. Already suffering from a severe attack of automotive dropsy, occasioned by concussion with a telephone post, the bumpy roads of this state proved too much for the fragile fixture, consequently it fell off.

Much as we hate to admit it, several town marshalls in Louisiana suspected us as rum agents. At Ruston our car was thoroughly searched, but all the town officials found was gas and ketchup. Delay and inconvieniences of this nature prompted us to deck the Ford with two prominent signs reading: "WE ARE NOT BOOTLEGGERS."

In parts of New Mexico water sold at five cents per pail. It hasn't rained in those places for three years. There's where our radiator sprung a leak.

Going down a steep mountain grade one dy the steering apparatus on the Ford became defective. Straight over a precipice we headed, only to be stopped by a mighty pine tree a few feet over the brink. The total damage amounted to nothing more than a broken headlight.

Needles, California registers about 110 in the shade these days. Do you wonder that we crossed the Mohaue Desert at night?

Our great ambition across the southern states was a sojourn into Mexico to attend a bull fight and perhaps sip a glass or two of lager, but friends informed us that bull fights are staged on national holidays only. Inasmuch as this is the slack season on Mexican holidays, we concluded to visit the Grand Canyon instead.

Among the many interesting things we stopped to see on the great transcontinental trip are included the Vicksburg National Cemetery, the Petrified Forest, prehistoric cliff dwellings, the Grand Canyon, and a carnival near Muleshoe, Texas.

Our $250 stake looks like $85 now, therefore, as soon as we find a good mountain stream in which to wash our clothes, we will scout around for a job in order to earn enough money to get home with.

So until lawn mowers are sold in Arizona, I am yours for prohibition in Mexico.

Sincerely,
Seegar Swanson.

P. S. Met O'Connor, formerly of the extension division of the U of Wis., at St. Petersburg, Fla. He cherishes the fond hope of raising a watermelon in his own back yard, something he couldn't do in Northern Wisconsin with any assurance of success.

Ashland Daily Press, May 21, 1925

Elliott's chalk embellishes Good Ship Wanderlust.

WE ARE NOT BOOTLEGGERS
ASHLAND, WISCONSIN
KEEP THAT SCHOOLGIRL COMPLEXION

In bold white letters we printed on both flaps of the Ford's hood the words, "WE ARE NOT BOOTLEGGERS." In equally bold letters we wrote on the right front door, "KEEP THAT SCHOOLGIRL COMPLEXION," and on the other, "WE ARE WARRIORS BOLD FROM THE NORTHLAND COLD." On the rear car doors Elliott printed, "ASHLAND, WISCONSIN," and drew scenic sketches of our home state.

Whether the "BOOTLEGGERS" inscription would ward off suspicious officers of the law only time would tell, but we did not mind that the "SCHOOLGIRL COMPLEXION" admonition was free advertising for Palmolive soap. It was a subtle way of emphasizing we were from Wisconsin where the soap was manufactured.

An evening hike into town led us to a theater where we attended a movie, *The Thief of Baghdad*, starring Douglas Fairbanks. The show was long and lively.

Having heard so much about the plains of Texas, we were agreeably surprised to find the eastern side of the state wooded. Roads in this area generally were satisfactory, varying from dirt to gravel, with some concrete pavement. One detour, however, randomly led through farmers' fields and pastures, and even through a swamp. It reminded us of Alabama.

Camped in a pasture near Terrel, we made an important decision. We would forgo a southern route into Mexico in favor of a northern route to the Grand Canyon.

Another vital decision involved the removal of ants from the large tin container in which we stored food. They had squeezed through the rim of the lid after we set the can on the ground before preparing for supper.

"That's what we get for camping in a pasture," Elliott said. He brushed several crawling ants off his bare arm.

The insects darted shiftily when we prodded them out of

the container. They stung both of us. Because our stock of food was low, the ants caused little damage.

We saw Dallas long before we reached it. As though we approached a mirage, we beheld its irregular skyline etched against a broad prairie. It was as if the city uncannily had been plunked down on the barren plain. The Ford drew closer. Tall buildings came into sharp focus. Suddenly we were in Dallas, hemmed in by its skyscrapers.

Driving about crowded streets for fully 15 minutes we found a side avenue to park the Ford. In our usual hit-or-miss fashion we hiked wherever fancy led us, entering big stores and office buildings, asking questions whenever opportunity afforded.

There was much to learn about Dallas, metropolitan and obviously growing. Its population, we estimated, already must be at least a quarter of a million. There was an air of being "big," perhaps rightly so. Situated as it is in the midst of the nation's great cattle ranches, petroleum centers and a rich agricultural area, the city clearly thrived on cotton, livestock, oil refineries, and grain elevators, all well-serviced by railroads. But not all was hustle and bustle. The pace was slower in the many aesthetic parks.

We were given conflicting information regarding the best route to the Grand Canyon, upward of a thousand miles to the west. The Chamber of Commerce was vague about its direc-tions, and referred us to the Automobile Club. There one of the girls, a brunette, recommended we travel via El Paso. "The roads are better," she said. Another girl, a blonde, advised we go via Wichita Falls. "It's cooler," she said.

We thanked the girls, but left with a sense our route to the Grand Canyon was a tossup.

Thirty miles west of Dallas we entered Fort Worth. It, too, had towering buildings, and teemed with activity. As in Dallas, traffic on its busy streets was well-regulated. Although its population was perhaps a hundred thousand less than Dallas, it obviously benefited similarly from the fabulous resources abounding in this part of Texas. Fort Worth, too, had inviting parks.

The new YMCA, we reasoned, would be the last for many miles. So we went in for a refreshing shower. We next located the Chamber of Commerce, hoping to get a definite routing to the Grand Canyon. Elliott said we first should test the girl behind the information desk to determine how reliable her routing would be.

"Can you tell us the best roads to take to Florida?" he asked.

The girl, a radiant young woman, gently smoothed her wavy brown hair. With twinkling blue eyes and a gracious smile, she turned our attention to a map she unfolded on her desk. She pointed out the route we had followed to reach Texas, giving an accurate account of road conditions as we had found them, including the need to pay toll to ride a raft across the narrow stream in Alabama. When Elliott asked how best to reach the Grand Canyon, we had no doubt about the route she recommended. She advised we start by way of Wichita Falls.

A high wind blew at the back of the Ford when we left Fort Worth. As long as we didn't have to face the wind, we didn't mind. If anything, the wind from behind pushed the car, giving increased gas mileage. We were on a hard-surfaced road, traveling through a fenced prairie land devoted to agriculture. After long miles of hills and trees, we thought the change of scenery was pleasant.

The day was hot, and adding to the discomfort of the heat was our feverish Ford. It had developed a new ailment, a leaky radiator. A pail of water obtained from a farmer's windmill reduced the car's temperature, but we knew the radiator should have been repaired in Wichita Falls. We procrastinated, however, hoping the leak was small and inconsequential.

Outside of Vernon we parked the Ford near a filling station. Early in the evening we strolled toward town to find a carnival drawing a crowd to its midway. It reminded us of the one we had attended in Millen, Georgia, except it was larger.

Carnival barkers outdid each other trying to induce Texans to buy tickets for attractions inside their tents. The westerners, we observed, spent money freely, but weren't recklessly throwing away their cash.

Of interest was the distinctive garb of the Texans. They wore ten-gallon hats, cowboy boots, wide belts, and other trappings peculiar to westerners. The hats, unlike the caps most men in other parts of the country wore, were reminiscent of William S. Hart movies. We particularly admired the tall physical stature of the younger men. We knew we didn't measure up to these westerners, even though we were beginning to gain the weight we had hoped for on our trip.

About 11 o'clock we joined the large gathering in front of a tent featuring a risqué song and dance show. A barker pointed a cane at a half-dozen girl dancers kicking their heels high in the air. Through a little brown megaphone he shouted, "Step right up and get your tickets now."

Without warning, a flash of lightning and a roar of thunder interrupted the barker's spiel. The crowd scattered. The frightened barker and the dancers jumped off their platform and lifted moistening flaps to duck into their tent.

Rain fell heavily as Elliott and I ran the mile to our car. The storm broke loose with full fury just as we climbed into bed. We made a clumsy effort to put on the Ford's frayed side curtains. Thunder, lightning, rain, and a powerful wind all but blew the car away. Not until the rain ceased at 10 o'clock the next morning did we get up.

"What a storm!" Elliott exclaimed.

The only storm on our whole trip, I reflected, except the tornado at the start of our journey. This wasn't quite a tornado, but was what we apprehensively had expected to encounter frequently in the West.

Texans, to our surprise, were happy about the storm, even if it caused some damage. The downpour ended a prolonged dry spell.

Stuck in a puddle when we prepared to leave about noon, the Ford refused to budge. With the aid of a borrowed shovel we dug a trench to give its wheels traction, but the car still wasn't in the clear when it was back on the highway. It wriggled through winding ruts made by other vehicles, struggling as far as Crowell. There the road became sand-surfaced and smooth.

Traveling as we were over miles of flat land, with settlements few and far between, we found that minor distractions helped relieve the monotony of travel in an area devoid of the unusual. Low hills west of Crowell, however, stood out in bold relief, but again sloped into a rolling prairie. Views of ranches helped provide diversion, as did the gates with cowcatchers that kept cattle from going through.

There were other minor, nonetheless interesting distractions. We helped a Texas cowhand get his Ford out of a ditch, donated gas to a motorist whose tank went dry near Paducah, loaned a jackknife to two youths repairing their car, and gave two ranchmen a ride to Tongue River. Jack rabbits hopped on the prairie towards evening, easy targets for anyone with a gun.

Usually we arose early in the morning, but took our time getting started. As a rule the Ford covered about two hundred miles a day. Texas seemed a larger state than we thought, so we were slow in reaching the Rocky Mountains. Without success, we strained our eyes to get an early glimpse of their foothills.

In the tourist camp in Matador a camper from California told us we soon would come to the foothills and then the mountains. The promise of hills didn't materialize the next day, however. Elongated stretches of the Texas plain were all we saw. Widely separated houses were flanked by windmills, and once we waved at a young girl we thought was waving at us. Looking closer, we knew she wasn't waving, just washing her hands and shaking them dry.

The plains came alive with snakes when we drove the Ford against the setting sun that evening. The sun's blinding glare through the windshield forced us to shield our eyes, but this didn't prevent us from seeing dozens of reptiles crisscross the highway. Some were so long they almost stretched from one side of the road to the other. We dared not stop, yet to run over the snakes would be rougher than driving on a corduroy road, to say nothing of the destruction of snakes. I slowed the Ford, braking continually to let reptiles wriggle across.

Knowing we might not reach a town for hours, we timidly set up camp off the road, treading gingerly for fear of more snakes. We reassured ourselves with the thought that perhaps the ones we just had seen on the highway were denizens of an isolated area.

The farther west we traveled, the fewer towns we saw. They were very small and rugged, like outposts for ranchers. For travelers there was a filling station, and generally a parking area for overnight camping. We made it a point to fill the Ford's tank in each town lest we get stalled miles from the next gas pump.

We thought of spending the night in Texico. Elliott noted,

however, that Central Time changed to Mountain Time at that point, and facetiously said, "that gives us an extra hour. Let's keep going."

Arriving at Muleshoe, a typical western Texas town of about 1,200 people, we walked aimlessly about, more interested in the name Muleshoe than what we saw. We thought maybe there was a blacksmith shop somewhere catering to unshod mules, but if so, didn't see one.

Our queries with regard to Muleshoe's name resulted in various explanations, most of which we considered far-fetched.

A townsman pointed in the direction of the Santa Fe railway station. "They hung a muleshoe over the depot door for luck," he said. "It brought so much business they named the depot Muleshoe. Then the town took on the name."

The most plausible explanation, we thought, came from a Texan with all the earmarks of a seasoned cowboy. "The town is named after the Muleshoe Ranch," he said.

The way the Texan told it, a cowhand kicked loose a corroded muleshoe partially embedded in the ground, where-upon the new ranch owner, E. K. Warren, changed the name of his recently acquired holdings to Muleshoe Ranch. Since the town he helped establish was located within the ranch, it logically was called Muleshoe.

Driving west on the highway leading out of Muleshoe was like meandering through the cotton fields of Alabama. Here, though, the highway dwarfed into a mere trail across ranches instead of plantations, and ran alongside railway tracks.

Now and then we met a cowboy on horseback who stopped to talk. Cowboys looked wonderingly at the Ford, concen-trating on its sleeping arrangement. I looked at one cowboy's horse, imagining how I would feel sleeping on the ground with the horse's saddle for a pillow.

Soon after crossing into New Mexico, we arrived in Clovis in time to drive about the city before settling down for the night in its fine municipal campground. Clovis, a sizable community of over 10,000 persons, appeared characteristically western. We hadn't yet left cowboy country as shown by spurred boots and ten-gallon hats. The city was a busy stop for the Atchison, Topeka and Santa Fe Railway, and we surmised its citizens and surrounding inhabitants were modernly entertainment-minded when we came upon the recently built Lyceum Theater. Other

Texas cowboys drive cattle herd.

new construction gave proof Clovis was an up-and-coming city.

Black clouds and a chilling north wind delayed our departure until one o'clock the ensuing day. Elliott utilized the delay by mending a rip on his shirt sleeve. I was amused to see him use our tire repair kit to patch the rip.

The Ford's leaky radiator worsened. We felt uneasy about asking for water at roadside homes after a housewife cautioned us not to waste any of the pailful she permitted us to dip out of a cistern.

"We haven't had rain for a long spell," she said.

When a rancher later charged us a nickel for a pail of water, we thought he was taking undue advantage of its scarcity. Finding a discarded one-gallon can in a ditch, we filled it with water trickling in an almost dried-up stream. Sparingly we poured the water from the can whenever we felt the radiator needed a drink.

The rear tires of the Ford had given us little trouble during our trip, but now the rear right one punctured for the first time since we were in Plymouth, Indiana.

"That spoils a pretty good record," Elliott said. He applied a patch to the inner tube. "I wonder how long it will take for the other back tire to give out."

As we often had done on the Texas plains, we drove off New Mexico's highway to play catch. When Elliott threw the baseball over my head, I leaped high in a vain attempt to catch it, and while retrieving the overthrown ball was startled to see an immense herd of cattle bearing down on me. I ran back to the side of the road to join Elliott. Though cowboys guided the cattle, we feared our presence might cause them to stampede. We were uneasy as we watched the herd slowly pass by. One cowboy waved at us, but this was not reassuring. It was, notwithstanding, a thrilling sight to see so many cattle on the move.

We had the notion that prairie schooners were a thing of the past. Yet, in New Mexico we saw several drawn by mules or horses. Each canvas-covered schooner, loaded with household effects, transported heads of a family and their children, and perhaps kinsmen. Unable to earn a livelihood, they left their homes to seek better opportunity elsewhere.

Also attracting our attention were adobe huts made of sun-dried bricks. From time to time we saw a burro trudging down the road, his back loaded with supplies, and led by a cowboy.

Water had an alkaline taste. In some parts of this semi-arid climate, it was so scarce it sold for 40 cents a barrel, according to a filling station attendant who made us feel he did us a favor quenching the thirst of the Ford's radiator.

Silver dollars circulated widely. If we tendered a 10-dollar bill to a storekeeper, he gave us silver dollars and smaller coins as change. It was the same at gas stations. Despite the fact that bulky silver dollars were like excess baggage, we gathered that here in the West this medium of exchange best served the silver mining industry anxious to broaden the market for its product.

In Mountainair we learned the area was noted for pinto beans. Production was down, though, because there had been little consequential rain for three years. A filling station employee recalled the year melting snow provided enough moisture to grow 50 carloads of the pintos.

A persistently raw northeast wind made traveling uncomfortable. It became more pleasant, however, when plateaus hove into sight. Before long, the Ford climbed lengthy hills, and at last we viewed the Manzana mountains, but didn't seem to reach them. The last 16 miles seemingly were endless, but we finally were at the Manzanas.

Stopping off the road for lunch, we counted our cash and traveler's checks. Our resources totaled $135, not as much as we expected.

"I hope it's enough to get us to California," Elliott said. He lowered his eyes contemplatively. "We probably won't find jobs until then."

— The Log, Sat. May 9, 1925

Chapter XIV
A Contrary Mojave Desert

WITH THE WESTERN PLAINS behind, we looked forward to mountain driving. The mountains in New Mexico, however, were not as majestically scenic as we expected. Devoid of trees and other green vegetation, peaks stood out in stark relief.

A short distance beyond Abo, signs indicated that on a nearby cliff were well-preserved paintings by prehistoric Indians. We studied these colorings on rocky walls, wondering when they were painted, how Indians obtained the colors, and what had become of these natives.

Detracting from the historic site were signs advertising modern day products.

"That's civilization," Elliott remarked wittily. Coming to the National Old Roads Highway, we pondered whether to continue by way of Gallup, New Mexico, or Socorro, and then

223

chose the latter route. A dried-up streambed served as a road for quite a distance. Its graveled bottom offered fairly good driving. Soon we traveled beside a muddy river originating in the mountains. Green vegetation fringed the river bank, contrasting with arid mountain sides. On this stream, the town of Socorro seemed like an oasis for its 3,500 inhabitants.

Beyond Socorro the Ford faced its first real test of mountain climbing. It performed satisfactorily over the six-and-one-half-mile road of the Blue Canyon Ridge. The highway then crossed a plain to Magdalena, a town the size of Socorro. Here we heard gasoline was 40 cents a gallon farther up the mountains. Acting on this helpful hint, we filled the Ford's tank at 32 cents per gallon.

That night we camped among small pines a few miles past Magdalena. To dispel a feeling of loneliness, Elliott built a

Elliott ponders route.

warming fire. The flames were soothing. He brought out his ukulele and played and sang his favorite song, "Wabash Blues." For some reason I couldn't explain, he abruptly switched to "He'd Have to Get Under, Get Out and Get Under," and just as he began singing "In My Merry Oldsmobile," the third string on the ukulele snapped. "Guess we should be singing songs about a Ford," he said, as he immediately replaced the broken string with one of the eight strings for which we had swapped our double-bit ax in South Carolina. We were pleased we had made the swap. We now had use for the ukulele string, but so far had no occasion to swing an ax.

Spring weather vanished during the night. It was so cold in the morning we huddled over a campfire all day. The feeling of loneliness persisted, but actually the mountains were not so isolated as we thought. We watched cars pass by at intervals, and again saw a covered wagon. Handling the reins of a mule team was a white-collared man who didn't appear to be forsaking the mountains.

"This fellow isn't leaving the country," Elliott said. He pointed toward scriptural passages emblazoned on the schooner's canvas cover. "He must be a preacher."

The last day of April was nippy and windy, but more cheerful whenever the sun broke through dark gray clouds. We resumed our journey westward, and as we traveled along a high mountain ridge, a cold rain pelted us. We weren't warmed, either, by snow-capped peaks in the distance.

At an elevation of about 8,000 feet we crossed the Continental Divide of the southern Rocky Mountains. Halting the Ford, we thought about the divide's significance, knowing that streams originating on the west side flowed toward the Pacific Ocean and those on the east side toward the Atlantic.

Across the divide we traveled through the Datil National

At last a tree in Pine Park.

Forest, largest in the nation, according to the ranger in charge of the government camp in Pine Park four miles west of Datil. The ranger invited us into a cabin to warm ourselves before a blazing fire in a stone fireplace.

Late in the afternoon we drove over the state line into Arizona, reaching Springerville by evening. Here we had a choice of campsites. The town had an unusual number of filling stations, and each offered free camping facilities. Gas, however, was 40 cents a gallon, as we were warned in Magdalena. We chose the campsite on the western edge of town.

While we purchased groceries in St. John the next day, a clerk asked whether we would give a Mexican peasant a ride to Concho, the first town down the road. We saw him standing at the end of the counter, attired like other Mexicans we had seen, and wearing a broad sombrero. We agreed, expecting to learn something about his way of life.

Crowded into the front seat of the Ford, his sombrero touching the roof of the car and its rim brushing against Elliott, the Mexican was untalkative. We learned nothing. Thinking he probably didn't understand English, I asked questions with my smattering of Spanish. It must have been my Spanish, because he merely mumbled incoherently. But when we stopped to let our passenger out in Concho, he handed Elliott 35 cents and insisted he keep it. He became extremely vocal, his large white teeth glistening, as he expressed appreciation in Spanish too rapid for me to interpret, except for "muchas gracias," and "adios."

Hungry after a morning drive in the invigorating mountain air, we looked for a spot to prepare lunch. The barren roadside was uninviting.

"The map shows we're getting close to the Petrified Forest," Elliott said.

Never having heard of the Petrified Forest, we envisioned trees growing there, and naturally thought it would be more pleasant to eat in the shade. Our hunger intensified as we continued traveling. Seeing no trees, we all but passed the Petrified Forest. Huge petrified tree trunks lying flat on the barren ground drew our attention. We saw no living trees, yet here was irrefutable evidence of what once had been a forest.

"Guess we got here too late for shady trees," Elliott said. He set up our camp stove. We brewed coffee, heated a can of hash, and sliced some bread. Leaning our backs against one of the petrified logs, we ate a scrumptious meal, topped off with rolls and a couple of doughnuts.

As we walked among tree trunks, some upward of five feet in diameter, we speculated how all this came to be.

No shade from petrified trees.

"This petrified wood tells a story," Elliott said.

A mystery story, I thought. I grasped for words to describe what we saw. Not spectacular, dazzling, nor gorgeous. Rather, wondrous, bewildering.

Mysteriously, why hadn't these trees just rotted into soil to nourish new trees? How did the logs turn into stone? If there were a forest here eons ago, why had the tree trunks broken apart when they toppled to the ground? Why were such amazing colors, like those of Lake Superior agates, exposed at the irregular ends where trunks had separated?

Signs said it was unlawful to collect petrified specimens within boundaries of the National Monument, but there were no restrictions posted against picking them up beyond the area.

Following a road until we saw several steers browsing on scanty vegetation, Elliott and I each found a broken section of a tree branch which we dug out of the sand. Perfect in size for mementos, the sections measured 10 inches in diameter and 6 inches long. We put the specimens in our car to take home.

The questions raised by the petrified tree trunks remained unanswered when we left the National Monument. Our continued conjectures concerning the forest mystery helped relieve the monotony of traveling through the desolate area that lay ahead. Finding no tourist parks in the widely separated settlements, we camped that night in a nook among rock formations near Diablo Canyon. There we read a sign inviting tourists to visit a nearby cliff dwelling and an Arizona zoo.

We went there. After collecting 25 cent fees from us and a small tourist group, a guide showed us a coyote chained to a stake, and then led us to a small cage in which horned toads and a Gila monster were penned.

So much for the zoo. The guide then took us to the edge of a big rock, pointing across a narrow gap to a diminutive niche in a wall of dirt and rock.

"That's a cliff dwelling," he said.

We and the other tourists looked at him dubiously. As if to dispel our obvious incredulity, the guide hastily led us to a six-foot wooden box containing a skeleton. He unabashedly

Guide displays Gila monster and toads.

claimed he uncovered the skeleton when he explored the cliff dwelling he had just shown us.

One of the tourists muttered something about a "flimflam, pure hokum." When we left, Elliott said, "At least we found out what a monster that little Gila was."

Arriving later at Walton Canyon, 10 miles east of Flagstaff, we knew we gazed at genuine cliff dwellings. Across the gorge we saw a lengthy recess on the side of a steep cliff, the recess divided into sections by man-made walls.

We descended to the bottom of the gorge, and with Elliott leading the way, climbed several embankments before reaching a rocky trail winding upward to the recess we had considered inaccessible. From the outer edge of the recess, a veritable cave in the cliff, we walked into a series of dwelling units separated by the walls we previously had observed.

It was apparent that prehistoric Indians constructed these

walls with stones gathered in the gorge, and skillfully plastered them with clay-like mortar. The walls were well-preserved, though front portions had crumbled. Pieces still lay on the floor, but stones probably had been tossed into the canyon or carried off as souvenirs.

The cliff dwellings were not as puzzling to us as the Petrified Forest. Obviously, a vanished tribe of Indians dwelt here peacefully centuries ago. The Indians undoubtedly felt secure from enemy attack, protected as they were in the impregnable rocky recess. They might have hung skin robes to shut off the open side from wind and sun, and to keep warm at night. We had no idea what they did to prevent children from falling off the cliff.

We comprehended that this part of Arizona was unsuited for raising crops, so it was reasonable to assume they relied upon wild nuts and berries and their hunting skill for food.

Returning to the government headquarters where we registered before probing Walnut Canyon, we asked the woman in charge about her conception of the cliff dwellings, and were glad her views were similar to ours. To a certain extent she also answered questions perplexing us since we left the Petrified Forest.

"The federal government established it as a National Monument in 1906," she said. "It covers 133 square miles, about 40,000 acres."

"What we don't understand," Elliott said, "is how so many trees could fall down in a forest and break into so many pieces, and then turn into colored stone."

The attractive young woman, clearly knowledgeable, turned toward Elliott. "There are different explanations," she said. "The one I think most likely is that there never was a forest around here at all."

Tramps climb to explore cliff dwellings.

She smiled as we showed signs of disbelief. "The theory is," she continued, "the trees grew many miles north."

Handing Elliott a folder, she marked printed paragraphs elucidating the theory. From the paragraphs she penciled, we gleaned that ages ago thousands of large trees may have been leveled by a catastrophe of nature, to be carried away by flooded streams. Bashed by raging waters, they might have been halted in the area of the present Petrified Forest by some natural barrier. Over a long period of time they possibly remained waterlogged in swamps, absorbing minerals until they hardened into stone of rainbow hues.

Resuming our journey, we discussed other explanations in the Petrified Forest folder, and set it aside for further reading. Of more immediate concern was the prospect of delay in reaching California. From reports we heard in the New Mexico mountains, we would be snowbound in the San Francisco Mountains of Arizona. Arriving in Flagstaff late in the afternoon, we failed to see snow, and were pleased to learn the highway to the Grand Canyon likewise was bare.

Flagstaff's tourist park, admirably situated in a cluster of pines, was the first pay camp we stayed in since leaving Florida. We did not object to the nominal 25 cents fee in view of the park's exceptional facilities. It was filled with tourists returning east after a winter's stay in California. Some, like us, planned a side trip to the Grand Canyon.

We eyed the surrounding mountain scenery. Forests were a gratifying sight after so many miles of treeless areas in Texas, New Mexico, and eastern Arizona.

This being Saturday, business establishments were open in Flagstaff during the evening, enabling us to stock up on provisions for our excursion to the Grand Canyon.

When two youths about our age visited us Sunday morning,

Elliott woozy on rim of Grand Canyon.

we realized we weren't the only ones relying upon a second-hand Ford to get around the country. Bound for Wisconsin, they said they purchased a Ford racer in California for $25 and intended to get home with it, although they admitted it wasn't in good condition. The racer needed constant tuning, they said, and like us, they had to stop frequently to fill a leaky radiator. Bad tires caused punctures and blowouts, and the brakes were poor. We wished the boys success, but looking at their dilapidated Ford, doubted it would get them to Wisconsin by the end of the week as they hoped.

Scenery bordering the 70-mile road to Grand Canyon National Park absorbed our attention, but our reaction was insignificant compared with the thrill of our first view of the Grand Canyon. The sheer depth and vastness of this tremendous cavity awed us. The canyon exceeded in grandeur the wildest flights of our imagination.

"The greatest thing we've seen so far," Elliott asserted. I lacked words to express a similar reaction.

Fascination of the spectacularly colored canyon was so magnetic we delayed seeking a campsite until we slowly drove eight miles along the south rim to witness the enormous gap from different vantage points.

"It's enough to make anyone woozy," Elliott said. I had the same feeling. Had it not been for the orientation to height we received while employed at the Flatiron Building in Melbourne, Florida, we surely would have been giddy peering over the edge of this deep gorge, a drop of three-fifths of a mile.

Winding up at the road we had followed from Flagstaff, we sighted the canyon village, and before attempting to reach it, located a public campground. We parked the Ford by some small trees. There was no charge for camping, but a daily fee of 25 cents was assessed for water.

Eager to view more of the canyon, we quickly warmed a pot of coffee and ate rolls for supper. Returning to the canyon, we paid more attention to endless rock formations and peaks in the gorge that extended from 18 to 20 miles across. Again, we had feelings of profound reverence.

Indian ceremony at Grand Canyon Village.

Colorful Indian costumes.

Before returning to the campground, we gave Grand Canyon Village the once-over. There we witnessed spirited ceremonial dances performed by Indians wearing feathered headbands, buckskins and beaded moccasins.

Inspired by the awesome splendors we had seen from the canyon rim, we felt an irrepressible urge to descend to the bottom. From rangers we learned the Bright Angel Trail was the only feasible means of descent.

"Don't hike," one ranger advised. "Ride a mule."

We elected to hike. At 10:45 the next morning we started down from the Bright Angel Hotel. At the outset we had to round a hairpin curve at the end of a rocky cliff. The path around the curve was extremely narrow, and since there was no railing to clutch, we hugged the wall, realizing how precipitous was the drop from the edge of the path. We saw that the narrow trail continued along the cliff, but not fazed by this beginning, we proceeded heedlessly down the winding path. The going was easy. We were heading downhill.

Riding on mules, a party of tourists came by the trail on its way back to the rim. We stepped aside, with scant room to spare. Leading the tourists, some of whom were women, was a guide. Having looked down from treacherous heights during our descent, we marveled how the mules unerringly kept on the trail with their steady, surefooted stride.

"Don't go too far," one of the women cautioned. "It's much tougher going up than down."

Three-fifths of the way below the rim of the canyon, about

Mule train ascends Grand Canyon.

View from descending trail.

3,000 feet lower, we came to Garden Creek, flanked by willow trees and other lush greenery, differing distinctly from the barren surroundings. Here we saw more tourists, resting before ascending back to the rim on mules. For awhile we considered returning, too.

"Let's not," Elliott said. He looked down toward the bottom of the canyon. "We haven't seen the Grand Canyon if we haven't been down to the Colorado River."

We didn't feel tired, so the hike to the river was easy. The trail was more gradual, not as steep and narrow as before. When we reached the stream, 2 hours and 50 minutes had elapsed since we left the Bright Angel Hotel.

We were about a mile below the level of the canyon's rim.

Now that we were on the banks of the Colorado River, our first impulse was to go swimming. Taking no chances with the swiftly moving current, we stayed in the quieter water near the shore.

Colorado River at Canyon bottom.

The invigorating dip, coupled with our hike, made us raven-
ously hungry. Unfortunately, we had brought only a frugal

lunch, two sandwiches, a roll apiece, and two oranges. So we faced a hungry climb as we began the slow ascent back to the rim.

As we were warned, going up was much harder than going down. We stopped for awhile when we came to the green vegetation, but were too hungry to tarry. We were compelled to rest frequently at turn-out points.

It was late afternoon before we reached the top. Utterly famished, and quite tired, we all but dragged ourselves to our camp a half-mile away. As soon as we devoured a couple of rolls, we opened cans of corned beef and baked beans to warm up for the heartiest meal we had enjoyed in a long time.

The next day a ranger told us we had hiked $8\text{-}1/2$ miles to descend to the Colorado River, and with the return trip, had covered 17 miles.

"Quite a hike, isn't it, even on flat ground," the ranger said. "Eight and a half miles is a long way to drop a single mile."

We recuperated rapidly after a good night's sleep, but this wasn't so with some of the tourists we had met riding mules. They limped about the camp complaining of aches and cramps. We supposed that in the first place they weren't in good enough physical condition to ride in a saddle. Nevertheless, we were glad our adventure on foot left us with no such discomforts.

The Grand Canyon had so much to offer we stayed five days. The lure of the rim was so irresistible we repeatedly hiked along its trail in both directions. As we stared across the broad expanse we hypothesized about the origin of the chasm with its myriad of cliffs, crags, peaks, and rock formations.

We asked rangers and other park employees for their opinions. One explanation was that over millions of years the Colorado River, aided by wind, rain, snow, and ice, carved the gorge, and in the process eroded soil to form the cliffs and peaks.

We talked with one ranger, however, who said he doubted this explanation.

"To me," he said, "it looks as if the canyon millions of years ago was level with today's rim, and for some reason sank a mile. The Colorado River dropped with it, and still flows as it always did, but now a mile deeper."

The ranger waited for his idea to register. "Or else the rim was lifted a mile high by pressure from the earth, the way mountains are formed," he added. "But don't take my word for it. I'm no geologist. It's just a thought."

Later in the afternoon, when low black clouds suddenly loomed over the canyon, we rushed to our camp. Seated in the Ford after putting on the side curtains, we were protected from pelting rain, but were leery about frightening flashes of lightning and the loud roar of thunder seemingly intensified by reverberations from the hollow canyon. The park's elevation was so high we had the awesome feeling we could reach for the lightning, and were at the very source of the thunder.

Author views crags glistening with slowly drying raindrops.

The storm was almost as brief as it was sudden. When the sun reappeared we saw a robin chirping merrily on a branch. A bushy-tailed squirrel with long ears chattered and frisked about, running up one tree trunk and leaping to another. A burro brayed as if glad the storm had ended. Returning to the canyon rim we saw changing colors of reds and yellows as peaks and crags glistened with slowly drying raindrops.

The second evening in camp Elliott and I purchased groceries in the small store located on the grounds. Elliott didn't count his change until we returned to our car.

"We're a dollar short," he said.

We went back to the store to show the owner the change. It wasn't surprising that he hesitated.

"I can't do anything about it now," he said. "If I find a dollar too much when I count my day's cash, I'll give it to you in the morning."

He beamed when we returned, and gave Elliott a dollar bill. The loss wouldn't have been terrific, and we could have been mistaken, but it was gratifying we dealt with a storekeeper willing to acknowledge the shortage in change was his mistake.

There was more to life than exploring the Grand Canyon, we learned. Camp life was rewarding, too. For added exercise Elliott and I played catch. With pupils attending the school adjoining the campground we played a knife game simulating baseball. Forest rangers sometimes stopped to talk while passing through. During evenings we visited with fellow campers, roasting marshmallows as we gathered around bonfires.

One of the park's rangers, a Mr. Plant from Maine, showed more than a friendly interest in our trip. He made several visits at our camp, and one evening invited us to his home where his wife served hot chocolate and delicious refreshments. They invited us to join them for a musical concert in the town hall, sponsored by the Santa Fe Company for park employees.

Mr. Plant discussed features of the Grand Canyon we had not observed, notably how varying layers of rock and sediment visible on walls of the gorge revealed different periods of time covering millions of years. For us he made more vivid the canyon's ever-changing colors, its reddish, golden hues, its delicate pinks, blues, and grays. He also told us what to expect when we came to other national parks. "Don't miss Yosemite," he said.

With Yosemite Park definitely in mind, we prepared to leave the Grand Canyon the morning of May 7. Loath to depart, we walked to the rim for a farewell look at the canyon, and then went back to the campground for last minute visits, particularly with Leslie Baker and Walter Mace, both from Evanston, Illinois. The young men had been with us several times since we first met them in New Mexico. There we had separated on the National Old Roads Highway when we chose to travel westward by way of Socorro, and they decided to go by way of Gallup.

We were glad they caught up with us at the Grand Canyon. Though they went their way about the park and we went ours, they joined us around the evening campfires. They said bad roads made travel on the Gallup route slow, and expressed regret for having missed the Petrified Forest and the cliff dwellings in Walnut Canyon.

Ready at last to leave, we remembered to fill the Ford's leaky radiator. A Chicago-bound tourist noting the pailful of water we poured in, came over with a can labeled "Radiator Compound."

"Try this," he said. We nodded assent, so he emptied half the can's contents into the radiator. "After you drive awhile this stuff will swell and plug the leak."

Appreciative, but not convinced, we left the campground at 2:45 P.M., hoping the radiator problem was solved. We drove fully an hour toward Flagstaff before stopping to make a check.

"It doesn't drip," Elliott said. To make sure, he ran his fingers up and down the radiator. The tourist who befriended us was right, I thought. The radiator compound plugged the leak.

En route to Williams we came to a deserted ranch. Driving in to look it over, we wondered what circumstances brought about its abandonment, probably drought or hard times. While we surveyed run-down ranch buildings, a broken windmill, and a decaying corral, I found a weather-beaten book of Washington Irving's writings. Had a ranch owner or a cowboy possessed it? I tossed the volume into the car, thinking I might later have time to brush up on Washington Irving.

Departing from the ranch, we were startled when the Ford went out of control at the outer gate. The Good Ship Wanderlust suddenly behaved as if it had lost its rudder. I was driving in loose sand, and as I turned the steering wheel to head west on the main highway, it failed to respond. Disconnected from the front wheels, the steering wheel spun freely while the Ford moved straight ahead. I stepped on the brakes to halt the car in front of a deep ditch.

To straighten the Ford on the highway, Elliott and I twisted the front wheels and pushed the car backwards. Our maneuvering apparently re-engaged the steering wheel with the front wheels. When we drove off, I had control of the car again.

In Williams, its population of 2,500 half that of Flagstaff, a curio shop drew our attention. It sold handicrafts and beadwork created by Navajo Indians. We each bought a bead necklace to send to our sisters, Jeanette and Myrtle.

While buying gas at a filling station we noticed the radiator dripping slightly. For a quarter we bought a third of a can of radiator compound, the same brand the Chicago tourist gave us at the Grand Canyon, with the hope this second dose of compound would seal the radiator for good.

Our Evanston friends drove into the filling station just as we were leaving. They said they made a sudden decision to leave the Grand Canyon shortly after we left. We thought it would be fun to camp together that night. The four of us stopped at a sheltered opening three miles beyond Williams. Carefree, we sat around a campfire, humming tunes and talking until midnight. When we told our friends about the strange behavior of the Ford at the deserted ranch, Baker said, "Your car jackknifed. In other words, it turned turtle. This sometimes happens to Fords."

The term "jackknifed" was new to us. Baker said the radius rod under the Ford came loose, probably when it wriggled through the loose sand we described. He corroborated what we had inferred by saying, "You got the rod working again when you straightened the wheels and jockeyed the steering wheel."

Baker walked over to the Ford. Testing the steering wheel and the radius rod, he said, "It's all right now."

Reassured, we dismissed thoughts the car might jackknife again.

Although we were up at eight o'clock the next morning, three hours went by before the Ford was on the road. At Seligman we set our watch back an hour as Mountain Standard Time became Pacific Standard Time. This was a gratifying moment. We now had been in all four time zones of the country.

The mountain descent was gradual, almost unnoticeable,

but we dropped over 4,000 feet by the time we camped by a parched river bottom two miles west of Kingman. Our Evanston friends overtook us there, so we didn't spend the night alone in the deserted area. For the second night we sat beside a campfire under a moonlit sky. This time our discussion became more serious. We exchanged views about war, the Ku Klux Klan, and the League of Nations.

Two small gold mining towns, Gold Roads and Oatman, intrigued Elliott and me during our Saturday drive. We saw men, each with a gold nugget dangling on his watch fob. One man, probably a mining official, pulled out his watch to note the time. Unlike our dollar Ingersoll, it too was gold.

The day was hot, 95 degrees above zero. Sweltering in the heat, we walked slowly, but miners we talked with gave no hint they minded the torrid weather. From our talks we learned how shafts were sunk on the mountain range to mine gold. Though the miners said there was a wealth of gold, we saw no modern improvements in the two communities.

As Elliott said, "This is rough-and-ready country."

The Ford lacked power climbing the steep mountain road. Elliott blamed the heat when the right front tire went flat three miles before we reached Needles, where a gas station attendant said the temperature was 94 degrees above zero.

"It's a cool day," he understated as Elliott paid him a dollar for four gallons of gas. "There's a fresh breeze blowing."

In Needles we had come to California, the third corner state charted for our trip. Recalling the cold reception that greeted our entry into Florida, we couldn't help noticing California's torrid reception. And ahead was the Mojave Desert.

We feared for the Ford. Already it had struggled in heat as high as 98 degrees. What would it do in the hotter desert?

Elliott suggested we wait in Needles until evening and travel by night across the Mojave. It was a good idea, I thought, because the temperature dropped 10 degrees by the time we started, and no doubt would get lower after dark.

Our plan was to take turns driving, enabling one of us to doze against the seat cushion. The road was rough at first, but improved after we traveled 40 miles. The air cooled to the point where driving was comfortable. About midnight we tired of night driving, so turned off the road to sleep. By now the heat had turned to cold. We appreciated the warmth of our blankets.

Two hours later the glare of headlights wakened us. Our friends from Evanston had pulled off the highway to park their car near ours. They said they, too, had decided to cross the desert at night, and seeing our Ford parked along the road, thought that if we could withstand the desert heat the next day, they could also.

We arose early in the morning, hoping to avoid some of the soaring temperatures. Instead, the day turned so cold we donned warm clothing.

"Who would think it?" Elliott remarked. "A desert with winter weather."

It still was cold when we approached Daggett, and though the below-normal temperature was disagreeable, we were happy the desert, contrary to expectations, had not sizzled.

At Daggett, officials of the California Department of Agriculture stopped all vehicles for inspection. They waved several motorists through after random glances at their cars, but ordered us to pull aside after one of the inspectors noted our Florida license plate. Occupants of two other cars waiting their turns, grinned when they saw the "WE ARE NOT BOOTLEGGERS" inscriptions chalked on the hood of the

Ford.

"We're not looking for moonshine," an inspector assured us. "Do you have oranges in your car?"

"A few," Elliott said. In Florida we ate so many we didn't crave all the oranges we brought with us when we left the state. Instead, we bought apples, quite expensive, usually five cents per apple.

The inspector pointed to a spot 50 feet from the Ford. "Dump your oranges there," he said.

We did as ordered, though it seemed we were wasting a half-dozen good oranges. California, apparently, didn't want its orange groves infected by Florida fruit.

With other motorists looking on, we were embarrassed when the inspector next directed us to unload all contents of the Ford for a thorough brushing. We thought he was making sure we made a clean entry into California's fruit belt. We were convinced he was making absolutely sure when he told us to unroll our bedding to shake the blankets. He then signaled us to drive on.

At Barstow we turned south, and at Victorville the temperature was so warm we removed the jackets we had worn on the desert. But not for long. Halfway up a rather steep mountain road it grew so cold we again put on the jackets.

In Cajon Pass, the majestic beauty of the mountain scenery was so overwhelming we stopped the Ford several times to appreciate it fully. The view was as breathtaking as any we had seen. It pleased us that the gradual descent of the mountain made the distance down seem long.

Arriving in San Bernardino shortly before sunset, we drove through outlying areas seeking a campsite for the night. We came to a vacant building, and figuring no one would disturb us there, parked by the rear wall. A shout from under a tall tree farther down the street excited us. We saw our Evanston friends parked under its branches, waving enthusiastically.

In a city as large as San Bernardino, population 35,000 or so, we knew it would be indiscreet to build a campfire. Nevertheless, warmly wrapped in jackets, we ate supper together and chatted until a late hour. When we parted company the next morning, we bade farewells, sensing our paths never would cross again.

Chapter XV
Irresistible Yosemite

ROLLING ALONG on concrete pavement was so relaxing Elliott held the Ford to 20 miles an hour. To be on concrete was a pleasurable relief from the rugged, often rocky roads we so often traversed. Viewing trees bearing ripe oranges was like being in Florida again. At Glendora Elliott jumped out at a roadside stand to buy a pailful for a quarter.

The day was mild. Unhurried, we spent several hours in Pasadena, aware we had come to an area more populated than any we had seen since Dallas. Pasadena, with its 75,000 inhabitants, was only the beginning, however. We were within 10 miles of Los Angeles, the metropolitan city of 1.25 million residents.

Situated as it is in the valley below the San Gabriel Mountains, Pasadena's beautiful setting affected us greatly. Much of our attention focused on its scenic, commercial, and residential areas, clear indication of economic growth.

Aside from these resources, however, the city plainly took even more pride in its annual Tournament of Roses Parade, and the New Year's Day collegiate football game. Although the 1925 game had been played five months earlier, Pasadena gridiron fans still talked about it. That was the year the famed Notre Dame football coach, Knute Rockne, drove into town with his undefeated "Four Horsemen and Seven Mules" to ride roughshod, 27-10 over Coach "Pop" Warner's unvanquished Stanford Cardinals, the Pacific Coast champions. We would have been especially interested in Stanford's team because its star player was Ernie Nevers, of Superior, Wisconsin, the stellar athlete we often had watched compete against our Ashland High School football, basketball, and track teams. He now is enshrined as a charter member in the Pro-Football Hall of Fame in Canton, Ohio, next to the number one selectee, Jim Thorpe, the all-around Indian athlete of Carlisle University. Nevers earned this distinction after his spectacular career with the former Duluth Eskimos and Chicago Cardinals. In one game with the Cardinals he scored a record 40 points against the Chicago Bears, in a 40-0 victory.

Traffic mounted as soon as we left Pasadena, and gained momentum the closer we came to Los Angeles. Though I was puzzled about where to drive, we followed signs, and with experience gained since Chicago, had no problems.

We entered the city on Huntington Drive and Mission Road, then drove through part of a bustling business district, eventually parking the Ford a few blocks behind Hope Street.

Wandering on foot, we came upon the imposing YMCA building. We spent much of the afternoon inside, getting showers, badly needed haircuts, and eating supper. In the gym we stepped on scales, gratified we both had gained weight, one of the objectives of our trip. Elliott, who weighed but 130 pounds when we started, now was a hefty 149 pounds. My weight registered 150, eight more than in Ashland.

"Travel agrees with us," Elliott said, noting we had shown slight gain at the time we wintered in Florida.

We wondered how large Los Angeles would become. All about huge buildings were being constructed, including the immense city hall. Houses were going up at a rapid rate. On our drive toward the city we had been amazed how widespread the residential areas were. The population expanded daily, the city boasted, because of the influx of newcomers seeking better job opportunities in a warmer climate. There was no manifestation of long-time Californians resenting the newcomers, but they did regard themselves as native sons and daughters, and made the distinction clear.

The diminutive Ford contrasted sharply with the large flashy automobiles whizzing to and from Hollywood. Knowing there likely would be no tourist parks in Hollywood, but wishing to visit movie studios the next day, we camped on a boulevard at Bronhally Park near Hollywoodland. We suspected movie stars and Hollywood "big-wigs" dwelling on close-by estates wouldn't want campers on the boulevard, and expected a traffic officer or some other minion of the law would order us off. Oddly enough, not even the penetrative smell of bacon frying on our camp stove drew attention. We had an uninterrupted night's sleep.

Despite its diminutive size, unwieldy top, bootlegger signs, and a missing fender, the Ford drew scant attention when we parked it the next morning by the Warner Brothers' studio.

"Guess they think it's part of a movie," Elliott said.

In the studio we observed how scenery was set up and props arranged, but had chosen the wrong day to see movie stars. We saw no celebrities in Universal City, either.

Before leaving Hollywood we made another tour of its streets hoping to spot a Mary Pickford or a Charlie Chaplin. Seeing no stars, we left Hollywood's glitter to head north into the serenity of the mountains.

Whatever the reason, the Ford climbed steep slopes in high gear. Encouraged by this show of power, we favored the car by stopping to cool its engine several times. By a roadside fireplace beyond Sanberg we fried eggs for lunch, and during the afternoon reached an elevation of 4,200 feet at Tejon Pass. Beyond this we came to a desert-like valley, large in extent, where irrigation made possible the cultivation of grapes and agricultural products.

A dense cluster of derricks hove into sight as we drove toward Bakersfield. There we had a close range view of oil being pumped from dozens of wells. With so many derricks in operation, we thought Bakersfield's prosperity would be short-lived.

"We don't worry about that," said the attendant of the filling station where we bought gas. "We'll be pumping oil for years."

We didn't know whether oil wells in Bakersfield had anything to do with lower prices at the gas pumps, but the cost per gallon was only 19 cents, and a quart of oil 20 cents.

In Porterville I cashed one of my $10 traveler's checks in the Home Bank. We had walked about two blocks down the street when an excited bank teller ran up from behind. Waving my traveler's check before my eyes, he deplored, "I shouldn't have cashed it. The bank in Florida didn't sign it."

He waited, expecting me to return the $10 bill he gave me in the bank. Elliott, however, produced the checks he carried. All had been signed. He wrote his signature on one and gave it to the teller, who promptly returned mine.

To mail my remaining checks to Melbourne, Florida, for the bank cashier's signature was out of the question, we agreed.

"They're good, we paid for them," Elliott said.

At Fresno a Standard Oil station accepted my rejected check without question. I had two more, but decided not to try redeeming them in a bank.

Arriving in Madera we learned two roads led to Yosemite National Park, our immediate goal. Both were muddy after heavy rain. We chose the shorter Madera road with its 16 per cent grade. The Merced highway had a 24 per cent grade, probably too steep for the Ford.

As soon as we left the San Joaquin Valley we drove up gentle hills which gradually sloped higher. Past the town of Raymond we camped by a narrow rippling stream, a beautiful sight. As we often did, we tarried until late morning, knowing the fun of touring was enriched by time spent camping. Preparing a meal, washing dishes, airing clothes and blankets, or just plain loafing, that was the way to savor the out-of-doors. Or, from a poet's point of view, "hold back the scenery, don't let its charm flit by."

While we sat by the stream, wishing we could drop a line to catch trout, we detected a glitter on the bottom of the sparkling, clear water.

"It looks like gold," Elliott said, "but I doubt it." He plopped his arm into the stream to scoop up a handful of glistening flakes. "It's only fool's gold," he said, tossing the flakes back into the water.

Before long, mountain climbing began in earnest. Sharp curves were numerous, and spring rains had affected the road so badly we had to drive the Ford in low gear over the worst stretches.

Logger atop tree stump.

The mountain highway led us into a heavily forested area where trees rose to great heights and were large in girth. In a government reserve we noticed trees had been cut by selective logging. Roadside signs warned that no campfires should be built without permission from forest rangers.

Following a loop road off the main highway, we got out of the Ford to walk awestruck among giant sequoias in the Mariposa Grove of Big Trees. Here we saw the grove's towering trees of tremendous girth, trees 2,500 years old, or more. Among them we viewed the Grizzly Giant, oldest of all, at 2,700 years. We had read about these ancient trees, but being in their midst emphasized the stunning reality of their existence through so many centuries.

Driving our Ford through the trunks of two living sequoias, the Wawana Tunnel Tree and the California Tunnel Tree, thrilled us in a way we never could forget. The tunnels, about 10 feet high and nearly as wide, took us through the hearts of trees more than 25 feet in diameter. We had no fear of the giants collapsing. They had withstood the test of time, the Wawana Tunnel having been carved out in 1881 and the California Tunnel in 1895. We wondered how many thousands of other visitors had driven through the Sequoia openings. We had no doubt most did as we did, snapped pictures of their cars in the tunnels or at their exits.

After we left the Mariposa Grove, I frequently had to shift the Ford into low gear, particularly as we neared Yosemite Park. Steadily we climbed the mountain ridge beyond which lay the Yosemite Valley. Several times we passed other cars struggling to make the steep grade. We stopped to help some motorists push their vehicles. The driver of one Ford said he installed a Ruckstell axle booster to give his car added power, and he told us of a companion driver who carried a complete set of spare

parts in case his Ford broke down. We were gratified that our Ford went up the grades with no special device to boost its power.

Two rangers parked at the side of the road waved at us, and farther on a car of tourists joined us when we stopped to view the mountain scenery. They gave us some walnuts, which we cracked with our teeth and ate as we proceeded toward Yosemite.

To the left of the road we looked down into a gorge hundreds of feet deep, and as the Ford began a steeper climb around a horseshoe curve, I kept the car close to the cliff at our right. When I began to round the curve, the steering wheel suddenly became limp, spinning loosely in my hands without turning the front wheels. The Ford had jackknifed, just as it did in Arizona.

The front wheels moved straight ahead and went over the edge of the embankment before I reflexively turned off the ignition switch and stepped hard on the brake pedal. The back wheels skidded, and the left front headlight bent when it hit a tree growing on the side of the embankment. But the Ford held.

Elliott and I jumped out of the car, and as we did so, walnuts fell out of Elliott's shirt pocket. Never one who worried, he took his time picking them up. I helped him. One had bounced over the embankment, irretrievable at the bottom of the gorge. We then fixed our attention on the suspended Ford.

Plainly, the front wheels were too far over the embankment to allow us a foothold for a push. In an attempt to roll the car backwards, we futilely tried to twirl the rear wheels. Thwarted by this effort because the headlight was bent around the

Model T after driving through trunk of California Sequoia. (opposite)

slender tree trunk, we concluded there was nothing else to do but let the Ford pull itself out of the predicament.

Knowing there was no way to start the engine with the crank, I climbed onto the front seat, hoping the starter would work. Relieved that it did, I stepped on the reverse pedal, making sure not to engage the forward moving low band. Though the front wheels wobbled and the steering wheel still was listless, the rear wheels had sufficient traction to back the car against the side of the cliff.

We lifted the hood to check the steering rod. We pounded and jiggled it, and after helping Elliott straighten the front wheels, I leaned into the car to test the steering wheel. To my relief, I again had control of the front wheels. Whatever it was, perhaps the radius rod, something fell into place.

Expecting that the rangers who had waved at us would be coming along soon, we hastened to cover the tracks of the Ford. As Elliott remarked, "It wouldn't do for them to think we drove recklessly."

What a jackknife cliffhanger, I thought. The rangers never would believe it.

Cautiously, I steered the Ford around the curve, continuing slowly up the steep grade. We went several hundred feet before realizing we had overlooked a grim reminder of our mishap. We stopped to straighten the misaligned headlight.

While we were at the registration headquarters to pay a five-dollar fee to enter Yosemite National Park, the rangers drove by, again waving at us when they passed. The registration official assigned us parking space in Camp No. 7.

The grandeur of our descent into the Yosemite Valley stirred our innermost feelings. Since the car moved down an unusually steep grade, we stopped several times to cool its brakes, giving us more time to assimilate the beauty surrounding us. The panoramic view seemed like an overture, an introduction to transcendent scenic wonders. The peaceful valley below, hemmed in by granite precipices and waterfalls, was so enchanting we made no haste to reach the valley floor.

Once there, we took our time browsing about the Yosemite village tucked among tall pines and other stately trees. The small grocery store, bakery, garage, the Yosemite Falls Studio, and several other enterprises no doubt looked forward to another busy season catering to Yosemite Park visitors.

In the grocery we bought two oranges costing 15 cents apiece. This far higher price than we ever had paid, was caused, we figured, by transportation costs over California mountains. We paid 10 cents for a two-cent newspaper.

To reach our campsite we crossed the Merced River. The spot assigned to us was beautifully situated along the tree-lined bank of the clear water stream. The site afforded an excellent view of Half Dome and Liberty Cap. Nearby we saw the Upper and Lower Yosemite Falls with their combined drop of 2,425 feet.

It was Friday, May 15, early in the season, and although there were many visitors in the valley, it was not crowded. The first person to stop at our camp was an enterprising, business-like man in his mid-thirties who introduced himself as editor of the *Yosemite Tourist.* He interviewed us briefly, and said we could obtain copies of the Sunday edition of his publication by calling at his print shop in the village.

"This is the most wonderful up-in-the-mountains place I've ever seen," our visiting editor said. "If you want to appreciate it as I do, first study it in the valley, and if you have time, climb the trails to see the peaks and falls one-by-one."

He spoke glowingly of sights visible in the valley, Vernal Fall, Bridalveil Fall, Nevada Fall, Yosemite Falls, Half Dome, Liberty

Cap, Sentinel Rock, The Three Brothers, El Capitan, Glacier Point, and Cathedral Spires.

"Follow the valley trails," he said. He recommended we visit Mirror Lake at sunrise for an awe-inspiring experience.

Sunday morning we walked to the village to buy two copies of the editor's *Yosemite Tourist.* In the eight-page paper stapled inside a brown cover, we read brief write-ups of tourists he had interviewed. Our interview was headed, "On Extended Tour," and referred to us as "two boys from Ashland, Wisconsin, who are having the time of their lives 'roughing it.'"

We were amused by some of the articles the paper contained. One described an admirer of Yosemite disgusted with two ladies "wondering why the hotel at which they stayed the night before didn't have lace curtains." We chuckled over another item which said, "Yosemite is the only place the California promoter has not exaggerated."

The *Yosemite Tourist* served as an introduction to neighbors in our camp. They asked questions about our trip, and we were interested in their travels, too. Tourists were mostly from California, but some had license plates from such distant states as Massachusetts, New York, and West Virginia. One car bore a sticker, Duluth, Minnesota.

We had many friendly visits with our immediate neighbors, Mr. and Mrs. George Hansen of Oakland, California, and their niece, Ruth Rodger of Piedmont, California. They invited us to join them at various functions sponsored for tourists.

Observing a fisherman one morning wading the Merced River in hip boots, we asked if he had any luck.

"Not yet," he said. He cast his fly toward the opposite bank. A trout hit, but wriggled free. With renewed anticipation, the fisherman cast his fly again. "In Yosemite you never know when a big one is going to strike," he said.

Close behind was another sportsman in hip boots. From him we learned fly fishermen were competing in a contest, the angler catching the largest trout to be awarded a trophy.

That evening the Hansens invited us to attend an outdoor program in front of the hotel-camp Camp Curry.

"Bring your flashlights," Hansen said. "The woods will be dark when we come back."

A path winding among tall pines led us to the hotel-camp. Opposite the rustic lodging establishment we had a thrilling view of Glacier Point, more than 3,000 feet above the valley below. Cradled on top of the point was a huge boulder, a large part of the rock jutting out over the valley.

"That's Balancing Rock," Hansen said. "Some call it Overhanging Rock. They say that Douglas Fairbanks did a handspring on it." One could only quiver envisioning the daring actor out on the rock, walking on his hands with his feet

Elliott atop Glacier Point.

over his head.

A big crowd had assembled in front of a wooden platform in front of the hotel. We arrived in time to hear the master of ceremonies extend a welcome on behalf of businessmen of Stanislaus County sponsoring a good-will tour in Yosemite Park. He introduced a Junior Chamber of Commerce quartet which opened the evening program by harmonizing "When You and I Were Young Maggie," and "Does the Spearmint Lose Its Flavor on the Bedpost Over Night?"

A group of fishermen then was called to the platform. The anglers each wore a felt or straw hat bedecked with colorful trout flies. They gazed expectantly at a large trophy held up by the master of ceremonies so the crowd could have a clear view of it. After moments of suspense, he announced the winner of the fishing contest, the angler we saw lose a fish on the Merced River. He later had caught a seven-inch trout, the trophy winner.

The crowd applauded. The man standing beside us, however, responded with a snicker. "Imagine that," we heard him say, "a six-foot trophy for a seven-inch trout."

A seven-piece string ensemble played a medley of Victor Herbert melodies, "Gypsy Love Song," "Moonbeams," "Toyland," and other favorites, and accompanied several male and female vocalists. We especially enjoyed a soprano solo, "Waters of Minnetonka," sung by a beautiful young woman gowned as an Indian princess.

As darkness came on, a man remote from the crowd broke the stillness of the night air by shouting upward across the valley to signal another man atop the rim. There was a pause. Then an echoing response was followed shortly by glowing embers cascading down the mountain wall like a waterfall. As reddish coals slowly streamed down the 3,000 feet to the

Firefall of
Yosemite Ends
After 97 Years

YOSEMITE NATIONAL PARK, Calif. (AP) — After 97 years, the famed firefall of Yosemite is no more.

The firefall cascaded from Glacier Point for the last time Thursday night. The tourist attraction was ended because it was too popular, producing traffic jams and crowded conditions.

"It is a kind of travesty on nature to push glowing embers over the cliff when Yosemite provides such great natural spectacles," said David Condon, assistant park superintendent.

Associated Press, January 1968

bottom, a violinist softly and sentimentally accompanied the Indian Princess romantically singing the "Indian Love Call." The firefall and the music held the crowd spellbound.

Having completed much of our exploration of the Yosemite Valley floor, we decided the next morning to begin hikes above the valley. We asked a ranger how to reach Glacier Point.

"Follow the ledge trail," he said. He indicated where it started. "But you might have trouble climbing it," he added, telling us three couples made an unsuccessful attempt the day before.

"They were stranded halfway up the trail by snow and ice," the ranger said. "No one knew they were there until they built a fire to signal for help. We brought them down in the dark."

Despite the ranger's note of caution, we started up the trail, well-stocked with rolls and sandwiches. In places the going was rough, especially when we came to the snow and ice where the three couples had built a fire to signal for help. Several additional inches of snow had fallen during the night, but the temperature was agreeably mild. We wandered off the trail, tossing snowballs at each other. It was like winter in Wisconsin, except it felt much balmier.

From Glacier Point we had a commanding panoramic view

of much of the tree-covered Yosemite Valley. Yosemite Falls, Vernal Fall and Nevada Fall were plainly visible among Yosemite's craggy peaks, and Half Dome stood out in bold relief.

We did not hesitate to walk out far enough on Glacier Point to look down over its edge, but were cautious about going out on Balancing Rock resting in a niche at the top of the point. The rock was a challenge, though. Elliott was first to venture toward its outer end. I snapped a picture of him, and then warily went out on the rock myself. I wasn't concerned about the height, but it did cross my mind this might well be the unlucky moment for Balancing Rock to totter and fall into the valley.

A short distance beyond Glacier Point we talked with a forester stacking wood for the fire that would provide embers for that evening's firefall.

"This has been going on for many years," he said. "They ran out of wood long ago. We have to haul it in."

"Who originated the firefall?" Elliott asked.

The forester stacked more wood. "A hotel man named Jim McCauley," he replied. "He ran the Mountain House up here on the rim."

We decided to be at Camp Curry to see that evening's firefall, a case of start to finish. We spent most of the day scouting other wonders of the summit as we casually hiked an 11-mile trail back to camp.

Continuing exploration of the "high country" the next morning, we ascended to the top of the 317-foot Vernal Fall, and then visited the 594-foot Nevada Fall, and the 620-foot Bridalveil Fall.

Vernal Fall presented an unforgettable sight. We saw a rainbow form in the misty spray of its plunging water, and

Tramps doubled in Mirror Lake.

instead of arching into the sky, the rainbow curved slightly above the contour of the ground, its brilliant colors brightening the rock-strewn slope.

We thought Nevada Fall was spectacular, too, but not as much as Bridalveil Fall where we again saw radiant colors of the rainbow reflected in its spray.

Delaying our return to camp, we followed several trails leading to splendid lookout points where we studied different parts of Yosemite Valley.

We arose before dawn the next morning to witness the sunrise at Mirror Lake. With no clouds in the sky, the sun rose gradually, and soon the smooth still water of the lake vividly mirrored not only the trees and shrubbery of its shoreline, but the steep rocky walls in the background, as well.

"The lake is like a looking glass," Elliott said. He stroked his chin. "We should have brought our razor for a shave."

Mirror Lake inspired us so much we went back for another sunrise visit the following morning.

When we returned to our Ford, the Hansens told us that during the night bears roamed the campground, but not in our area. In their search for food, the bears created quite a disturbance, the Hansens said, and frightened campers wakened in their tents.

Aware that on some future night the bears might prowl around our campsites, we and the Hansens decided to keep flashlights by our pillows, knowing a flashlight was an ideal weapon to keep bears at a distance.

In hopes of seeing some bears, we made several trips that day to an area near Sentinel Rock where rangers fed garbage to the animals as they came out of the woods. Our timing was poor, however, for we saw no rangers nor bears.

But toward evening we had close contact with a deer.

Unafraid, the buck approached the Ford. Elliott held out a doughnut, enticing the deer to snatch it with his mouth.

In Yosemite, of course, deer were more or less a common sight. We had seen 8 on our Glacier Point hike, and on our way to Yosemite Park Elliott tried to take a picture of a herd of 16 which scattered when he walked toward it.

We learned much about Yosemite's plant and animal life on tours conducted by government naturalists.

The guide on our initial tour was a pleasant young man, spick-and-span in his green forestry uniform. By way of opening his lecture, he pointed to a coyote crossing a meadow. He then set the stage for the tour by briefly explaining the origin of Yosemite National Park.

Concerning the park's name, the guide said, "the valley was named Yosemity in 1851 by Dr. Lafayette Bunnell when he sat by a campfire with other members of the U.S. Mariposa Battalion, the first white men known to enter the valley. Yosemity was the name of a tribe of Indians that fearlessly killed grizzly bears. In their Indian language, Yosemity meant 'grizzly bear.'"

The guide paused, waiting for his explanation to sink in. "Yosemity later was spelled Yosemite in an army lieutenant's report, and that's how it is spelled today."

Continuing, the guide said, "As for the park itself, it all began in 1864 when President Abraham Lincoln took time during the Civil War to sign a bill that gave California the Mariposa Grove of Big Trees and many acres in the Sierra Nevada Mountains for a state park."

"California later ceded the property back to the federal government," the guide said, "which in 1890 established Yosemite National Park."

However, the guide that Elliott and I listened to didn't

allude to President Lincoln as the founder of Yosemite Park. "John Muir is regarded as the 'father of the Yosemite,'" he said. "Through his writings and campaigning he was the one who most influenced Congress to create Yosemite National Park."

The guide quickly passed his eyes over his intent listeners. "Anyone here from Wisconsin?" he asked. Elliott and I raised our hands.

"You can be proud of John Muir," he said. "He lived on his father's farm in Wisconsin, and was a student at the University of Wisconsin four years before coming to Yosemite at the end of the Civil War. You also can be proud of Dr. Bunnell for naming Yosemite. He lived in Homer, a small town in southern Minnesota, cross-river from Wisconsin. In your state, he was surgeon for a military regiment."

In 1903, Muir and President Theodore Roosevelt camped together in Yosemite Valley, the guide said. He took us to the spot where the two had conferred on the importance of establishing more national parks and wilderness areas to preserve America's scenic wonders. It was quite close to our campsite on the other side of the Merced River.

"After Muir and Teddy Roosevelt had viewed the valley attractions, Muir led the president up to Glacier Point," the guide said. "Roosevelt needed no more convincing," he added. "Before he left Yosemite Park he described it as 'the most beautiful place on earth.' From then on, Roosevelt exerted an even more powerful force to conserve the nation's natural resources," the guide said.

The guide next drew our attention to Yosemite's wild flowers, discussed bird and animal life, and completed the tour by identifying pines, cedars, conifers and other magnificent trees in the valley. We saw boulders and splintered rocks lying at the base of granite walls. The guide explained they had broken off precipices, evidence of timeless changes continuing almost imperceptibly in Yosemite Park.

In camp that night I felt the nature tour had aroused in me greater respect for wilderness, but lacked words to describe my introspective mood. For the words I lacked, I referred to the letter I received in Cocoa, Florida, from Harriet Rymer, our former high school teacher. She wrote:

> Perhaps on the highways you will not
> experience the feeling I have for the West,
> the silence and the solitude of the open
> spaces, which fill one with awe and rever-
> ence. But if you do not experience the
> loneliness and solitude of an Arizona desert,
> or the feeling of your own insignificance in
> the depths of a great forest, you will have
> missed a great real experience.

Not all our time was spent in exploration. We shopped and visited in the village and took it easy in camp. For a literary diversion I managed to read Washington Irving's *Alhambra* in the discarded volume I had picked up at the deserted Arizona ranch.

A tourist from Pennsylvania gave us several books he had finished reading, plus a few thin paperback novels. Though our high school teachers had frowned on dime novels, contending they would lead to the downfall of American litera-ture, Elliott and I devoured those the tourist gave us. I got a kick out of reliving the exploits of Shacknasty Jim, especially the one where he plucked a bullet out of the air with his fingers before it could enter his heart. I also enjoyed reading such flapdoodle as "considerably more of less than less of more."

While engrossed with one of the novels the tourist gave us, I recalled the time my 10th grade English teacher thought I was concentrating too deeply to be doing school work. She came up behind me in the study hall as I was slumped over, holding a novel low behind the seat in front of me so no one could see what I was doing, and snatched it out of my hands.

"For pity sakes," she said, "what's this you're reading?"

I knew she was right and sincerely intended I wouldn't read dime novels instead of studying Shakespeare. Feeling guilty, I didn't ask her to give me back my book. Consequently, I never did find out how the story ended.

Campers leaving Yosemite gave us dishes, a dishwashing mop with a can of Dutch Cleanser, soap, and generous supplies of food, including milk, bacon, eggs, butter, sugar, cocoa, coffee, canned goods, pancake flour, and syrup. We were glad to receive a single-bit ax to replace the ax we traded for ukulele strings in South Carolina. It would be handy to chop wood for campfires.

The only incident that marred our stay in camp was the search by rangers for a woman doctor missing since the night before. They found her body in the Merced River a few feet below our camp. A ranger said the woman probably fell into the stream while walking in her sleep.

Much as we hated to admit it, Yosemite's mesmeric hold on us had to end. Harsh reality hit when we counted our cash. It had diminished to $58. On Saturday, May 30 we packed to leave, only to be delayed when the Ford refused to start. The battery had run down too low.

"Let's try the Armstrong commencer," Elliott said.

We took turns with the crank, but the car's magneto failed to provide the spark needed to start the engine. We tried pushing the car in gear. That effort, too, was futile.

Elliott raised the hood. After we checked the spark plugs and wire connections, we saw the timer was badly worn. Two Los Angeles college students gave us a ride to the village garage where we purchased a Ford commutator and roller for 80 cents. The new commutator, however, wasn't enough.

We hiked back to the garage, taking the car's coils with us to have them tuned, knowing we also needed to purchase new points, a further one dollar drain on our meager cash. Several hours and a lot of labor later I held my breath as Elliott cranked the Ford. This time it started.

About one o'clock we began climbing the Big Oak Flat Road which we knew would be steep and perhaps slippery. We had traveled but a short distance when the Ford sputtered and its low band stuck. There was nothing to do but turn around to seek help at the garage.

We returned to our camping spot after a mechanic advised us to fix the car ourselves. "It's Memorial Day," he said. "We have to charge you time-and-a-half for labor, three dollars an hour."

Loosening the low band was accomplished easily, but determining the cause of the Ford's sputtering wasn't that simple. We removed the top of the engine to scrape off a thick coat of carbon, adjusted points on the spark plugs, and tinkered with the motor in general. All this required time, so we decided to remain in camp until Monday. Campers offered solutions, but not until a tourist from Port Angeles, Washington drained water from the carburetor did the car cease sputtering.

The delay in departure gave us two extra nights to remain in Yosemite, a rather pleasant prospect, we figured. We continued visiting neighboring tourists, and were invited to share meals with them, some around the cheery glow of campfires.

Unexpectedly, we gained another night's stay when a downpour of rain wakened us Monday morning. We knew the mountain road out of Yosemite would be unsuited, even unsafe, for travel.

Rain in the valley tightened bonds of fellowship. The Yoder family of Seattle, Washington invited us to their appetizing pancake breakfast, and when rain still came down late in the afternoon, we had supper with them in their tent. The rain was light enough to allow their campfire to burn, so we had a savory meal of roasted wieners, with scrumptious lemon pie for dessert.

As a matter of fact, it was Saturday, June 6 before we thought it advisable to leave Yosemite Valley. It rained on and off during the entire week. With reports of treacherous mountain roads, we did not venture forth.

In a way, this added delay was to our advantage. Some last-minute mail arrived which we otherwise would have missed. We had received quite a few letters during our long camp-out in Yosemite, and wrote as many ourselves. Now we had an opportunity to write final notes to let our families know we would be on the road again.

It was early morning when we once more started out. Descending downhill into Yosemite Valley had been one thing, climbing up and out was another. We counted on the Ford to get us up, but about the only assurance we had was a full tank of gas. We took the precaution of filling the tank on Memorial Day, surprised that so remote in the Sierra Nevada Mountains the cost was only 28 cents a gallon. The price for a quart of oil was but 25 cents.

Facing problems at the very beginning, the Ford strove to climb slippery inclines, steep and often curved. Though the car frequently stalled in oozy ruts, we eased it out of moist and spongy muck by pushing with all our might. We made such good progress we caught up with three other Fords having the same trouble.

Acting upon the suggestion of one of the drivers, we agreed the four cars should travel together, so all occupants could join in pushing. The plan worked so well that when we reached the ranger checking station we lined up the four Fords for a picture.

One of the motorists pulled out his watch. "It took 4 hours and 15 minutes to travel 18 miles," he said.

"Then let's call this spot Ford's Rest," another driver added. We all concurred.

Successfully out of the Yosemite Valley, Elliott and I now could relax as we continued to drive through miles of magnetic Sierra Range scenery. It had to end, of course, and by late afternoon we were in the foothills of the 1849 California gold rush. Evidence of the hectic gold mining days was mostly gone, but here and there were traces of placer mining, abandoned sites where prospectors panned for the precious metal.

By evening we came to a deserted-looking area designated on our Rand McNally road map as Chinese Camp. The name intrigued us. We parked the Ford behind a dilapidated red brick building, little suspecting its significance during the gold rush days.

Delaying supper, we walked over to the structure, noting its walls were caving in, and that its heavy steel doors, front and back, dangled loosely. Amazed, we read a sign, "Wells Fargo Express."

Entering the crumbling building, we peered into a massive vault, its steel door wide-open, to see where gold brought in by successful miners was deposited to await shipment by Wells Fargo Express to San Francisco or Sacramento. Scattered about were papers, broken chairs, and much debris of nondescript nature. Though the interior was totally in shambles, it was easy to comprehend what a busy place it must have been during the feverish gold rush days. But 75 years or so of abandonment and reckless ransacking had taken their toll.

Chinese Camp bore other marks of a miners' settlement. A few cabins remained, but we saw nobody living in them. Shrubbery grew in neglected yards.

From back in the hills came the strains of a fiddle, "Darling Nellie Gray," melancholically played by someone I imagined to be a lonely miner, perhaps dreaming he someday would uncover a "Ben's Nugget," as narrated by Horatio Alger Jr. Then, as the tune dolefully changed, its words ran through my mind:

> In a cavern, in a canyon,
> Excavating for a mine,
> Dwelt a miner, Forty-Niner,
> And his daughter Clementine.

The next morning as we were about to leave, we learned the area was not as deserted as we first thought. We talked with an elderly prospector who said miners still dwelt in the region, panning for gold. "We don't expect a bonanza," he said, "but we keep at it."

*Certainly have enjoyed ourselves immensely in
Astoria. 2 parties given in our honor. <u>Ahem!</u>
Worked several days @ union wages, $5.50 per
8 hrs. So instead of $8.00 for a traveling stake, we
left Astoria about noon with $50.03. Right front
tire picked up tack beyond Newport. Crossed
Columbia River on ferry @ Ranier, cost $1.00.
Scenery beautiful in Wash. Our ambition achieved.
We have been in the 4 corner states of the Union.*

— The Log, Mon. June 29, 1925

Chapter XVI
The Last Milestone

AFTER LEAVING Chinese Camp we stopped our Ford on a flat stretch of ground by the roadside for breakfast. Preparing meals like this we found pleasurable. We took our time, pumping air into the quart-sized cylindrical gas tank of our Coleman camp stove to provide pressure for the two burners, and then leisurely cooking whatever struck our fancy.

On this occasion we chose pancakes for breakfast, and rather than baking them in orthodox fashion, took turns flipping them out of the frying pan to see which of us could toss them highest in the air to turn them over into the pan. This drew the attention of passing motorists, judging by the tooting of horns. To us, it was just a matter of fun, a way better to enjoy meals as we sojourned through the country. Needless to say, the whiff of freshly-brewed coffee always added zest to the meals.

The weather in Yosemite Park had been so moderate we were unprepared for the hot temperatures we encountered after departing from Chinese Camp. They were in the high 80s.

Stockton was the first city of comparatively large size we had seen since Bakersfield. Its attractive wide streets were inviting. We estimated the city's population was about 50,000, not quite twice that of Bakersfield. Being in Stockton after more than a month in the mountains gave us a sense of returning to the workaday world. We realized life in the wilds had been an interlude, a delightful escape from reality.

The heat became so intense during the afternoon we lowered the top of the Ford and drove bareheaded, with shirt sleeves rolled up, and shoes kicked off. The change, however, proved too sudden. Our arms and faces reddened, and I became so nauseous I couldn't eat supper. We thought about raising the top, but after a night's sleep, decided to leave it down. We suffered no more adverse effects.

In Sacramento, the roaring mining town of California's gold rush, we spent an hour touring the state capitol, surrounded by its splendid park. The city did not seem crowded for space. Its modern buildings and broad boulevards were spread throughout the city. We thought that industrially and shipping-wise, Sacramento was up-and-coming. It apparently was in the midst of a thriving agricultural region.

After a hot drive through the Sacramento Valley we noticed the Ford averaged 25 miles per gallon of gasoline, five miles higher than its usual average. In the mountains the average had been less than 18 miles per gallon. We surmised the increased mileage was due to concrete pavement over a flat surface.

Fruit was cheap, oranges as low as six for 10 cents in

Sacramento. In Red Bluff we had an enjoyable change in diet, eating strawberries for the first time since Florida. They were but 25 cents for two heaping quart boxes. Two pounds of apricots cost a dime. In Redding, on the other hand, gasoline was quite high, 22 cents a gallon.

All through the San Joaquin and Sacramento Valleys the Ford flowed flawlessly over concrete pavement, but in the hills beyond Redding travel became more difficult over a chucky gravel road, and was further slowed by construction crews. Through both valleys we gazed over numerous orchards and grain fields, and had our first view of rice in cultivation.

Parked that night in an open field beyond Dunsmuir, we hiked down to the Sacramento River for a cooling swim. With the Ford's top still lowered, we slept soundly under a blanket of stars.

Tuesday, June 9 marked a gradual change in scenery. The air cooled as the Ford ascended slopes. Before saying good-bye to California, we descended to the Klamath River, and soon were in mountainous country similar to New Mexico and Arizona, arid, reddish, and abounding with rugged rocks.

For at least a hundred miles our attention centered on 14,000-foot Mount Shasta, the snow-capped, inactive volcano of the Cascade Mountain Range. For what seemed endless hours it was to the right of us, never closer, never farther away. We thought it would be fun to find a forest road to see how high up the mountain we could climb, but gave up the notion as we drew closer to the Oregon border.

Oregon greeted us with concrete pavement, tree-covered mountains, and valley meadows teeming with wild flowers. Small communities were centers of logging activities.

In Ashland the Ford aroused curiosity when we parked it in the business district. Passers-by saw the words, "ASHLAND,

WISCONSIN," on its doors. Some asked about our Ashland, showing interest as we told them about its shipping activity on Chequamegon Bay, then quickly extolled their own Ashland with its temperate climate in the forested state of Oregon.

The city, its population half of our Ashland, had a tourist park rivaling the allure of our Prentice Park and its artesian springs. It's gasoline price, though, was high for western states, 25 cents a gallon.

Tourist parks in Oregon were frequent, their fees ranging from 25 to 50 cents per night. We, however, preferred to camp alone in forest openings by the side of the road, enjoying tranquility in the midst of spiraling evergreens and giant Douglas firs.

Near Eugene we stopped at a wayside to pump up a slowly leaking tire. Parked near us was a Chevrolet with a goat fenced-in on the running board.

"We carry the goat for milk," the driver said as he stepped out of the car, lifted the goat to the ground and tied it to a tree. Squatting beside it with a pail, he milked her.

"Me and my family aren't tourists," he said. "We just go from town to town looking for jobs," He said they did anything from repairing sewing machines to sharpening saws. He reminded us of the versatile piano tuner in South Carolina.

We spent the night behind a schoolhouse. The Ford stubbornly refused to start the next morning, resisting repeated cranking.

"We've got to get out of here," Elliott said. "The teacher and school kids will be coming soon."

With considerable exertion we leaned against the sides of the Ford to push it forward, and with Elliott guiding the steering wheel, we got the car out of the schoolyard and onto the highway. But it failed to start. We began to worry. Was the

Author leans toward giant Oregon tree.

Ford about to call it quits in Oregon?

"That Ford!" muttered Elliott. "It might help to scrape carbon off the cylinder head," he suggested. We tried this after pushing the Ford up the road a way to park it on the shoulder. The diagnosis was wrong, however, because at five o'clock, despite this and other corrective measures, the Ford remained defiant, refusing to respond to both the self-starter and the crank.

A helpful carpenter we saw working at the schoolhouse during the day spared us from sleeping that night by the side of the road. He hooked a chain on the front axle of our car and towed it several hundred feet. He then signaled Elliott to throw the Ford into gear, and in less than a minute the motor started.

"Good luck," he said, driving off to his home.

The Ford, however, acted up again, proceeding by jerks. After we camped for the night on a high hill beyond Albany, it still misbehaved the following day. We concluded it was time to look for jobs if we expected to have the car overhauled in a garage.

Encouraged when we read a roadside sign, "Help Wanted to Pick Loganberries and Strawberries," we inquired at the farmhouse a short distance off the highway.

"The pay is two cents a quart," the fair-haired man of the house said, "but the berries won't be ripe for a couple of days."

We left, seeing little prospect of earning much at two cents a quart, and certain we would eat up the wages waiting for the berries to ripen. At that, we figured, two cents a quart was a high wage for the berry grower to pay, when at Woodburn we bought three full quarts of strawberries for a quarter.

Portland was getting ready for its widely-publicized Rose Festival as we entered Oregon's largest city. We traveled on the west bank of the Willamette River surrounded by gorgeous

scenery. To view the city's beautiful residential area we climbed
a gently sloping incline. We admired the attractive homes
where roses bloomed profusely on well-trimmed lawns. In the
distance we had a clear view of snow-topped Mount Hood
rising majestically east of the Willamette River to an elevation
of 12,000 feet, and of Mount St. Helens across the Columbia
River in the state of Washington.

In the Portland surroundings the lower-lying Willamette
River engrossed much of our attention. We visited a sawmill,
hoping to find jobs.

"Our men are skilled workers," the mill foreman said.
"They're steady and don't quit their jobs." He said he couldn't
offer us work.

With sawmills on the river, it was logical for us to assume
that tall timber close at hand would have been cut down, but in
Portland such was not the case. Towering firs and other big
trees had been spared for parks.

In Portland's business district, where we had some difficulty
finding our way about, we stationed the Ford at the top of an
incline eight blocks from the YMCA, where we had showers
and weighed ourselves. Elliott still was gaining, tipping the
scale at 152 pounds compared with my 148.

The downtown area was decked in holiday fashion for the
Rose Festival on June 15-20. Our Ford hardly lent color for the
gala occasion. It started, but through heavy traffic Elliott had
to manipulate the choke and hold down the steering wheel
throttle while I steered and kept my foot on the accelerator.
The car almost stalled in the middle of intersecting streets, and
once it bumped the car ahead, but we were going too slowly to
cause damage. The driver, however, leaned out to glower.

In Portland our cash reserve was so low we had to decide
about getting jobs. We abandoned search for work in sawmills,

knowing we didn't qualify as sawyers, carriage riders, trimmers, or edgermen. We felt, though, there must be other work in a prospering city of 300,000. We saw foreign and American ships loading and emptying cargoes along the river banks. With so much lumber, canned salmon, manufactured goods, and agricultural products being handled, we thought surely there was need for workers. Elliott, however, suggested we travel on to Astoria to seek employment there. "I visited my uncle's home in Astoria three summers ago," he said, "and I'm sure we can find jobs."

Weeks of travel had disheveled our clothes, so Elliott recommended we splurge for new outfits. We were spared expenditures for caps, since in the West men went bareheaded, for neckties because it was sporty to wear open-collared shirts minus ties, and for garters because they were becoming a thing of the past. The low moccasin shoes we purchased in Florida still were in good condition, but our trousers showed signs of wear. Having observed that whitish corduroy trousers were in vogue, stylish without ever being pressed, we each bought a pair for a total of $10. This reduced our treasury to $12.

That evening the Ford limped into a free tourist camp in St. Helens. A handyman camper offered to help us check the rebellious car.

"Your trouble is the carburetor," he said. "I'll fix it for a dollar." He looked at us for approval.

We told him to "go ahead," and rather than stand around watching him, we walked into St. Helens to see a movie featuring comedian Ben Turpin in *The Shriek of Araby*. There was no audience except us. Apparently deeming it unnecessary to provide music for two spectators, the piano player left his bench to curl-up on a seat to nap during the performance.

It was three o'clock the next day before the handyman had

the carburetor functioning, but not until he dispatched us to town to buy three needle points. We paid him his stipulated dollar, aware it was a small fee, but with which he appeared satisfied. We were pleased that the Ford started when we left camp just as it began to rain.

Ships plying the Columbia River attracted our attention as we traveled toward Astoria, a drive of about 100 miles west from Portland. Both sides of the river were forested, with a small town now and then forming a break in the verdant scenery.

The Ford faltered on several occasions, causing us to ask mechanics what the trouble might be. At Svenson the labor charge was 7 cents for a wire adjustment. Previously we paid a mechanic 25 cents for erroneously telling us we needed a new timer. At the other price extreme, a farmer charged us 35 cents for a gallon of gasoline when the Ford ran out of gas in front of his gate.

With less than eight dollars in our pockets, we and the temperamental Ford arrived in Astoria Sunday morning, June 14, to be welcomed at the home of Elliott's uncle and aunt, Mr. and Mrs. Julius Benson, and Elliott's younger cousin Marguerite, who greeted us with a radiant smile.

The Bensons invited us to sleep in their home as long as we wished, but we declined, explaining we thought it unwise to break our habit of sleeping outdoors. They suggested we park the Ford in their spacious back yard. The family listened with rapt attention when we responded to questions about our trip. They said we could expect to see more new sights in the Astoria area.

The following afternoon Elliott and I began a search for jobs. Along the waterfront we saw a "Men Wanted" sign posted near a ship which had just docked with a cargo of cement. We were among the dozen men hired to remove heavy sacks of cement from the hold of the vessel, and to pile them on the

Tramps with one of Astoria's pretty girls.

dock. The exhausting work lasted three and a half hours.

"What's the pay for this kind of work?" Elliott asked the man in front of him.

"Dollar an hour," he replied. The worker exaggerated, I thought, but to our surprise the paymaster gave each of us $3.50 cash when the cargo was emptied. Astoria, we learned, was a union town where higher wages prevailed.

Instead of continuing a random quest for jobs, we asked Mr. Benson if he knew places where we could apply. He directed us to Astoria's union headquarters, and said he, as a union member, would speak a good word for us.

At union headquarters we joined a group of men gathered for job assignments. The union secretary said we would have to become members, but that he would start us out on temporary common labor jobs to earn money for sign-up fees.

Our first assignment was for a Catholic school improvement project, helping carpenters who also had been directed there.

We worked at the school two days and were paid $11.00 each.
To us, wages of $5.50 per day were unbelievable, considerably
higher than our previous earnings. On succeeding mornings
we received more assignments.

Astoria reminded us of Ashland. Its population was about
the same, and its spring weather had the warmth of our
summers, with a hint of coolness to ward off sweltering heat.
Elliott's cousin introduced us to several girl friends, including
Dorothy Nillson, Lydia Benson, and Gertrude Kankanin.
Thanks to the girls, we absorbed much information about their
city and its surroundings.

For one thing, we were told Astoria was named for John
Jacob Astor, known to us as the pioneer fur trader who established trading posts on Lake Superior. We were unaware his
far-reaching activity had extended to the Pacific Coast where
his trading post in Astoria handled vast amounts of furs from
the Northwest in the early 1800s.

During evenings the girls packed into the Ford and guided
us to scenic lookouts. Conversation, of course, didn't center
mainly on Astoria. Nevertheless, they showed us the salmon-
canning plant in which they worked, and as we drove along the
wide Columbia River, they pointed out foreign and domestic
ships docked at piers along the waterfront. They likewise
showed us boats of sportsmen and commercial fishermen that
contributed to Astoria's recognition as one of the world's
greatest salmon canning centers. The girls told us, however, that
salmon canning wasn't Astoria's only commercial enterprise.
There were mills sawing lumber for export, and ships carrying
agricultural products abroad and to American ports as well.

Of historical interest was nearby Fort Clatsop, winter
campsite of Lewis and Clark after their adventurous journey up
the Missouri River and ending at the Pacific Ocean.

One evening the girls arranged a picnic on the Pacific Ocean beach. Adding delight to the picnic was swimming in the ocean. Elliott and I thought the water was cooler than in the Atlantic Ocean at Cocoa and Palm Beach, but similarly invigorating.

On the way back to Astoria, the girls directed us to Clatsop Beach to view the wreck of the *Peter Iredale,* the British sailing vessel grounded in sand during a violent storm at the mouth of the Columbia River in October 1906.

The ship's masts, broken off as the vessel was buffeted by terrific wind and waves, were visible on the deck. We wondered whether any sailors lost their lives, but the girls said all 20 crew members were rescued.

On other evenings we took the girls to movies, after which we ate in restaurants, or enjoyed sundaes in ice cream parlors. They invited us to two parties in their homes.

Tramps conclude Pacific Ocean cooler than Atlantic.

The Ford behaved reasonably as we drove it in and about Astoria, yet we knew it was not shipshape. Still haunting us was the uneasy feeling we might have to abandon it and work until we could buy another. Still indisposed to give it up, we made fundamental repairs on days when no jobs were available, such as grinding valves and tightening connecting rods. Starting the car, however, had been our main problem. "Let's see what the Ford manual says," Elliott suggested. He opened his suitcase to get out the booklet of instructions.

"If the engine doesn't start there are nine possible causes, it says here," Elliott said. Reflectively, he turned a page of the manual. "If the engine lacks power and runs irregularly, there are eight possible causes." He flipped another page. "If the engine stops suddenly there are eight more possible causes."

We began a systematic checking of causes, most of which were minor. But since starting the car had been our major difficulty, we concentrated on those causes. Eventually we concluded the commutator contact was imperfect, or the magneto contact was short-circuited by some sort of obstruction. We remedied the commutator problem, and then found the magneto contact indeed was obstructed. With some effort, we removed the obstacle, and to our amazed delight, the motor started as soon as Elliott turned the crank. With the magneto functioning once more, we hoped that henceforth we would not be compelled to rely only on the Ford's battery, often run down, to spark its engine.

Although we reported each morning at Astoria's union headquarters for potential job placements, assignments became fewer. When we received none at all, we judged economic conditions in Astoria were as unfavorable as elsewhere in the nation.

"There just aren't any more jobs," Elliott said. "Let's pull up stakes." He counted our cash. "We've got $50.30," he

Nearing journey's end, the Manual finally consulted.

Summary of Engine Troubles and Their Causes

ENGINE FAILS TO START

1. Gas mixture too lean.
2. Water in gasoline.
3. Vibrators adjusted too close.
4. Water or congealed oil in commutator.
5. Magneto contact point (in trans. cover) obstructed with foreign matter.
6. Gasoline supply shut off.
7. Carburetor frozen (in zero weather).
8. Water frozen in gasoline tank sediment bulb.
9. Coil switch off.

ENGINE LACKS POWER—RUNS IRREGULARLY

At Low Speeds.

1. Poor compression—account leaky valves.
2. Gas mixture too rich or too lean.
3. Spark plugs dirty.
4. Coil vibrator improperly adjusted.
5. Air leak in intake manifold.
6. Weak exhaust valve spring.
7. Too great clearance between valve stem and push rod.
8. Too close gap between spark plug points.

At High Speeds.

1. Commutator contact imperfect.
2. Weak valve spring.
3. Too much gap in spark plug.
4. Imperfect gas mixture.
5. Vibrator points dirty or burned.

ENGINE STOPS SUDDENLY

1. Gasoline tank empty.
2. Water in gasoline.
3. Flooded carburetor.
4. Dirt in carburetor or feed pipe.
5. Magneto wire loose at either terminal.
6. Magneto contact point obstructed.
7. Overheated—account lack of oil or water.
8. Gas mixture too lean.

ENGINE OVERHEATS

1. Lack of water.
2. Lack of oil.
3. Fan belt torn, loose or slipping.
4. Carbon deposit in combustion chamber.
5. Spark retarded too far.
6. Gas mixture too rich.
7. Water circulation retarded by sediment in radiator.
8. Dirty spark plugs.

ENGINE KNOCKS

1. Carbon deposit on piston heads.
2. Loose connecting rod bearing.
3. Loose crank shaft bearing.
4. Spark advanced too far.
5. Engine overheated.

added, "enough to get rolling."

Monday morning, June 29, we left Astoria, $42 richer than when we arrived 15 days earlier. "The fund would have been more," Elliott commented, but then, as he said, "we had met the girls." I wondered how far $50 would take us.

Bidding good-bye to relatives and friends was quite emotional. They all had made our visit extremely pleasant. We said farewell to the girls while they were at work in the canning plant. When we drove slowly by a house near the edge of town we heard a phonograph playing, "Till We Meet Again."

From Astoria we retraced the Columbia River Highway to Rainier, about halfway to Portland. Along the way we had our second view of an appalling waste of trees and scenery, the black, charred debris of an extensive area devastated by a forest fire.

At Rainier we boarded a ferry to cross the Columbia River into Washington. The cost was a dollar. With a deep sense of exuberance we drove the Ford off the ferry. We had reached the fourth corner state of the Union, the goal of the Good Ship Wanderlust.

But to complete the circuit of the outer rim of the U.S.A., we still had more than 1,500 miles to go.

Chapter XVII
Adding Horsepower

TO ENTER LONGVIEW we drove under a gateway of huge logs, symbolic of the community's lumber activity, obviously its chief industry. Longview seemed to us to be a model city, its streets excellent, its residences home-like, and its public buildings reflecting municipal pride. It was a unique experience to drive under another gateway of large-sized logs when we left the city.

Rain wakened us the next morning as we camped by a stream near Olympia. The damp air was so cool we put on sweaters and drank extra cups of hot coffee. Rain, nonetheless, didn't hinder us from visiting the state capitol in Olympia. By afternoon it stopped, and a bright sun raised the temperature into the mid-70s.

By the time we reached Tacoma we understood why Washington was known as the "Evergreen State." Its picturesque mountains were covered with firs, hemlocks, and pines, and its fertile valleys were verdant with croplands and orchards. As if in contrast, snow and glacier-covered Mount Rainier rose over 14,000 feet in the distance.

At Tacoma we had our first view of Puget Sound, and saw ocean vessels in its deep harbor. The city of 100,000 boasted of its hundreds of manufacturing plants, chiefly lumber and paper mills. We thought hills rimming the harbor added charm to the city.

Ever since Texas, the left front tire of the Ford punctured frequently. Annoyed by the need to patch its inner tube so often, we were so exasperated when the tire again went flat in Tacoma we hunted for a secondhand tire shop, aware we could ill-afford to buy a new one. Fortune smiled on us because we bought a replacement for $1.75, less than a third of the price of a new tire. We did not purchase a new inner tube, however, deciding to use the old one, even though it had two dozen patches. Both of us ventured the opinion that it would puncture within a couple hundred miles, but the durability of the fragile tube surprised us.

It was the last day of June when we camped on a vacant lot on the outskirts of Seattle. Elliott had been in the city before, and expressed misgivings about driving the Ford into it.

"Let's take a streetcar," he said.

After a hastily prepared supper of scrambled eggs, we boarded a trolley as Elliott suggested, and headed into Seattle. In the city we spent the evening visiting places familiar to Elliott. In a metropolis of 360,000 it naturally was impossible to comprehend the extent of its activities, but Elliott knew his way around. One of the distinctive features he showed me first was Seattle's high Indian totem pole.

Stores were closed, but we window-shopped. At a newsstand

selling newspapers from all parts of the country we bought a copy of the *Superior Telegram* for a dime, and in its Chequamegon Bay section read news about Ashland's preparation for its annual Fourth of July celebration, always a big event. We caught a late streetcar for our return to camp, resolved to cover more of Seattle the next day. Exposed as it was on a vacant lot, the Ford readily might have been ransacked while we were gone, but the thought never entered our heads.

Determined to see as much of Seattle as possible, we drove the Ford into the heart of the city early the following morning. Parking the car near the totem pole, we admired the remarkable Indian statue again. In a curio shop we bought replicas of the pole to mail home as souvenirs.

Walking to the waterfront we looked at wharves where big ships attested to Seattle's fame as a Puget Sound seaport. Residents with whom we talked told us of the city's industrial growth. Yet, when we asked about job opportunities, they conceded work on the Pacific Coast was scarce because of the lagging national economy.

A burly lumberman, however, cited Seattle's timber industry. "We're number one in the country," he said proudly. He also let us know its salmon production likewise had top ranking.

Returning to the business district, we were pleased to find a low-priced place to eat. In Woolworth's we paid 25 cents each for a plate lunch and a cup of coffee.

At the post office we inquired for mail at the general delivery window, but only one letter was there. It had been forwarded to me from Astoria. We considered this fast service since it seemed only hours since we had been in Oregon.

After shaves and showers in Seattle's YMCA, we drove about

the city's rolling hills, respecting its modest residences, and noting attractive churches, schools, and public buildings. The Ford ran unruffled over smooth streets.

About one o'clock we left Seattle, cognizant of the grim reality our remaining $35 was not enough to assure completion of our journey. Throwing discretion to the winds, we headed east, confident we would find work somewhere. Meanwhile, we drove complacently, aiming to enjoy more scenic marvels of the West.

In a short while, the Ford rolled bumpily on a gravel highway, jolting us into a realization we were leaving the concrete pavements of California, Oregon, and Washington, as far as Seattle. Nevertheless, we were enthused to be in a heavily forested mountain region again. For the night's camp we selected the free government park at Denny Creek in the Snoqualmie National Forest.

Our map indicated the forest covered many miles of the Cascade Mountains, northward, and to the south toward Mount Rainier, but the park, so near a main-traveled highway, provided an exceptional and convenient sampling of this vast public domain.

Glad to be on foot in a forest, we hiked into a grove of towering trees, and kneeled to drink cool water from a clear mountain stream. We felt so exuberant we made our evening meal a festive occasion. The tantalizing scent of bacon frying in the pan must have penetrated far into the forest, perhaps tempting bears. With the bacon we ate boiled eggs and fried potatoes, and for dessert, cinnamon rolls with piping hot coffee. After the supper we even felt good washing clothes.

The exquisite beauty of the Cascades induced Elliott to drive slowly the next morning. We took pictures of Keechelus Lake, beautifully enriched by its dark blue water and snow-

Cascade Mountain stream.

capped mountains in the background. We expected the Ford's radiator would boil over as the car climbed Blewett Pass between Ole Elum and Wenatchee, but the car ascended the grade without a whimper.

In the Wenatchee area we saw many of the orchards contributing to Washington's recognition as a leading apple-growing state, home of the shiny Delicious apple popular throughout the country. Here the orchards were irrigated. Recalling our apple picking experience in New York State, we thought about seeking work, but made no application, realizing fruit was not yet ready for harvest.

We had experienced so much temperate mountain weather we were unprepared for the abrupt rises in temperature which first hit us at Ole Elum and rose higher as we traveled eastward. Adding to our discomfort was the dusty gravel road.

The heat affected the Ford, too. It hit on three cylinders several times, forcing us to adjust the misses. On a steep six-mile mountain grade near Waterville several Ford drivers stopped to cool boiling radiators, and larger cars got hot, too. The Wanderlust, for some unaccountable reason, made the ascent without boiling over.

When we camped that evening by a dance hall past Waterville we were in the midst of grain fields, a sure indication the forested mountains of the Pacific Coast were behind us. We drove with the Ford's top lowered most of the day, and didn't raise it at night.

"It's sure great to sleep under the stars," Elliott said. We looked for, and identified constellations, and then drifted off for a blissful night's repose.

The sun rose early the next morning, and so did we, at 4:30 A.M. The heat also rose. In the hot grain belt the only food with appetizing appeal was hardtack. This appeared to be a staple food in this warmer part of the country. In other areas we seldom had found hardtack stocked by grocers.

In Spokane the arid heat was so oppressive we failed to appreciate fully the attractiveness of the city of more than 100,000 inhabitants, situated as it was in an obviously rich agricultural and timber producing area. We cooled off in Spokane's YMCA swimming pool, where many others also sought relief from the heat.

Choosing not to travel nor to stroll about the city, we spent much of the day in the Y reading newspapers and magazines. In the lobby a sign caught our eye.

NORTHERN STATE STAMPEDE
July 4th Celebration
COEUR d'ALENE, IDAHO

A rodeo such as this was one of the attractions we had hoped to attend in the West. This, our first opportunity, had double appeal, tying in with a Fourth of July celebration. We cut short our visit in Spokane, and in the heat, departed for Coeur d'Alene at four o'clock.

Once more the Ford was on concrete pavement. As the arid landscape changed to mountains covered with tall trees, the temperature cooled noticeably. We were but a few miles from sizzling Spokane, yet the temperature change was so sudden we might as well again have been back in Florida.

We thrilled at our first glimpse of the vivid sky-blue water of Lake Coeur d'Alene. It struck us as extraordinarily beautiful, its shores absolutely inviting.

"A mountain paradise," Elliott said. "What a place to celebrate the Fourth of July."

A drive through the city convinced us it also was singularly exceptional. We spent the evening in its lakeshore park. As though tuning up for the Independence Day celebration, the city band presented a lively concert on the lakefront. After a stroll about the holiday carnival grounds we drove several miles west of Coeur d'Alene to camp in an ideal wooded spot we noticed on our way into town.

For its Fourth of July celebration Coeur d'Alene's population of 10,000 more than tripled. A preponderant abundance of Washington license plates indicated most visitors were from Spokane and its vicinity. Doubtless influenced by the rodeo, many wore cowboy boots and wide-brimmed hats.

The day was sunny and pleasantly warm. Crowds formed early for the morning parade featuring flag bearers, marching bands, colorful floats, and clowns.

After the parade, hundreds assembled in the city park to hear a stirring address by William Edgar Borah, Idaho's popular Republican U.S. senator since 1907, and recently named chairman of the Senate's Foreign Relations Committee. His patriotic speech, liberal in tone, was applauded enthusiastically.

While the senator spoke, another big crowd reflected the American spirit by cheering loudly at a nearby baseball game. About these simultaneous events I wrote in my log: "While Senator Borah was applauded, a batter in the ball park connected with the ball. The roar of cheers and applause all but drowned-out the ovation given the senator. The batter must have made a greater 'hit' than Senator Borah."

During the noon hour the lakeshore was lined with families eating picnic lunches.

The afternoon stampede lived up to its advance billing, well-worth the $1.25 admission charge we each paid. The rodeo, conducted five miles out of town, drew a capacity crowd. From our standpoint, it was an excellent show of cowboy skills, but for spectators around us it also was an occasion to cheer for favorite contestants.

"That a boy, Slim," shouted a rooter next to us. He swung his Stetson wildly, jumping excitedly.

Women cheered loudly for Bonnie Gray, trimly garbed in a cowgirl outfit. They yelled when some of her daring feats eclipsed those of cowboys.

We thought the most exciting events were bulldogging, steer roping, bronco busting, and wild horse racing.

"Those cowboys would make great football tacklers," Elliott said as we watched them leap from saddles onto galloping steers to bring them to the ground.

Spectators cheered cowpunchers who roped running calves, brought them to the ground, and shackled them. There were "ohs" and "ahs" if they missed.

Humoring the crowd were clowns mimicking antics of the cowhands, but not as dangerously as it seemed because to avoid injury it was evident they had to be well-trained as riders and ropers. Nevertheless, they evoked considerable laughter.

The rodeo had grim aspects, too. Three men were injured during the show, one painfully, and a steer was hurt when his back feet tangled with a six-foot fence he failed to leap over.

With coveted awards at stake, it was natural that most of the onlookers applauded regional contestants, but a deafening roar greeted Breezy Cox of New Mexico when the announcer awarded him a silver-adorned saddle and proclaimed him "the world's greatest cowboy." To earn the award, Breezy Cox provided many thrills, notably his daring leap from a speeding automobile onto the back of a rampaging steer.

Coeur d'Alene's celebration ended with a stirring band concert and picnics in the city park. As darkness came on, fireworks lit up the sky, superseding daytime firecrackers. That night Elliott and I sat up late discussing the rodeo and the day's other thrilling events. In the dark we had stumbled upon an ideal campsite below the summit of July Fourth Hill. Close at hand was a gurgling spring.

Sunday, scenic mountains held our attention all day. The highway was good as long as we were in Idaho. At Kellogg we came to a gold-mining town. Its prosperity was apparent when we drove on an eight-mile strip of concrete. Signs said the mining company built it "to encourage good highways."

"They must mean that for Montana," Elliott said. As soon as we crossed the state line the road became rough, narrow, and rocky, "the worst yet," as Elliott said.

The rugged surface didn't make for smooth driving up the steep mountain grade confronting us beyond the border crossing, nor the steeper Camel's Hump past Cabin City.

Halfway up the Hump the Ford stalled. There was gasoline in its tank, but not enough to feed the engine on the sheer grade. When the car came to a halt, Elliott said, "I remember reading a story in the *Saturday Evening Post* about a folk song written in Montana called "The Stalled 'Flivver.'" he said. "Well, here's another stalled flivver in Montana."

Elliott turned the car around and coasted downhill to Cabin City where the charge for gasoline was high, 32 cents a gallon.

A spare tire rolled off the rear of a Ford that passed us on the other side of the Hump. Knowing we couldn't overtake the car, we waited for its driver to return, but no doubt unaware of his loss, he did not come back. A couple of our own tires were in poor condition, so we kept it.

"Rocky Mountains, rocky roads," Elliott said wryly. He stepped lightly on the gas pedal, not to minimize the bumpy ride but to avoid puncturing tires. The front ones were in such precarious shape they blew out frequently. We replaced one with the tire that fortuitously fell off the passing Ford near Camel's Hump.

Compensating for the nuisance of flat tires was wondrous scenery. The wooded mountains, as we beheld them, were a resumption of the captivating views of the Pacific Coast. This was Rocky Mountains greenery we had expected to see in New Mexico, but didn't.

As we resumed travel on the jagged road the next day, we realized our Ford wasn't the only vehicle whose tires were damaged. By the roadside we saw tires other motorists had discarded. We stopped to examine them, and occasionally found one which appeared in better condition than ours. Such tires we tossed into the Ford, and after future punctures substituted them for our poorer ones. This spared the need to buy new tires, a vital concern now that our fund had dwindled to $20.

Making such use of tires other motorists threw away brought to my mind the poem I had read in my American Literature class. It was "Opportunity," by Edward R. Sill, wherein an English prince, bereft of his sword, picked up another flung away by a soldier as useless, went back into battle, and won.

We camped that evening on a Montana riverbank a few miles east of Superior. Here we had a splendid view of the setting sun, and watched cattle grazing in the valley. We thought this river country resembled the Mohawk Valley in New York State. Before retiring we realized we now were in the Mountain Standard Time Zone. So I turned my watch hands ahead an hour.

Near Missoula forested mountains became sloping hills, and by the time we reached Drummond they almost were devoid of trees. Herds of cattle on rolling green landscape extending far into the distance gave evidence we were in Montana ranch country.

Mosquitoes had not bothered us much since Florida, but now they again were a nuisance. At night we sat up late around a campfire to drive them off with smoke smudges. When the night cooled, the high-pitched buzzing of the mosquitoes ended.

Cozily covered in our blankets, we listened to the chugging of a locomotive pulling a long string of freight cars. We dozed off to the click-clack of wheels on rails, and the wailing sound of the engine whistle gradually fading in the distance.

During daytime we had close-range views of both freight and passenger trains roaring by on transcontinental tracks paralleling the highway. Hoboes riding in freight cars sometimes waved from open doors. Apprehensive about the endurance of our Ford, we pondered whether we might have to get home by doing as the hoboes did, by riding the rails.

It was, however, but a fleeting thought. Elliott frowned. "We'd better look for work before we're dead broke," he said.

We began by applying at ranches, spaced far apart. The first two attempts were failures, but the third held promise because we were advised to try the Charles Williams Ranch. We located it a dozen miles south of the main highway, only to have hopes quashed again.

"Try the Bar-B-Ranch," Wilson said. "They have tons and tons of hay to cut."

When we finally located the ranch near Deer Lodge, it took another half-hour to find the owner. Regrettably, this was more time wasted. There were no jobs here, either.

Though we drove what seemed like endless miles, our road map showed we had covered little more than a third of

Montana. "It's a big state, like Texas," Elliott said. As in the Lone Star State, we noted changes in scenery. So far in Montana we traveled in mountains, hills, valleys, and now approached the barren landscape of Butte.

Prospects of obtaining work would be brighter in this city of almost 40,000 people, we thought. The Anaconda Copper Mines were here, and gold and silver mines in the area assuredly added to the mineral wealth. Yet when we applied for jobs at two employment offices, no work was available. The only job listed in one of the offices was for experienced teamsters, placement requiring an advance fee of $2.50. For this kind of work we did not feel qualified.

About 10 miles east of Butte we crossed the Rocky Mountains Continental Divide for the second time. A sign said the elevation was 6,200 feet. This time, though, we would travel in the direction of streams flowing eastward into our part of the country.

An open area by a mountain creek a short way beyond the divide was our campsite for the night. The solitude of the Deerlodge National Forest was relaxing.

We were getting closer to Yellowstone National Park, where we definitely intended to camp, but unless we found jobs, the admission fee would be too much. With determination we renewed our efforts when we rode into Whitehall the morning of July 8. Several men we talked with said they, too, were looking for work. When we bought stamps in the post office to mail postal cards home, we asked the clerk whether he knew of any jobs.

"No, I don't ," he said. The clerk thought a moment. "Look up Mr. Luther at the high school. He might know," he said.

Having no idea what a Mr. Luther might be doing at a high

school during the summer vacation, we nevertheless looked him up, and found him working on a renovation project.

"Maybe Mr. Lowe needs some help," he said. "He's a mule rancher at Renova. Jump into my car. We'll run over and see him."

Surprised that a total stranger would be so accommodating, we cheerfully accepted his offer. To our further surprise, after we arrived at the mule ranch Mr. Lowe said, "Sure, I can use a couple of hands to help with the haying." He hired us for the remainder of the week at a wage of $2.50 each per day with room and board.

We thanked Luther during the drive back to the high school to pick up the Ford. Returning to the ranch, we expected to sleep in the car as usual, but elected to sleep indoors, away from mosquitoes, when the Lowes showed us a screened bedroom on the upper floor of their two-story house. We parked the Ford by a fence near a big barn.

That afternoon we began work by cocking alfalfa. A 17-acre field already had been mowed and awaited stacking.

At supper we met the Lowes' teenage twin daughters, Hettie and Nettie. Demure and blue-eyed, they looked so much alike we could hardly distinguish them. They shyly asked questions about our trip, and showed keen interest in the Ford. We gathered, however, they preferred saddle horses as a means of travel.

The Lowes made us feel as part of the family, and working with Mr. Lowe was far from arduous. He taught us many things about ranch life in Montana. He said he would rather raise mules than graze cattle on his ranch because there was a year-round market for them. A profitable sideline, he said, was raising hogs.

Erecting a derrick to stack alfalfa was part of the second

Hettie and Nettie Lowe with horses.

day's work.

"I've got two poles, 36 and 42 feet, but have to know how long the third pole should be," Lowe said. "With your schooling, can you figure it out?"

We sat behind a haystack to reckon. Applying the Pythagorean theorem, we finally came up with a rough estimate of 55 feet. When we came from behind the haystack with our answer, we saw three poles erected. Lowe, without the benefit of our geometry, had calculated the right length, and had put up the derrick as well.

Friday was a scorching day, 100 degrees above zero. The only relief from the heat was watching a horse gallop by with Hettie and Nettie on its back. How these girls, 14 or 15 years in age, managed to hang onto the horse as it raced on narrow, brush-lined paths was a mystery to me.

"They should be in rodeo," Elliott said.

When we returned to the field after the noontime meal, Elliott brought his camera. He snapped a picture as the girls again rode by, their bobbed, blonde hair waving as their knees gripped the sides of the horse both were riding.

About quitting time, just as a few raindrops fell, a cowboy stopped by seeking lodging for the night. Lowe not only assured him of a room but invited him for supper. While Mrs. Lowe and her young daughters served hot cakes and bacon, the cowboy related his experiences as a Wild West performer of the Western Association in such major cities as Chicago, New York, and Boston.

"In Montana," he said, "I made $65 riding steers and

Hettie and Nettie Lowe "should be in rodeo".

broncos in the Fourth of July rodeo in Deer Lodge. I got $5 each time I hung on until the steers and broncs crossed the 'dead line,'" he boasted.

Waving his arm to demonstrate his skill with a lariat, he said he learned to rope steers by practicing in secret. "The ranch foreman wondered who was breaking horns off his steers," he said, grinning.

In his extroverted manner, the cowboy bragged he hailed from Texas, but said, "Montana is going to be my stopping place from now on. I'm going to get $6 a day and a dollar a head commission buying cattle for the packing house in Butte." We thought this was an exaggerated rate of pay, but saw no reason the cowboy shouldn't remain in Montana. He was by no means small potatoes.

Neighbors who came to visit Lowe during the evenings helped him repair machinery or aided him with chores. They eyed our Ford parked outside the barn. We were amused when one of the men asked, "How high are the mountains in Wisconsin?"

The haying was not completed by Saturday night, so Lowe asked whether we cared to work "a couple more days next week." Without hesitation we said "yes."

With more alfalfa mowed and ready for stacking, we thought Lowe would work Sunday to keep ahead of threatening rain.

"We never work on Sunday," he said.

Mrs. Lowe, whose cooking we admired, served breakfast an hour later Sunday morning. She baked tasty cinnamon rolls, and fried bacon and eggs. As the saying goes, "Man may work from sun to sun, but woman's work is never done."

As we withdrew from the table, Lowe asked, "How would you like to go fishing?" He said the stream flowing through the

Stacking hay with homemade hoist.

ranch had many good holes.

A fishing trip on a ranch was something Elliott and I never dreamed possible. Even the Texas cowboy asked if he could go along.

Lowe said he had only two fishing poles and lines, and offered one to us. We asked the cowboy whether he would like to fish while we watched. His face lit up. He said, "I sure would."

The four of us hiked toward the middle of the ranch to the crystal clear stream meandering through brush and tall grass. At first Lowe and the cowboy fished together, and then Lowe went off by himself farther upstream. We saw the cowboy toss out his line as though it were a lariat.

Hearing the clop of horses' hoofs, we turned to see Hettie and Nettie rush by on their saddle horse. They waved and soon faded out of sight, just as the cowboy was landing a fish.

"What is it?" Elliott asked.

"A mountain trout," the cowboy responded.

I thought it resembled a redhorse, a non-game fish of northern Wisconsin.

Toward noon, Lowe rejoined us. He showed us the four fish he caught, the same kind the cowboy landed. Mrs. Lowe served them for dinner the next day, deliciously fried.

When we stacked the last load of hay in 105 degree heat Tuesday afternoon, Lowe said he no longer needed our help, and that he would pay our wages in the morning. We hated to leave the Lowes and their ranch. Lowe wrote us a check for

Crew is proud of job well done.

Hauling last load of hay.

$27.50, and then saddled his horse to be gone for the day.

After saying good-bye to Mrs. Lowe and her daughters, we headed for the Ford expecting to make a quick getaway. Such was not the case, however. The left front tire was flat and the battery was too low to start the engine. Patching the tire was easy enough, but when the Ford didn't respond to repeated cranking we felt jinxed and stymied.

Elliott came up with a solution. "Let's ask Mrs. Lowe if we can borrow their horses to give us a tow," he said.

Lowe's team of workhorses was in the barn, but harnessing them posed a problem. Elliott said he had never tried it, and I had only harnessed smaller horses on my uncle's farm. The harnesses racked in Lowe's stable were heavy, but by trial and error I got them on Lowe's team.

With Hettie and Nettie wonderingly looking on, I hitched the team to the wide hayrack standing near the barn, and tied the Ford to the rear of the wagon with a chain I hooked to the front of the car. Elliott climbed up on the hayrack to take hold of the reins, and slowly the horses pulled the car out of the driveway onto the road. He then flapped the reins and shouted "giddap" to spur the team into a run. I sat in the car behind the wheel, opened the throttle and threw the motor into gear. The car responded with a chug and spurted forward. I stepped on the brake pedal so the car didn't ram the hayrack, yet dared not ease up on the throttle for fear of killing the engine.

Elliott untied the chain from the Ford and turned the wagon around. He got into the car to keep the motor running while I drove the team and hayrack back to the barn. After tying the horses in their stalls, I removed the harnesses.

"It's still running," Elliott said when I returned to the Ford. His eyes twinkled with a knowing look. "The extra horsepower did it," he said.

— The Log, Tues. July 21, 1925

Chapter XVIII
The Wobbly Wheel

IN WHITEHALL we were delayed because of difficulty in cashing Lowe's check.

"The check is drawn on the bank in Boulder," the teller in the Whitehall bank said. "I can't cash it without calling Boulder to find out if it's good. You'll have to pay for the telephone call."

The drive to Boulder would have cost more than the telephone call, so we paid the 25 cent toll. The Boulder bank confirmed validity of Lowe's check.

"There's another hitch," the teller said. "You're strangers here. You'll have to show proper identification."

We showed him our YMCA membership cards and some letters addressed to us. These failed to convince him. "Do you know anyone in town?" the teller asked.

The only person we knew in Whitehall was Luther. We

315

found him at the high school just as he prepared to leave. He cheerfully drove to the bank with us and endorsed our check so we could get it cashed.

At last we were on our way to Yellowstone National Park, knowing we now could afford to pay the $7.50 entrance fee. The road was fair. After we turned south it reminded us of parts of Texas and New Mexico, cutting across ranches, and of Alabama, winding wherever cars could travel best.

Population was sparse. Mosquitoes, on the other hand, were numerous. When we camped that night in the Beaverhead National Forest we resolved to buy mosquito dope for future camping. We had made sure to park the Ford on top of a hill. It was a good thing we did, because it chose not to start the next morning until I shifted it into gear while Elliott pushed it down the incline.

As we continued traveling, we found gasoline and oil prices to be higher in the mountainous area, 27 cents a gallon at Jefferson Island, and 30 cents for a quart of oil. Naturally, we let the gas tank run low.

Wondering what to expect in Yellowstone Park, we asked a man buying groceries in the store at Ennis if he could give us information.

"All I can tell you is to drive past West Yellowstone until you come to it," he said. He told us he lived this close to the park all his life, but never had been in it.

At West Yellowstone we replenished our grocery supply, and along with other tourists, visited curio shops and other stores catering to park visitors.

After a night's sleep off the highway beyond West Yellowstone we arose early to enter the national park. At the admission booth we paid the required $7.50 fee and received a map and guidebook showing campsites and how to get to the hundreds of attractions in the vast park of 3,500 square miles.

The map showed the park to be mostly in Wyoming, the "Equality State," the first to grant women the right to vote. We had added another state to our travels.

Our entrance into Yellowstone did not present immediate spectacular sights as in the Grand Canyon and Yosemite National Parks. Having no conception of what to look for, we stopped at the first turnoff we came to for perusal of our map and guide folder. It became immediately apparent the thickly forested park had so much grandeur we would have to concentrate on its major attractions to gain the best perspective our limited stay would allow. Fortunately the map clearly showed the Grand Loop Road which would provide such highlighting. For a starter, we chose the Lower Geyser Basin.

As we drove along the tree-lined road we encountered several large black bears. They ate food tossed out by motorists ahead. Elliott idled the Ford and two bears gulped pieces of bread and rolls we threw out to the side of the road.

"We've got to get pictures of this," Elliott said. He reached toward the back seat for his camera.

We stepped out of the car, and while a bear stood on his hind legs and pawed for bread I held out to him, Elliott snapped my picture. I then took a similar snap of him feeding another bear.

Before we got back into the Ford, the driver of a Buick ahead ran toward our car with a camera in his hand.

"Would you mind taking my picture feeding a bear?" he asked. "My wife is too scared to do it." His tremulous approach as he handed his camera to Elliott gave me a feeling he, too, was timid.

Warily, he held out a cookie toward an oncoming bear.

"Let go of the cookie before the bear grabs for it," Elliott

Bear begs for bread.

warned, "or he'll sideswipe you." Elliott snapped the shutter
just as the bear reached up for the tidbit.

The man thanked us jubilantly, but in our minds we weren't
sure whether we had done him a favor, or had allowed him to

be exposed to the swinging paw of a bear.

More bears appeared as we continued into the park. One we didn't stop to feed. "He's too big," Elliott said. By the time we had disposed of a loaf of bread and a half-dozen sweet rolls, we drove on.

Choosing an ideal spot at the first designated campground we came to, we ate a hasty lunch, meanwhile mapping strategy for exploring the park. Elliott suggested we drive around at random to view the many points of special interest.

Tourists were everywhere. We joined a group to observe Riverside Geyser spew steaming water on the Firehole River, and marveled at the Cascade of the Firehole, and the Grand

Elliott pets Yellowstone bear.

Prismatic Hot Spring reflecting colors of the rainbow. We lingered by the Mammoth Paint Pots, transfixed by their bubbling and gurgling oozy clay.

From various other vantage points we soon comprehended the vastness and uniqueness of Yellowstone Park. Contributing to this feeling of vastness was the beauty of Yellowstone Lake, 20 miles long and as deep as 300 feet. Beyond its shore we focused attention on a towering range of snow-capped mountains.

We halted the Ford whenever we found opportunities to walk for better views. This gave us better sights of the Lower Falls of the Yellowstone River, plunging more than 300 feet into the gorge forming the Grand Canyon of the Yellowstone.

We spent several hours observing the splendor of the canyon. The temptation was to descend to the stream at the bottom, but sheer walls from 1,000 to 2,000 feet looked too formidable. We had excellent distant views of the Lower Falls. Our longest stop was at Inspiration Point, appropriately named we thought, because from here the canyon view was exceptionally awe-inspiring.

The sight of elk and bears near the roadside in lower parts of the park caused many motorists to stop their cars to take pictures. Some said they had seen moose, but we weren't so fortunate. When we heard the park had buffalo, we went in search of them.

To reach a herd we spotted in a corral we had to descend a steep mountain grade. The herd was large enough to give us a clear idea what the West was like before the buffalo almost became extinct. We dared not go inside the corral for close-up pictures, but were able to snap distant shots from the fence.

On the way back, a Ford in front of us stalled on the steep grade. Elliott and I jumped out to help by pushing, and when this failed, the driver said, "Let's turn the car around and I'll drive up the hill in reverse. That way I'll get better traction." Thus, to our amazement, the Ford successfully ascended to the top. As for our Ford, it climbed the grade straightaway.

More steep mountain grades had to be negotiated as we resumed our exploratory tour. Driving conditions were safe enough, although on some slopes signs warned motorists to keep cars enmeshed in gear. When the car ahead stopped suddenly, our motor died as Elliott braked the Ford. In an effort to pass the stalled vehicle he stepped on the starter, but the car's engine was too hot to get going. We saw several other cars behind us at a standstill.

Two young men sped by all the vehicles in a light-weight Ford racer. Once at the top, they walked down to help those who were stranded. With their aid, everyone finally got up the incline. The young men, so concerned about the plight of

Fishing near bridge and falls.

others, did not identify themselves, but we noted by a tag on their racer they were from Muskegon, Michigan.

Parking our Ford at Junction Camp for the night, we hiked to Fishing Bridge to watch fly fishermen landing 12 to 18-inch trout from the banks of the Yellowstone River. We talked with several of them. They showed us the artificial flies they whipped over the stream, Joc Scots to Royal Coachmen, most of which lured the trout.

"Fishing is good here," one angler told us, "but it gets better if you go deeper into the park."

Mosquitoes became pesky that evening.

Elliott shook a small bottle. "It's a good thing we bought this mosquito dope," he said. We both rubbed on an oily mixture with a distinct odor of citronella. The air chilled about 10 o'clock. Free of mosquitoes, we had another good night's sleep despite the lingering scent of the citronella.

Off to an early morning start, we drove back to the campsite at West Thumb to enjoy another view of Yellowstone Lake. A rain shower added to the picturesqueness of the scene. The shower, however, forced us to raise the rooftop of the Ford, but we lowered it again when the sun came out later.

Retracing the Grand Loop Road to Fishing Bridge at the upper end of the lake, we headed for the geysers of the Upper Basin. When we arrived at Old Faithful, the renowned geyser had just finished erupting, giving us 65 minutes to hike to other geysers, some of which spouted steaming sprays while we stood beside them.

By the time Old Faithful was due for its next display we mingled with hundreds of other tourists gathered together like spectators along sidelines of a football game. Cameras clicked all around when the geyser slowly began to gush.

For over five minutes we were enthralled by a stream of hot

water shooting upward to be capped high above by a single white cloud of vapor. Descending to the ground, the cloud narrowed into a continuous stream creating the effect of a second geyser at the side of Old Faithful.

Impressed by what we saw, we decided to remain for the next display by the famed geyser. Taking advantage of the intermission, we hiked to geysers we missed during our first walk. Signs by the gushers indicated they bore names peculiar to their formations, such as the Giant and Giantess, Beehive, Castle, Grand Cornet, Sawmill, and Lion and Cub.

Enhancing the thrill of witnessing Old Faithful in action for a second time, was another geyser behind it. Unexpectedly, it also spurted water and steam high into the sky, as if attempting to steal the show from Old Faithful.

Providing an attractive setting for the geysers was Old Faithful Inn, a rustic-styled log building. We entered its lobby

Witnessing Yellowstone geysers.

and, while scouting for souvenirs, were surprised to hear one of the girls employed in the curio shop call us by name. She was Mary Ellen Kerr, who lived a few doors from my home in Ashland. Though she could spare but a few moments from her work, she said she knew about our trip, "but I never dreamed of meeting you in Yellowstone Park." She briefly told us the latest hometown news.

When we pulled in at the Mammoth Springs tourist camp near Gardiner we met two more Ashlanders, Mr. and Mrs. Kleinfeldt, who were about to leave for their first view of Old Faithful and a tour of the Upper Basin. They already had spent a day in the Mammoth Springs area, and recommended we see places we otherwise might have missed. It was good to hear more news about Ashland.

We drove to several hot springs during the morning, and spent the afternoon in the Mammoth Springs camp to wash clothes and tidy up the Ford.

Scores of campers gathered around a forest ranger that evening to hear a nature talk pertaining to Yellowstone Park. He began with a warning about bears, too late for us. Citing injuries to bear-feeding tourists, he cautioned against teasing the animals while holding out food for them. "The safest way," he said, "is not to feed them at all."

The ranger's talk gave us a better understanding of the park attractions we had seen but not fully comprehended. We had been aware of the vast coniferous forest, its pines, spruces, and cedars, but unfamiliar to us was the lodgepole pine, gracefully tall and slender, the trees growing closely together. We knew we should have taken time to locate the Fossil Forest of the Lamar River, when the ranger said petrified trees stood upright, and not flat on the ground as in other petrified forests in the West.

Flowers, too, had been of interest to us, but we did not realize how many varieties grew wild in the park, including, among many others, the Indian paintbrush, violets, lilies, iris, phlox, lupine, geraniums, orchids, and shooting stars.

We had seen many kinds of birds, but nowhere near the 200 or more species the ranger said existed in the park.

"Watch for bald eagles, ospreys, pelicans, trumpeter swans, whiskey jacks, and mountain bluebirds," he told his listeners.

Nor had we seen some of the animals the ranger described, "grizzly bears, coyotes, antelope, and pronghorn and bighorn sheep."

Concluding his talk, he said, "If you want to see more of Yellowstone, follow the trails, get away from the crowds."

We dilly-dallied the next morning, and looked back longingly before we halfheartedly left Yellowstone by way of Gardiner, Montana. We knew we couldn't stay longer. Our cash was down to $27.50.

The Ford exerted all its power to get up steep mountain grades between Gardiner and Livingston. We helped by making mechanical adjustments, particularly when the car squirmed its way over the rutted and rocky highway between Big Timber and Billings. Before reaching Billings, we rested awhile after eating lunch at Pompey's Pillar, the unusual rock formation so-named by Meriwether Lewis during the Lewis-Clark expedition.

"I wonder whether Lewis ate lunch here and how long he stayed before he thought up a name like that?" Elliott asked me.

Probably quite awhile, I told him. I was sure Lewis didn't want to leave a sight like this any more than we did.

A few miles beyond Pompey's Pillar a pertinent sign at a railroad crossing caught our attention. It read: "Keep your hands on the wheel, let the girl hug herself."

Beautiful mountain scenery.

Driving that day had its problems, so we didn't relax until evening when we found a splendid camping site, a wild-looking spot on a high bank overlooking a stream and a railroad track.

The following day was one of utter frustration. The Ford ran smoothly, but seemingly was falling apart. To begin with, the dashboard holding the coils and wires came loose. After we tightened it, the steering rod slid down, drawing a chain so taut it opened the gas-feed wide open. The car spurted forward, compelling Elliott to slam on the brakes.

Tires gave us trouble, too. The right front one went flat three times. The third time we threw it away to put on a discarded tire we had picked up along the highway. To aggravate the situation, we ran out of tire patching. So we walked two miles to Hysham for a new supply before we could patch the inner tube.

We were glad, however, when the rear right tire punctured. Had it not flattened, we would not have noticed that the wooden spokes of the wheel were loose. We had to throw away the tire and use one we had picked up several days before.

"It looks like the spokes are ready to cave in," Elliott said. "We'll have to buy a wheel."

Finding a wheel for sale was not as simple as buying a new tire we soon found out. We shopped in several towns, but no garage or filling station had one in stock. This was not strange, we realized, considering that few cars, if any, had need for one.

"All we can do is keep driving," Elliott said. He looked critically at the faulty wheel, and kicked the rim gently. "Let's hope it holds up."

Despite the day's frustrations and slower driving, considered advisable because of the rear wheel's condition, we traveled 170 miles. Signs along the highway made us aware our troubles were insignificant compared with those a century ago. We were driving through the Montana region where the U.S. Army battled Sioux Indians, and where General Custer and his valiant soldiers fought to their deaths.

We added North Dakota to our list of states when the Ford crossed the border several miles east of Wibaux. Needless to say, leaving Montana was with a feeling of regret. The vast mineral resources of the "Treasure State," its copper, gold, silver, and other ores, didn't mean much to us, but we did value its other treasures, mountain scenery, forests, and ranches. Most of all, Yellowstone Park was far behind.

Soon we noticed an unmistakable change in scenery. We were in the North Dakota Badlands, where barren and eroded formations extended to the Black Hills of South Dakota. We camped for the night on top of a hill overlooking a railroad track alongside the Badlands.

The evening cooled as the intense heat of the day moderated with the setting sun. We thought we were alone in the weird wilderness, but the deadly silence broke suddenly. From atop the hill we watched and listened as two young men strolled down the railroad track singing, "The Red River Valley." As their harmonious voices trailed off with "Let Me Call You Sweetheart," we had a sense of yearning.

"What a scene for a movie," Elliott said, "but no way to film those voices."

The next day immense wheat fields bordered the highway once we left the hilly country of Medora and Mandan. Judging by the luxurious growth we observed, North Dakota was about to harvest a bumper crop.

Generally, the road was in fair condition. Nevertheless, we kept close tab on the Ford's defective wheel. So far, it held up, although we heard swishing sounds for many miles. Now that we drove on North Dakota's level land, we thought there would be less strain on the spokes. Our apprehension did not ease, however, because added to the swishing was an occasional clicking sound.

Elliott voiced admiration for the attractive bridge spanning the Missouri River on the western side of Bismarck. To avoid driving in sweltering heat we idled several hours in the capital city, devoting some of the time in the state capitol, the last we would visit on our journey. In Bismarck I moved my watch ahead an hour. We had reached our own time zone, Central.

Late in the afternoon we drove 25 miles beyond Bismarck to camp in a vacant field. The condition of the back wheel had worsened, we had only six dollars left, and had no more dope to battle pestiferous mosquitoes.

Notwithstanding, we continued driving slowly the next day, and camped that night in a gravel pit a few miles short of the Minnesota border. There were fewer mosquitoes, so we built a fire around which we discussed our reaction to the trip across

North Dakota. Striking was the vastness of its grain and hay fields, we agreed, and likewise were the few cities we traveled through, ideal "small town" places to live, with populations in Dickinson, Jamestown, and Valley City less than 10,000 each.

There was nothing attractive about the gravel pit, but the morning was so refreshingly cool it was noon before a late start brought us to the Minnesota border. It felt good to cross the Red River at Fargo to arrive in Moorhead, knowing only one state now separated us from Wisconsin.

If only the shaky wheel wouldn't cave in. Such was our thinking as we drove without incident as far as New York Mills. There, however, the rear right tire blew out. We hated to throw it away because the tire had punctured only twice before since the start of our trip. Worse yet, for the second time it warned us that all was not right with the wheel from which we removed it. While replacing the tire with a picked-up spare, we saw that a spoke had dropped out of the wobbly wheel, and that several more were on the verge of falling off.

Elliott pointed to an auto sales building two blocks up the street. Frowning, he said, "We've been driving with three fenders, but we won't get far with three wheels." He kicked the faltering wheel. Another spoke fell out.

"There's little chance of buying a secondhand wheel," Elliott said. "The only thing we can do is have that garage order a new one."

Discussing the crisis at length, we realized this meant waiting days for a new wheel, and that we would have to find jobs to pay for it.

As it turned out, we were crossing a bridge before coming to it. When we told the garage manager of our need for a rear right wheel, he caught us by complete surprise.

"Could you use a secondhand one?" he asked. He led us to

a corner in the garage and held one up. "It's the only wheel we could save from a wrecked Ford," the manager said. "We took it off the back axle, on the right side." He tested the spokes to show they were firmly in place. "Like the wheel company says, a wheel is no stronger than its weakest spoke. Okay, you can have the wheel for a dollar," he said. At first he had asked two dollars.

Jubilant over this fortunate turn of events, totally unexpected, we were on the road again, relieved not to hear the swish-swish of a swaying wheel. It also was pleasant to move beyond the grain and potato fields of western Minnesota once more to see the spruces, poplars, and maples of wooded areas. A warm rain was a welcome change from days of hot dry weather.

At Aitkin we crossed the Mississippi River, observing how narrow it is compared with our mile-wide crossing into Louisiana.

"We've slept in many odd places, but never beside a haystack," Elliott said as we parked for the night five miles east of the river.

On this, what might be the last night we would sleep in our Ford, it rained hard, but not with the gusty wind, thunder, and lightning that greeted us on our second night's sleep at the start of our trip. For supper we ate dry bread and hardtack, the rationed diet to which we limited ourselves for several days.

We left the haystack early in the morning, in the unrelenting downpour of rain which continued for hours. For some reason we didn't understand, the Ford's engine ran much smoother than in dry weather. The same could not be said for the tires, however. They punctured nine times, partly due to roughness of the highway, but mainly because of their worn-out condition. Patching them in the rain was disconcerting, yet alleviated somewhat by skill we had developed.

We worked as a team. As soon as we had a flat, Elliott raised the wheel with a jack so I could remove the tire with a metal pry bar. Together we put a patch on the inner tube, wedged it back into the tire, restored the tire on the rim, pumped it up, lowered the jack, and were set to go.

At Tamarack we were so hungry we bought a dozen sweet rolls for a change in our restricted diet. Two more tire punctures slowed our progress, but the rain ended before we arrived at the skyline overlooking Duluth and Superior.

Here we had the thrill of again seeing Lake Superior, the first time in almost a year. We lingered at the top of the hill for a protracted look at the engrossing scene, a view we thought paralleled most we had encountered on our trip.

With understandable interest, we watched lake vessels arriving with cargoes of coal to deposit at Duluth's and Superior's huge docks, and carriers departing from docks with iron ore mined in northern Minnesota. Through my mind ran:

> By the shores of Gitche Gumee,
> By the shining Big-Sea-Water.

After descending partway down the long winding highway into Duluth, we drove to the house where we purchased our Ford, but finding no one at home, wondered what the car's original owner would have thought about its tour around the nation.

Industry, grain elevators, and navigation continued to draw our attention as we proceeded slowly through Duluth traffic. We cheerfully paid 20 cents toll on the Interstate Bridge, knowing it would be the last toll on our trip, and that we were crossing into Wisconsin, our home state.

In Superior we saw extension of rail and waterfront activity. After a drive down Tower Avenue, the city's main street, we located the YMCA on 14th Street, where we shaved and showered. We also checked our weights. Elliott had attained 157 pounds. My weight increased to 153 pounds. As Elliott put it, "fit as a fiddle."

Before leaving Superior we stopped at a gas station to check the battery, and found it needed no distilled water. This was a procedure we had followed throughout the trip. Most filling stations provided water free, but some charged 10 or 15 cents. The systematic checking resulted in the car's generator having only occasional trouble keeping the six-volt battery charged.

At the gas station I made the final entry in our expense book:

> 3 gal. gas $.73
> 1 qt. oil $.25
> The End

At 4:30 P.M. we began the final lap of our journey, a distance of about 70 miles. As though giving us a warmhearted send-off, the whistle of a vessel leaving Superior's "world's largest iron ore dock" emitted a drawn-out low-pitched blare.

"Remember how we started out big with the world's largest broom-handle factory?" Elliott asked me. "Now we're ending with the world's largest ore dock."

The last lap, however, was anything but a mad dash for home. The gravel road, though scraped by graders, was ragged and ridged like corduroy. Rain had ceased, but several times we skidded sideways through slippery mud, the Ford swinging close to the ditch.

Crossing the Brule River Bridge we saw several fishermen wading Wisconsin's famed trout stream. The road improved considerably as we came to the sand barrens east of Iron River. We were in blueberry country when we drove by Topside, Spider Lake and Ino, as I well knew from blueberry-picking trips I often made.

We aspired to reach Chequamegon Bay in time to see its glorious sunset, but twilight closed in before we came to Moquah. A few miles later we had our first glimpse of the bay. Passing the site where the French explorers and fur traders, Radisson and Groseilliers, had built the first white man's habitation in Wisconsin in 1659, we soon were at the Fish Creek slough which held fond memories for both of us. Here, at the mouth of Fish Creek, our favorite trout stream, flashed recollections of fishing trips, duck hunting, viewing of swans and geese, and paddling a boat through reeds and cattails into Prentice Park, remarkable for its bubbling springs in the midst of spiraling evergreens.

We were home at last, July 24, 1925. It was after nine o'clock and getting dark. Elliott flashed a smile and said good night when he got out of the Ford with his luggage in front of his home on Ninth Avenue West and Fifth Street. I completed the journey of the Good Ship Wanderlust by parking it in front of my home on Third Avenue West and Seventh Street, at the very spot from which our trip had started.

Just as I drove up, I spotted Bill Lynch, strolling by. He rushed over to greet me, and the "heap of junk." After we exchanged pleasantries, Bill chuckled and said, "guess I'll have to go crow hunting."

I drove the Ford to Elliott's house the next morning. Although we both stayed up late after being welcomed home by our families, we were wide awake. About nine o'clock I stationed the Ford in front of the Chamber of Commerce office on Ashland's main street. As soon as we stepped into the

Chamber office, Oscar King and his secretary, Tillie Resnick, a high school classmate of ours, greeted us cordially. Expressing surprise, King said he thought we still were on the mule ranch in Montana, from where I last wrote to him.

"We're broke," Elliott said, "but thanks to our Ford we made it."

King's brow furrowed. "Broke, but richer," he interjected.

He walked to the front window to look at the Ford. "It seems to be in good shape," he said, "except for that missing fender."

We assured King that our Ford, in spite of eccentricities displayed in the course of our trip, actually was in good running order. Its body, Elliott pointed out, was intact, its original battery and generator seldom gave us trouble, the engine ran smoothly, the top was rigid, and the folding bed was as comfortable as when we first slept in it. We had to replace three of our original tires, but the Ford still rode on its rear left one.

While discussion about our adventures continued, John Chapple of the *Ashland Daily Press* dropped in on his round for news. I thought he vicariously shared our trip as he jotted notes for a homecoming story.

Meanwhile, King telephoned Clarence Pfefferkorn at his

'Ford Bums' Back Home

Ashland, Wis.—These Ashland "Ford bums" have just returned from a 15,000 mile trip embracing the four corners of the United States.

Seegar Swanson (left) and Elliott Nystrum, left Ashland 11 months ago for a See America First tour. Swanson was employed before his departure as secretary to the secretary of the Chamber of Commerce, while Nystrum worked as clerk in the Ashland National bank.

Their entire capital, like that of Mutt and Jeff, was $100. At several places they stopped and worked to add to it. In one place they remained four months.

During the trip they visited Maine, Florida, California and Washington.—Pfefferkorn photo.

Milwaukee Journal, *August 16, 1925, runs photo and article announcing* Tramps *return. (above and opposite)* photo studio suggesting he take our picture standing by the Ford. A small group of people gathered as he focused his camera for a photo that later would appear in the *Milwaukee Journal* and the *Superior Telegram.*

That afternoon the *Daily Press* published Chapple's front page story headlined:

"FORD TRAMPS" ARE
HOME AFTER TOUR
OF ENTIRE NATION

Half regretting our trip finally was over, Elliott and I wondered what its benefits would be. With his usual thoughtful expression, Elliott said, "Well, at least we set a goal and stayed with it. Stick-to-itiveness, you might say."

Chapple summed up the end result in his editorial headed, "Ashland Tramps Home Safe and Sound." He wrote:

> We are glad to shake the hands of
> Seegar Swanson and Elliott Nystrom on
> their return from ... auto trip they made.
> We admire their spunk in seeing thirty three
> states in the Union with very little money.
> They will never regret the trip, and the
> experiences they went through will be lived
> over again and again as the years roll by.
> They took the trip at a time when they were
> fancy free and had no one to say when to
> get back or how long to stay. The result was
> that they had a good time, saw their country
> from one side to the other and returned
> healthier and happier than when they left
> Ashland.

"FORD TRAMPS" ARE HOME AFTER TOUR OF ENTIRE NATION

Seegar Swanson and Elliott Nystrom Complete 15,000 Trip With 32 Cents in Their Pockets.

AMAZING ADVENTURES

See Historic Bunker Hill at Boston, Everglades of Florida, Grand Canyon, and Many Other Places.

After 15,000 miles of touring which took them to the four corners of the United States and through 33 states, Ashland's "Ford Tramps," Seegar Swanson and Elliott Nystrom,

With this omen of encouragement, they commenced the long tour.

At Evanston, Illinois. they parked their car on the main street, and slept in the car each evening, spending the days exploring Chicago. The third morning of their stay the Evanston police decided their car was an abandoned one, and were just going to haul it away when Swanson and Nystrom appeared, jumped into it and lit out for Niagara Falls.

When they reached the New York fruit belt they were broke, for the first, but not for the last time on the trip. They got a job picking apples and slashing cabbages, working there a month.

Then they hit for Maine.

In zero weather, facing a fierce snowstorm, they entered Portland, Maine on November 20, heavily bundled and wearing big mittens. Then they motored down to Boston, and saw historic Bunker Hill and other places. From here they went to New York.

Five days in New York left them

to catch the water so they could use it over again.

At the Grand Canyon they followed trails eight and one-half miles to the bottom of the canyon and took a bath in the muddy but famous Colorado river. They viewed the petrified forests and the prehistoric cliff dwellings.

Then aboard for California, where they visited Los Angeles and went out to Hollywood to look over the movie stars. They slept on a boulevard in Hollywood but got away without being nabbed by the officers.

They visited Yosemite National park, but it rained after they got there and the roads were so slippery that they did not dare to leave so had to stay three weeks till the roads dried.

Up the Pacific Coast, they finally took in the famous Rose Festival at Portland, Oregon At Astoria they got a job unloading cement from boats, and then joined a pick and shovel gang. Their finances rose from $8 to $50 so they started east.

Fourth of July was spent at Coeur d'Alene, Idaho, where they are home.

With 32 cents between them, they drove into Ashland at nine o'clock last night in their car "The Wanderlust," battered, repaired, and mud-spattered.

On the car were written the names of some of the principal cities they have visited, including New York, Miami, Florida; Los Angeles, Portland, Oregon; and other places. The windshield was plastered with stickers of some of he famous scenic spots of the country, including the Yellowstone, the Grand Canyon of the Colorado, and the Yosemite National park.

The two boys left Ashland on September 20. Seegar had been assistant to the secretary of the Chamber of Commerce and Nystrom had been working in the Ashland National bank. They had about $100 between them and decided to see the country.

They left Ashland, and the next day, which was the day of the Marengo Valley cyclone, two trees crashed down beside their car as it was near Glidden.

with only $30, so they headed for Florida.

They landed in Florida on Christmas day, stone broke again.

Without even enough money to go to a restaurant, they went fishing and caught some yellow-tails and sea trout which they cooked for Christmas dinner. The next day they got a job picking oranges and grapefruit and a little later became carpenters' helpers and finally cement mixers.

In April they crossed the Everglades of Florida and headed west.

They visited the national cemetery at Vicksburg, Mississippi, and in Louisiana, were arrested as suspected bootleggers.

In Texas they stopped at Muleshoe, where they took in a carnival and sized up the big westerners from the plains. The country was flat and uninteresting, and the mountains of New Mexico were a relief.

Here their radiator started leaking, and water was five cents a pail. Whenever they stopped the car, they put a pail under the radiator

witnessed the big Northern Idaho Roundup. In Montana, broke again, they got a job on a ranch. Their first experience was being thrown off the backs of bucking bronchoes while the ranch owner locked on and laughed.

Yellowstone park was next. and with $19 in their pockets and a thousand miles to go, they decided Ashland was a good place to be.

Hard tack and raisin bread comprised their food for the last few days, as they saved every cent for gasoline. With 800 miles to go one wheel came off and they finally bought a second-hand one for a dollar and started on again.

Thursday night they were at Aitken, Minnesota, and going strong. They reached the Ashland city limits at 9 p. m. last night. Another fifty miles and they would have had to go to work again, as they had only 32 cents.

Swanson's and Nystrom's plans for the fall are not definite, but they may both go to college this year.